**ST ANDREWS STUDIES
IN PHILOSOPHY AND PUBLIC AFFAIRS**
Founding and General Editor:
John Haldane, University of St Andrews

Values, Education and the Human World
edited by John Haldane

Philosophy and its Public Role
edited by William Aiken and John Haldane

Relativism and the Foundations of Liberalism
by Graham Long

Human Life, Action and Ethics: Essays by G.E.M. Anscombe
edited by Mary Geach and Luke Gormally

*The Institution of Intellectual Values:
Realism and Idealism in Higher Education*
by Gordon Graham

Life, Liberty and the Pursuit of Utility
by Anthony Kenny and Charles Kenny

Distributing Healthcare: Principles, Practices and Politics
edited by Niall Maclean

Liberalism, Education and Schooling: Essays by T.M. Mclaughlin
edited by David Carr, Mark Halstead and Richard Pring

The Landscape of Humanity: Art, Culture & Society
by Anthony O'Hear

*Faith in a Hard Ground:
Essays on Religion, Philosophy and Ethics by G.E.M. Anscombe*
edited by Mary Geach and Luke Gormally

Subjectivity and Being Somebody
by Grant Gillett

Understanding Faith: Religious Belief and Its Place in Society
by Stephen R.L. Clark

*Profit, Prudence and Virtue:
Essays in Ethics, Business & Management*
edited by Samuel Gregg and James Stoner

Natural Law, Economics, and the Common Good

Perspectives from Natural Law

Edited by Samuel Gregg and Harold James

St Andrews
Studies in
Philosophy and
Public Affairs

ia

imprint-academic.com

Published in the UK by Imprint Academic
PO Box 200, Exeter EX5 5YX, UK

Published in the USA by Imprint Academic
Philosophy Documentation Center
PO Box 7147, Charlottesville, VA 22906-7147, USA

ISBN 9781845403119 paperback
ISBN 9781845403102 cloth

A CIP catalogue record for this book is available from the
British Library and US Library of Congress

Cover Photograph:
St Salvator's Quadrangle, St Andrews by Peter Adamson
from the University of St Andrews collection

Contents

Contributors

Philip Booth is Editorial and Programme Director at the Institute of Economic Affairs and Professor of Insurance and Risk Management at Cass Business School, London. He has previously worked in the investment department of Axa Equity and Law and as a special advisor to the Bank of England on financial stability matters. He is a Fellow of the Institute of Actuaries and of the Royal Statistical Society.

Samuel Gregg is Director of Research at the Acton Institute. He has written and spoken extensively on questions of political economy, ethics in finance, and natural law theory. He has authored several books including his prize-winning *The Commercial Society* (2007), *Wilhelm Röpke's Political Economy* (2010), and *Becoming Europe: Economic Decline, Culture, and America's Future* (2012). He is a Fellow of the Royal Historical Society.

Harold James is Professor of History and International Affairs at Princeton University. His previous books include *The Creation and Destruction of Value* (2009), *The End of Globalization* (2002), and *Family Capitalism* (2006).

Gerald P. O'Driscoll is a widely quoted expert on banking and monetary policy. Previously director of the Center for International Trade and Economics at the Heritage Foundation, O'Driscoll was senior editor of the annual *Index of Economic Freedom*. He has also served as vice president and director of policy analysis at Citigroup, vice president and economic advisor at the Federal Reserve Bank of Dallas, and as staff director of the Congressionally-mandated Meltzer Commission on international financial institutions.

Louis W. Pauly holds the Canada Research Chair in Globalization and Governance at the University of Toronto. He is a leading scholar in the field of international political economy. He is the author of *Global Ordering: Institutions and Autonomy in a Changing World* (2008).

Emma Rothschild is Professor of History at Harvard University and a Fellow of Magdalene College, Cambridge. She is the author of *The Inner Life of Empires: An Eighteenth-Century History* (2011), and *Economic Sentiments: Adam Smith, Condorcet and the Enlightenment* (2011).

Ludger Schuknecht is head of the Economic Policy Directorate General at the German Ministry of Finance. Before that he worked for the European Central Bank, which followed assignments at the World Trade Organisation and the International Monetary Fund. His recent research focuses on public expenditure policies and reform and the analysis of economic boom-bust episodes. He is co-author of *Public Spending in the 20th Century: A Global Perspective* (2000).

Amity Shlaes directs the economic growth project at the Bush Institute, and she writes a syndicated column with Bloomberg. HarperCollins plans to publish her biography on Calvin Coolidge in 2012. She teaches the economics of the 1930s at the New York University Stern School of Business and is the author of two national bestsellers, *The Forgotten Man* (2008), and *The Greedy Hand* (2000).

Edward Skidelsky is a lecturer at the University of Exeter. He is the author of *Ernst Cassirer: The Last Philosopher of Culture* (2009) and co-author of *How Much is Enough? Money and the Good Life* (2012). He writes on the institutional theory of art, the intellectual roots of neo-conservatism, and the ethics of capitalism.

Lord Robert Skidelsky is emeritus Professor of Political Economy at the University of Warwick, a fellow of the British Academy, and a crossbench peer. He is the author of the acclaimed three-volume biography of the economist John Maynard Keynes, and most recently *Keynes: The Return of the Master* (2010).

Craig Smith is a lecturer in the Department of Moral Philosophy at the University of St Andrews and is the author of *Adam Smith's Political Philosophy: The Invisible Hand and Spontaneous Order* (2005). He is director of the Politics and Economy Project at the Centre for Ethics Philosophy and Public Affairs.

Benn Steil is director of international economics at the Council on Foreign Relations. His book *Money, Markets and Sovereignty* (2010), co-authored with Manuel Hinds, was awarded the 2010 Hayek Book Prize.

James R. Stoner, Jr., is Professor of Political Science at Louisiana State University. He is the author of *Common Law and Liberal Theory* (1992), and *Common-Law Liberty* (2003), and editor, with Samuel Gregg, of *Profit, Prudence and Virtue: Essays in Ethics, Business and Management* (2009).

Arthur Waldron is the Lauder Professor of International Relations in the Department of History at the University of Pennsylvania. A specialist in Asian history, he was educated at Harvard, and he has previously taught at Princeton, Brown, and the Naval War College. He has written several books in English, including *From War to Nationalism: China's Turning Point, 1924–1925* (2003), and edited four books, including two in Chinese. His works have been translated into Chinese, Italian, Korean, and Japanese.

John Haldane

Preface

In 2009 St Andrews Studies published a volume entitled *Profit, Prudence and Virtue: Essays in Ethics, Business and Management*, edited by Samuel Gregg and James Stoner. This originated in a project developed by the Social Trends Institute in New York in collaboration with the Witherspoon Institute in Princeton, NJ, which led to a conference convened in Princeton in 2007. In addition to essays deriving from that meeting, *Profit, Prudence and Virtue* contained a number of chapters commissioned subsequent to the banking crisis and recession of 2008.

Evidently, those events, or more accurately processes, continue to have effects. One such has been to call into question the role of large financial institutions, particularly in relation to money-market mutual funds and other credit instruments. What was said to have begun a few years earlier as a growing threat of unrecoverable mortgage-debt, quickly revealed extensive leverage schemes and other forms of commercial-asset speculation: and these had produced levels of indebtedness that simply could not be covered by capital available within the traditional banking system.

Beyond that, however, it became clear that public deficit and debt within major western economies threatened their capacity to borrow in international credit markets and that national and international banks might lack the resources to provide relief. Vast International Monetary Fund, European Central Bank and governmental loans were provided to Ireland, Greece, Portugal, Spain, and Italy in an effort to assure the bond markets that these countries would be supported in their borrowing efforts, but those markets took their own view of some national economies and the required returns on sovereign bonds rose to unmanageable levels.

Having once borrowed to invest, and then to cover temporary deficits, nations such as those mentioned have been borrowing to pay back the interest on prior borrowing. So it has continued to the point where it has become impossible for some to borrow at all, and sovereign credit default has begun in Europe. Not only has the credit worthiness of some of the smaller, recently developed economies been destroyed but that of major Western nations has been questioned. The largest sovereign credit rating agencies have reduced the long-term evaluation of the debt securities of major countries, including the United States and France. As nations implement fiscal plans designed to curb or cut expenditure and/or increase tax revenue, so growth is diminishing and with it the potential to earn a route to debt freedom. A further slowdown in economic activity has begun and a major and protracted downturn is increasingly likely.

There have, of course, been many factors at work in bringing the international economy to this point, but a major one is the borrowing and lending of money. In his *Politics* Aristotle gives a speculative account of the development of money, according to which it first arose in order to ease the exchange of goods, allowing for a separation of the circumstances of exchange beyond those involved in direct barter. This gives an essentially instrumental justification, and Aristotle believed that the acquisition of money for its own sake has no natural purpose and is thereby irrational. Elsewhere he makes the point more generally arguing, in the *Rhetoric*, that wealth consists in using things rather than merely owning them. These are among the earliest philosophical reflections on economics and its relation to human good; but as with so much else in his philosophy Aristotle's ideas influenced Western thought particularly through their appropriation by major figures such as Aquinas. This indeed constituted a major part of the tradition that has come to be known as *natural law ethics*.

Aware that the earlier project on ethics, business and management raised questions of a fundamental nature that needed to be addressed further, and conscious of the impact of the debt crisis on confidence in the financial system, the

Social Trends Institute along with the John M. Templeton Foundation, and with the aid of the Witherspoon Institute convened further gatherings of academic and other experts to discuss some of the central issues surrounding economic practices, and to consider as Aristotle had done their relation to the human good, in particular the common or social good. Here again these reflections are brought to a wider audience through the publication of a set of papers edited by Samuel Gregg of the Acton Institute in this case in collaboration with Harold James of the Woodrow Wilson School, Princeton University. It is a privilege to publish these valuable essays as a further volume in St Andrews Studies, a series committed to bridging the gap between academic analysis and argument, and the interest of the educated public in matters pertaining to human well-being.

Samuel Gregg

Introduction

'Money... economics... the common good... natural law.'
What, many will ask, have these things to do with each
other?

As the 2008 financial crisis and subsequent recession
demonstrated, the well-being of the financial industry in
North America and Europe is crucial for the economic,
political, and even ethical character of life in modern
developed nations. It is in fact an important component of *the
common good*. This phrase is widely used today but historically finds its most concrete definition in the tradition of
natural-law moral reasoning associated with figures such as
Aristotle and Thomas Aquinas. Broadly speaking, natural
law understands the common good as the sum total of
conditions that help people to pursue human flourishing. In
natural-law reasoning, however, expressions such as 'human
flourishing' have very concrete content; they are not whatever we want them to be. But even for those accustomed to
thinking about human development and progress in less-
specific terms, the notion that all societies require certain
habits, institutions, and procedures to exist before civil-
izational growth can occur is unlikely to arouse controversy—save among radical cultural relativists.

Some of the conditions embodied in the common good
are relatively static. The absence of rule of law, for instance,
makes it very difficult (though not completely impossible)
for human flourishing to occur. Governments perform particular functions that all but anarchists would deem essential
duties. Other aspects of the state's contribution to the common good, however, depend on transitory conditions. The
precise degree of direct government intervention in the economy, for instance, is not fixed. There is no moral principle,

positive law, or economic insight that tells us that the state's control of 21 percent of gross domestic product (GDP) is intrinsically better than 20 percent or 22 percent.

That said, it is difficult to disagree that money and a dynamic, wealth-creating economy play essential roles in promoting the common good in large, complicated social orders. Money itself may be an instrumental good, inasmuch as it does not provide an ultimate, self-evident rationale for human choice and action. But without money as a means of exchange, a store of value, and a unit of account, the opportunities for human flourishing would be limited by the realities of life in a barter economy. Likewise it is more difficult for most people to pursue the good life in conditions of abject material poverty.

The roles played by money and the economy in contributing to the development and maintenance of the common good are not without their controversies. They are complicated, for instance, by questions raised about the state's responsibilities vis-à-vis money and economic activity, the macro- and micro-roles played by government in economic life, and even the different influences exerted by competing economic and monetary theories.

With the onset of the 2008 financial crisis and the subsequent measures taken by governments in North America and Western Europe to address its causes, fallout, and associated recession, debates about subjects ranging from the state's economic functions to the nature and purpose of economics have intensified. Much of this discussion has focused on the empirical merits of different policies adopted by various governments in the wake of the financial crisis and recession. At the same time, the *principles* that ought to inform the state's economic role have also been receiving attention and reconsideration that was not so evident in public discourse between 2001 and 2008.

The United States, for example, witnessed the emergence of a discussion concerning the extent to which government approaches to the economy since the time of Woodrow Wilson represented departure from the principles of the American founding. Obviously the American economy of 2012 is very different in composition, size, and technical complexity from the American economy of 1910 (let alone the colonial economies of 1776). Yet while these differences and changing circumstances obviously affect the character of the state's involvement in and effects upon economic life, they are not at the heart of contemporary debates. Instead many of the arguments concern the principled *reasons* that ought to inform the government's economic role, regardless of the circumstances: matters such as the respective degrees of emphasis given to economic liberty versus economic security, or the rightful autonomy of individuals and free associations versus the state's particular responsibilities for the common good.

The role and function of money has prominently featured in these controversies. In part, this reflects a focused critique of monetary policy in the financial crisis and associated recession. Yet it is also indicative of divided opinion concerning the functions of money in the economy, money's character as an economic good, and the value of policies adopted by central banks.

In many senses, these are not new debates. But what often seems absent from such discussions is a *principled* framework for thinking through relevant questions. This is not to suggest that utility considerations are unimportant. As John Finnis writes in *Natural Law and Natural Rights*, there are many contexts in which we may reasonably calculate, measure, and weigh the consequences and efficiency of alternative choices. An obvious example, Finnis notes, is a market for those things which may legitimately be exchanged and in which a common denominator (i.e. money) allows comparisons of profits, costs, and benefits to occur. Finnis also observes, however, that making utility calculations or consequence assessments the primary or only points of moral reference is, strictly speaking, irrational.[1] Indeed, *all* forms of utilitarianism and consequentialism are incoherent, because they assume the impossible: that humans can somehow know and weigh all the present and future consequences of particular actions or rules. The world still awaits a coherent response to this critique.

This collection of papers — produced through the generous support of the Social Trends Institute and the John M. Templeton Foundation, and with the assistance of Harold James of Princeton University, Luis Tellez of the Witherspoon Institute, and John Haldane of the University of St Andrews—brings together philosophers, historians, economists, monetary theorists, and policymakers who recognize the importance of thinking about questions of economics, money, public policy, and the common good from a more-than-utilitarian perspective. As will become evident, not all the contributors adhere to natural-law thinking or even agree about the precise content of natural law. They do, however, share the view that considerations for utility—while important in any discussion of economic policy—are not sufficient for a full understanding of the myriad debates and discussions reopened and, in some instances, intensified after 2008. Whether it is expounding on concerns for property-rights, distinct views about the nature and ends of economic science, arguments about the proper scope for government intervention in the economy, worries about the possibilities for virtuous living in a highly financially-oriented modern capitalism, or the moral and fiscal implications of high levels of private and public debt and government deficits, the contributors point our attention to the issues at stake which, in many ways, underlie and transcend questions concerning the relative effectiveness and efficiency of different policy choices.

To elaborate upon these points while also drawing out specific questions requiring more detailed attention, the papers in this collection are divided into two parts.

Part 1, *Natural Law and Economics*, seeks to underscore the long-standing connections between natural-law reflection and the development of economic thinking. In 'Faith, Enlightenment, and Economics', historian Emma Rothschild alerts us to the fact that eighteenth-century thinkers—such as Adam Smith, David Hume, and Baron de Montesquieu—who exerted enormous influence upon the development of modern economics (including its ethical assumptions), had far more complicated understandings of faith, religion, and reason than is generally appreciated. Rothschild also illustrates the assumption of a shared human nature pervading the writings of such scholars, which in turn had tremendous implications for the particular notions of equality that came to be emphasized in emerging market economies, not only in Europe but also on a global level.

Some of these themes are further developed by philosopher Craig Smith. In 'Adam Smith and Natural Law', he squarely challenges the widespread notion that the thought of this founder of modern economics marked a radical rupture with natural-law concepts and concerns. He maintains that Adam Smith recognized that his social evolutionary account of morality could be read as facilitating moral relativism—something that Smith was deeply worried about. He goes on to illustrate that attributing a type of consequentialist morality to Adam Smith constitutes a misreading of his thought and has led many to associate a materialist and consequentialist ethic with the market economy and economic science more generally. Both of these problems, he argues, can be resolved through attention to the place of natural law in Adam Smith's thought. He points to the influence of Protestant modern natural-law thinkers such as Hugo Grotius, Samuel von Pufendorf, and Gershom Carmichael upon Smith, and how Smith combined their insights with Newtonian methods of enquiry, the emphases associated with other Scottish Enlightenment thinkers (such as Smith's tutor Francis Hutcheson and Lord Kames, both significantly influenced by natural-law thought), and the ideas of Smith's great friend David Hume. The result was a conception of a universal human nature pervading Smith's thought that drew upon the vocabulary of natural law and qualified Hume's emphases upon utility.

In any discussion of natural law, there is a tendency to associate it with the West. In one sense, this is legitimate, given that, historically speaking, both natural-law reasoning and modern economic thinking have developed most extensively within Western Europe and North America. This, however, can distract us from attentiveness to non-Western settings in which natural-law principles and methods of reasoning have developed, including with regard to economic issues. This is the subject of Arthur Waldron's paper, 'China, Natural Law, and Economics'. Waldron's thesis is that the emergence of many economic ideas and concepts in China occurred in ways that reflected the influence of natural-law thinking.

Referencing the *Discourses on Salt and Iron,* authored by Han-dynasty scholar Huan Kuan, Waldron illustrates the long conflict throughout Chinese history between state-orientated approaches to economic policy (the modernists) and those relying more significantly upon 'bottom-up' social and economic development (the reformers). A full reading of the text, Waldron suggests, bears striking similarity to the debates between physiocrats and mercantilists in eighteenth-century France. Waldron also observes that the debates were (and are) partly about the best way to realize the common good. This concern has translated into arguments about the efficacy of monopoly, the effects of government control of money, and the merits of private versus public ownership of property. Waldron goes on to underscore the role played by natural-law concepts in clarifying the terms of these debates. He also highlights two emphases pervading these texts: the necessity of economic and social life being grounded upon people choosing to order their lives correctly—even virtuously; and a view that moral order is embodied in the nature of things which can be known through human reason.

'Natural Law and Property Rights', authored by Samuel Gregg and James Stoner, begins by examining the history of natural-law reasoning with regard to one of the institutions highlighted by previous authors: property rights. They outline how several natural-law traditions treat the issue of property, underscoring the contributions of Aristotle, the Roman jurists, Thomas Aquinas, later scholastic thinkers, early-modern natural-law scholars, and a number of natural law-Scottish Enlightenment authors. These traditions are contrasted with the more modern approach, which begins with John Locke before drifting into utilitarian rationales. Gregg and Stoner then explore how natural-law considerations might influence contemporary policy discussion, using the examples of government regulation and intellectual property. In doing so, they illustrate how applying natural-law principles can help develop the internal consistency of particular policy positions.

Taking our discussion to the level of the international economy, Benn Steil traces the influence of natural-law ideas upon the different movements shaping the emergence of financial and economic globalization. In 'Globalism and Natural Law: A Brief History', Steil's focus is specifically upon the ancient Greek traditions of natural law, especially

Stoicism, and how notions such the *ius gentium* were used by early-modern natural-law thinkers such as Francisco Suarez and Hugo Grotius to produce a formidable case for free trade and the free movement of persons. Steil also illustrates the connections between natural law and the development of the *Lex Mercatoria*, which shaped international trade in the medieval and the early-modern period. He further demonstrates that ideas that have developed within the natural-law tradition — such as protections and entitlements accorded to private property, the practices associated with contracting in good faith, the acceptance of responsibility for harm to another, and the application of sanctions in accordance with harm done — have enabled people from very different cultural backgrounds and understandings of the good life to trade and exchange with each other over vast distances.

The philosopher Edward Skidelsky examines how normative positions derived from the standpoint of virtue ethics influence attitudes toward money. In 'The Emancipation of Avarice', he explains how the often incoherent popular and elite responses to the 2008 financial crisis have reflected moral-cultural dispositions toward money and economics that are generally part and parcel of post-Enlightenment ethics and thought. These dispositions, Skidelsky suggests, had eclipsed more ancient Greek and Christian traditions, which viewed money as an instrumental good rather than an end in itself. According to Skidelsky, avarice — greed, or love of money for its own sake — was once treated as intrinsically *unworthy* of human beings, regardless of any beneficial side effects that might flow from a single-minded pursuit of wealth. This does not mean, Skidelsky cautions, that commerce and trade were considered inherently problematic. Rather the Greek and Christian traditions insisted that such activities involved significant *risk* to one's moral well-being. This ethical and cultural setting, however, changed significantly with the eighteenth-century Enlightenment, under the influence of scholars ranging from Mandeville and Montesquieu to Hume and Smith. The word 'avarice', Skidelsky maintains, was slowly supplemented by particular conceptions of self-interest. One effect was to shift notions of public good from attention to virtues and the end state of affairs toward its being understood as a side effect of many private actions. Another was to effectively empty reflection about money and economic thought more generally of any substantive moral content. Skidelsky argues that the same post-Enlightenment views of money and economics helped facilitate the rise of consequentialist thought. Confined at first by Adam Smith to the realm of economics, consequential ethics soon escaped these limits and began to permeate the entire social order. In this light, Skidelsky suggests, no one should be surprised that economics shifted in 'an increasingly formalistic direction, eclipsing Smith's own ethical and sociological concerns'.

Developing some similar themes, albeit from a somewhat different perspective, the historian Harold James maintains in 'The Financial Crisis and the Disciplinary Challenge of Natural Law' that particular aspects of the financial crisis can be traced back to particular deficiencies in contemporary economics, not least among which is the excessive mathematization of mainstream economics and an associated lack of attention to issues of institutional design, especially when compared to economics in previous centuries. But one of the deeper lessons of the 2008 financial crisis, James argues, is that values and principles matter far more than many economists and policymakers are willing to acknowledge. And, he adds, this raises the question of what values and moral goods ought to inform the workings of financial and economic globalization. Previous ages, James maintains, were by no means as relativistic as our own when it comes to such matters. For centuries, empirical economics was combined with serious ethical reflection; there was no assumption that combining these was somehow 'unscientific'. James concludes by illustrating the types of questions that a post-financial crisis world may be more open to considering. These range from whether it is good to be in debt at all to the differences between exploitative debt and a debt that assumes obligation to the potential benefits and burdens of entrepreneurial risk. In James's view, natural law can serve as an important corrective to those forms of political and economic thinking that purport to be 'value-free'. It can also contribute to the development of a coherent and morally robust inner logic to economic activity, which he believes has been lacking for some time.

Part Two of this collection of papers, *Economics and the Common Good*, shifts the discussion towards public policy considerations and seeks to underscore some of the normative issues operative in these discussions. Gerald P. O'Driscoll's 'Monetary Order for a Free Society' takes us to the heart of the relationship between money, freedom, and social order. Part of O'Driscoll's concern is to illustrate the influence of particular conceptions of natural law on these matters. He particularly notes that early-modern natural-law thinkers, such as Juan de Mariana, criticized the state's interference in matters of coinage on both economic and moral grounds. In exploring these issues, O'Driscoll suggests that the contemporary state's ongoing efforts to establish a monopoly of the money supply in the name of order actually undermines the market economy's ability to realize both freedom and order — especially through central banking's distorting effects upon the system of price signals and its coordinating effects within the economy. Until, O'Driscoll argues, we are willing to face up to this central issue, we will not be able to engage in fundamental reform of the monetary systems whose flaws were underlined by the 2008 financial crisis.

In 'Money and Its Future in the Global Economy', Samuel Gregg examines the different normative priorities shaping the past, current, and possible future of monetary policy. Certainly, different monetary approaches depend much on the corresponding priorities assigned to various functions of money in modern market economies, as well as the views taken of money by competing economic theories. These functional considerations, however, cannot disguise the often-competing moral commitments — whether to equality of economic outcomes, to formal equality before the law, or to limited government and the promotion of liberty — that form much of the background to such decisions. According to Gregg, these normative positions contribute to a range of monetary policy options, which are grouped under the categories of state-orientated and market-orientated money, and to the options of internationalizing or decentralizing money. This touches upon questions of sovereignty and the wisdom — or otherwise — of governments exercising a monopoly of the minting and supply of money. The irony, according to Gregg, is that from the standpoint of long-term history, the

2008 financial crisis did not raise any substantively new ethical or economic questions concerning the functions and purpose of money. It did, however, illustrate the continuing saliency of moral and political considerations in shaping government attitudes toward money's role in an increasingly globalized economy.

A somewhat different approach is articulated in Louis Pauly's 'Supraterritorial Obligations, the Global Economy, and the Changing Politics of Responsibility'. According to Pauly, the world that is constantly being shaped and re-shaped by the various processes associated with globalization presents unprecedented challenges for how we think about the exercise of political authority. Drawing on natural-law reasoning to explore the concept of political responsibility, Pauly links this concept to the principles of what he calls individual and collective autonomy. He then proceeds to draw a comparison between the ideas of responsibility and accountability in order to highlight how this operates at the level of international relations, especially when it comes to efforts to regulate global markets, particularly during periods of crisis and instability. Unlike Steil, Pauly is less confident that global economic problems can be resolved by the unintended solutions produced by market transactions and institutions. Whether we like it or not, Pauly maintains, the will to power exercises—and will continue to exercise— considerable influence, especially with regard to people's tendency to resort to violence to resolve problems. The reality that Pauly seeks to describe is not one of global government. It is rather more ad hoc in nature, inasmuch as the global political order and global economy is likely to be governed by a small number of states that become used to working together, primarily through making domestic decisions that are cognizant of external political and economic considerations. Despite its less-formal character, Pauly suggests, this approach has real potential to manage international crises of a political, economic, and financial character.

Moving to the realm of the appropriate stance of economic policy in situations of severe crisis, the definitive biographer of John Maynard Keynes, Robert Skidelsky, takes us through broadly monetarist and Keynesian diagnoses of the 2008 financial meltdown in 'The Great Recession: Causes and

Cures'. He notes how both explanations involve close attention to the role played by monetary policy. For the monetarists, 'the causation runs from a collapse in the money supply to failure of the "real economy"; in the Keynesian story, the causation runs from the failure of private-sector investment demand to the collapse of the money supply'. Likewise, the cures offered by both schools flow from their competing explanations. The Keynesian response is to increase the amount of aggregate spending; monetarists, by contrast, believe that a sufficient cure for the recession is to increase the supply of money. It is Skidelsky's contention that the monetarist approach was illustrated to have failed, based on the experience of Britain between 2007 and 2009. In economies marked by low levels of confidence, Skidelsky argues, government must embark upon programmes of fiscal stimulus to re-spark growth. In exploring these arguments and competing claims, Skidelsky points to real differences among economists concerning government's responsibilities for the common good in times of economic distress.

A quite different approach to understanding the 2008 financial crisis may be found in Amity Shlaes's 'The Limits of Cardiology: Forgotten Factors in the Great Depression and the Current Period'. Bringing an economic historian's eye to bear upon the American economy in the 1930s — especially the Roosevelt administration's interventions — Shlaes demonstrates how factors such as an ingrained hostility to business, tax increases, a bias toward the interests of labour unions, the systematic violation of property rights (something that natural-law theory generally regards as deeply problematic), and a pattern of arbitrary behaviour by the state (also rigorously criticized by natural-law theory) made the Depression last longer than it might otherwise would, magnified its economic effects, and undermined a number of liberties. Many of these same problems, Shlaes suggests, manifested themselves in the wake of the 2008 financial crisis, with equally negative implications for the economy as well as human freedom. Analogizing the economy as a victim of heart failure, Shlaes calls for a broadened perspective from policymakers who are seriously interested in the patient's long-term recovery.

Knitting together economic analysis with ethical reflection, Philip Booth also examines the 2008 financial crisis in 'The Crash of 2008: A Discussion of its Causes and their Relationship to Ethical Issues'. Booth begins by making the case for the role played by government intervention and regulation in driving, wittingly and unwittingly, many of the dynamics that contributed to the financial crisis. Serious attention to these factors, he maintains, should make us hesitate before we simply ascribe the crisis to the greed of bankers and to insufficient regulation. Booth lays particular stress here upon the effects of moral hazard — that is, effectively sheltering market participants from the consequences of imprudent and excessive risk-taking — in encouraging private individuals and much of the financial industry down the path of a financial Armageddon. Booth also illustrates the ways in which perverse incentives, often created by well-meaning regulation, can facilitate unethical behaviour. He cautions, however, against assumptions that a restoration of moral coherence in people's choices and actions will automatically prevent such problems from re-occurring in the future. Building a robust moral culture is valuable for its own sake. But, Booth says, it should be accompanied by a concerted effort to re-establish links between risk, reward, failure, and responsibility that have been broken by policies that limit the fallout from failed financial enterprises.

Our last paper, Ludger Schuknecht's 'Booms, Busts, and Fiscal Policy: Public Finances in the Future', spends some time examining the contributions of monetary and fiscal policy to the 2008 financial crisis. He also, however, devotes attention to the challenges in the future created by excessive government spending in the past and present. The policy measures he advocates include: (1) significant fiscal consolidation to bring deficits and debt back on a sustainable path; (2) reductions in public spending that (in contrast to Robert Skidelsky) he believes will 'help reinvigorate long-term economic growth'; (3) Social Security reform to address the rising costs associated with ageing populations; and (4) structural reforms 'to reduce incentives for the recurrence of booms and busts'. Sound public finances, Schuknecht maintains, are far more important for the economic component of the common good of nation-states than many realize. The implication is that inaction on the part of government when it comes to addressing debt and deficit issues is now inexcusable.

So where does this leave us? A common theme linking many of these papers is the futility of trying to separate concern for the good life from economic theory and practice, particularly when it comes to the role played by money in our global economy. Disciplinary distinctions are important; in many instances, they help to facilitate analytical clarity. At some point, however, concern for the common good demands these different perspectives be brought together.

In most instances, natural-law theory is better at illustrating what should not be done as a matter of principle when it comes to policy guidance in the face of economic problems and crisis. That, in itself, is quite consistent with the natural-law tradition inasmuch as its negative absolutes are understood to be binding in all instances. It tends to be less prescriptive about what *should* be done in economic or monetary matters (though even here the principles do give more than simply a general orientation).

But whether the subject is the dynamics of money or the role played by central banks and governments in the economy, natural-law perspectives do have the potential to take us beyond purely positivist conceptions of reality and remind us that the purposes of money and economy activity are not to be found in themselves. The application of natural-law principles to these issues also furnishes us with a consistent inner logic that itself is derived from the ends that natural law identifies as intrinsically good for human beings. Lastly, natural law informs us that the choices about money and the economy made by individuals, businesses, and governments have more-than-technical dimensions. While many will disagree about the general content of human flourishing, few are willing to claim that it is limited to material prosperity or decline. Natural law is a perpetual reminder of the elemental truth about the non-material dimension of human existence, even in the midst of the world of supply and demand.

1   John Finnis, *Natural Law and Natural Rights* (Oxford: Clarendon Press, 1980): 111–18.

Part 1

NATURAL LAW AND

ECONOMICS

Emma Rothschild

Faith, Enlightenment, and Economics

The relationship between faith and economic life is not only a matter of religiosity or religious observance. The faith I would like to discuss in this paper is not particularly religious. But it is a very important part of the earliest ideology of laissez-faire and of the market economy, or of the Enlightenment origins of so much of our contemporary way of thinking about economic life.

The Enlightenment has been parodied, at least since the 1790s, for being irreligious and anti-religious. The extensive scholarship about the relationship between religion and the Enlightenment presents a different picture.[1] John Witherspoon was himself a figure of the American and indeed the Scottish Enlightenment—and a man of religion. The milieu of clerical scholarship was one of the most important of the environments of enlightenment, together with printing and the law. But even some of the most secular philosophers of the Enlightenment were considered to be religious, in the specific sense that they made man into a sort of deity.

The theorists of the Enlightenment, particularly Adam Smith and David Hume, are celebrated for their coolly realistic view of human nature. Hume, who was very much closer than Smith to being anti-religious, wrote a marvellous essay about luxury—'Of Refinement in the Arts'—which in many ways is an essay about Florence, or about what one could call the Florentine model.[2] The essay was enormously influential in the European ideology of commercial enlightenment, because in it Hume defends luxury, which is not an easy thing to do. He outlines an almost idyllic future in which progress in knowledge goes hand in hand with progress in industry, and with knowledge of what he describes as 'ethics'. He also outlines a progress of sociability in which men and women meet and have agreeable conversations. 'Mildness and moderation' advance, in turn, with the arts of industry and science. Florence, whose history Hume studied with intense interest, was an extreme example of an 'opulent republic': 'the Florentine democracy applied itself entirely to commerce.'[3]

I do not think it an exaggeration to call Hume's imagined society an idyll; a version of the Florentine model was at the centre of Enlightenment optimism about the progress of commerce and industry. But it was not an idyll that Hume was able to found, in any satisfactory way, on his knowledge — as an historian — of past societies. Nor was he able to found it on the science of human nature, or the philosophical psychology of human action that he tried for so many years to invent. It was an act of faith on Hume's part to believe that mildness and moderation would advance together with the progress of industry, commerce, and exchange.

Hume's essay on refinement was written in opposition to the Protestant asceticism of the eighteenth century, including the Presbyterian refusal of luxury that was later so important to Max Weber's theories of religion and capitalism. It was also written against Jean-Jacques Rousseau's idealization of primitive societies. But there is a more profound point that comes out in the essay, which has to do with Hume's faith. I think that this is the right word to use, even of Hume, as well-known as he is for his scepticism. For he expresses a confidence in his essay on luxury that knowledge, industry, and exchange will have an effect on how humans behave, such that they become milder and more moderate. This is an extraordinarily important idea, if one tries to evaluate the original ideas of the market economy and laissez-faire. Laissez-faire is itself, with its opposition to regulation, a powerful expression of confidence in humanity and in individual women and men.

Faith in Laissez-Faire

Something like the same faith can be seen on a much larger and more momentous scale in the idea that has been taken to be central to Adam Smith's economic thought: the invisible hand. Smith believed in reducing regulation not only by national governments but also by powerful private corporations, such as the East India Company, the established church, and local government and parochial institutions. His idea of laissez-faire was thereby the expression of his confidence that, left to themselves, individual human beings would arrive at an outcome that was not always wonderful but would be better than all of the alternatives.

This faith in the universal characteristics of human beings had an essential role in relation to the Enlightenment economists' reasons for confidence in what might be described as the economic system. There has been almost endless debate over what Smith meant by 'the invisible hand' of the market and why he believed that a capitalist system would work well in the end. Smith used the expression in a very fleeting way in *The Wealth of Nations* (1776). The celebrity of the expression was really an artefact of the late nineteenth and early twentieth centuries. It is clear that Smith did not have a providentialist or deist reason for his confidence; he did not believe that God had ordained a capitalist economy and that God was ensuring the outcomes would be satisfactory.

But there is nonetheless a large act of faith implicit in Smith's use of the metaphor of the invisible hand and, more importantly, in his support for laissez-faire, or letting people do what they want to do. The act of faith consisted in the belief that, somehow or another, things will turn out more or less for the best. And at the heart of that confidence, in Smith's case as in Hume's, was a belief that there is a universal human nature, which in general tends to mildness and moderation. This tendency can be distorted in difficult circumstances or when individuals are inspired to frenzy by national or religious enmities. But in the circumstances that Hume described, the quasi-Florentine circumstances, human nature will tend to be, if not virtuous, then at least moderate.

Hume and Smith made an effort, unsuccessfully in my view, to justify their presumption that there was a universal and innate human nature by recourse to empirical science.

The presumption was strongly egalitarian, in the sense that Smith asserted that every single individual—the philosopher and the common street porter, in Britain and in other societies—was born with the same universal nature. It was a matter of faith, and to some extent, of intuition and introspection. It was also a matter of imaginative transposition. This was, for Smith, the capacity that enables people to go deeper and deeper into themselves to find something that is universal and also to think themselves into the situation of other human individuals, however different they may be. It is the process that he described in *The Theory of Moral Sentiments* (1759). If one were to paraphrase Smith's conclusion, it would not be that human beings are basically good but that human beings, over the long term, are not really all that bad.

This is a very modest and also a very powerful idea. It is close to Hume's idea of mildness and moderation. It is also close to what James Madison found in Hume's analysis of the shortcomings of human nature, and of the conditions of a stable and balanced system of government. It is a faith in what individual men and women are really like, particularly under the sort of favourable circumstances that could be approximately described as Florentine.

Arguments About Equality

The fundamental act of faith implicit in the ideology of laissez-faire is connected in a very interesting way to issues about global justice and global inequality. The great Enlightenment theorists were preoccupied with inequality: Smith uses the words 'unequal' and 'inequality' forty-seven times in *The Wealth of Nations*, in a variety of different senses. Hume, in his essay 'Of Commerce', concludes that

> A too great disproportion among the citizens weakens any state. Every person, if possible, ought to enjoy the fruits of his labour, in a full possession of all the necessaries, and many of the conveniencies of life. No one can doubt, but such an equality is most suitable to human nature.[4]

Here, again, is Hume's not entirely scientific conviction that certain kinds of human relationships are particularly suited to human nature.

These arguments about equality were very much arguments about equality within a particular European society.

Rousseau, for example, used a celebrated metaphor which, in economists' terms, presumed that there was a single commodity in inelastic supply; he talked about the rich using powder on their wigs so that the poor have no flour for their bread. It was an image that captured the European imagination.[5] Even the younger William Pitt, the British prime minister, introduced a tax on luxuries that was known as the hair-powder tax. Individuals who wished to keep servants with powdered wigs were required to buy a licence, which cost a guinea, to be affixed to the gate of the parish church; the purchasers of these licences were known as 'guinea pigs'.[6]

The imagery in this case was of a national society. But one of the fascinating aspects of the period of the late Enlightenment was the extent to which individuals were beginning to reflect on relationships of justice and even equality across very long distances, including oceanic and terrestrial frontiers. These reflections can be seen vividly in the discussion of the abolition of the slave trade. There was a sense of the visibility of distant ills, a sense of causal relationships among oppressive actions in different parts of the world, a sense of the feasibility of taking action to prevent ills, including slavery, the slave trade, and British oppression in India. There was also a sense, which was very striking in the 1770s and 1780s, of incipient institutions of global justice. These institutions were imaginary and intangible, but the imagination is a large part of thinking about global political relationships. The political imagination of the times contributed to a very remarkable sense that there was something like a global political society, or that there might eventually be a global political society.

Hume's argument about the suitability of equality to human nature is an argument, again, about equality among people within a particular society. It was really a political argument, to the effect that if there is a political society with some people who are enormously rich and some who are extremely poor, it will cease to be a society. It will contain the seeds of its own destruction.

This was a familiar argument, discussed by Montesquieu and others. But when Smith, and to some extent Hume, was writing, there were glimmers of an extension of the argument to a much larger and virtually global society. People were beginning to think about what it would mean to have to extend Montesquieu's analysis of inequality to the relationships, for example, between people in India and people in Scotland or France. They were also thinking about the extent to which evil in distant places was becoming visible or audible to people in Western Europe. There was a sense that because of the expansion in communication and newspapers and government information, people actually knew what was happening in the world. There was an imposing time-lag, but people in Europe did eventually know what was happening in Africa or India. There was a sense, too, of causal relationships: the distant ills mattered to people in England or France, because English or French policy was causing terrible things to happen in relation to the slave trade or in the East Indies.

There also was a sense of feasibility: things could be done in England or France that would affect these distant ills. There were the great consumer movements of the 1780s and 1790s against the slave trade. There were the boycotts of sugar and tea because of slave cultivation in the West Indies and the oppression of the East India Company in India. So with all these prospects of visibility, causality, and feasibility, there was a glimmer of an understanding of the political institutions that could come into being, whereby people in Europe would actually be part of the same political society as people in distant countries. There were fantasies in the 1770s of global senates, where literally every part of the world would be represented.

These are questions of faith of a relatively nonreligious sort, and they had strong prudential or hedonistic components as well. In Hume's terms, it would not be agreeable to live in a society with very poor or very oppressed people. It would not be suitable to human nature. But the society of the late Enlightenment, by the time of Hume's death in 1776, was as wide as the world.

---

[1]   See Jonathan Sheehan, 'Enlightenment, Religion, and the Enigma of Secularization: A Review Essay', *American Historical Review*, 108 (October 2003), http://www.historycooperative.org/journals/ahr/108.4/sheehan.html.

2   See David Hume, 'Of Refinement in the Arts', in *Essays Moral, Political, and Literary*, ed. Eugene F. Miller (Indianapolis, IN: Liberty Classics, 1987): 268–80.

3   *Ibid.*: 271, 273, 275; David Hume, 'Whether the British Government Inclines More to Absolute Monarchy, or to a Republic', in *Essays Moral, Political, and Literary*: 47–53, 49.

4   David Hume, 'Of Commerce', in *Essays Moral, Political, and Literary*: 253–67, 265.

5   Jean-Jacques Rousseau, *Les Pensées de J.J. Rousseau, Citoyen de Genève* (Amsterdam, 1763): 119.

6   Peter Pindar, *Hair Powder; A Plaintive Epistle to Mr. Pitt* (London: J. Walker, 1795): 31.

Craig Smith

Adam Smith and Natural Law

In discussing the appearance of the idea of natural law in the thought of Adam Smith, my purpose is to engage with two problems related to his work. The first problem is one that Smith himself explicitly recognizes and attempts to engage: because his project of moral explanation is based on a social evolutionary account, he cannot provide an external perspective through which to pass judgment on the moral practices of other cultures. This is the problem that arises from conventionalist or sociological accounts of the generation of shared moral beliefs. It is the problem of a potential slide into moral relativism. When one explains moral beliefs as socially generated patterns of behaviour, this suggests that the content and bindingness of these beliefs is dependent upon their socially sanctioned status in a given society. And it appears to rule out the possibility of an objective moral order, robbing us of an outside perspective through which to criticize the moral beliefs of a particular society. Smith was deeply troubled by this lack.[1] The clearest example of this is his discussion of infanticide. He regards it as morally abhorrent yet admits that it was considered acceptable in even relatively civilized societies. Here he perceives the influence of custom combined with 'far-fetched considerations of public utility'.[2] It is a puzzle to him how such a 'particular usage' that shocks 'the plainest principles of right and wrong' can persist.[3]

The second problem is the misinterpretation of Smith as fostering a consequentialist ethic that eventually develops, by the hands of the economists who succeeded him, into a view of man as a rational utility-maximizer and ends up as a justification for rampant self-interest. This reading of Smith views him as a progenitor of the idea of man as an economic agent, and subsequently of the idea that morality can be reduced to utility calculations. The problem with this is that it reads back into his thought a series of later developments in moral philosophy and political economy. He is quite clearly not a utilitarian in anything like the same sense as Jeremy Bentham and James Mill. Indeed, he explicitly rules out this interpretation of his thought from the very start of *The Theory of Moral Sentiments,* where he describes his project as an account of morality that stresses the importance of assessments of motivation and character.

A Resolution

Both of these problems can be solved by appreciating the place of natural law in Smith's intellectual project. His own struggle with the danger of moral relativism, and the mis-apprehension of him as the intellectual forefather of a mater-ialistic and consequentialist ethics that underpins economic rationality, find their resolution in his development of a ver-sion of natural-law thinking.

Following on from the work of Duncan Forbes, Knud Haakonssen has argued that the key to understanding Smith's legal and political thought lies in his revision of the natural-law tradition.[4] Smith was certainly steeped in the tradition of Protestant natural-law thinking. His teacher at Glasgow, Francis Hutcheson, followed the work of his predecessor as professor of moral philosophy, Gershom Carmichael, and deployed the natural-law theories of Grotius and Pufendorf as a key part of his teaching.[5] Both Grotius and Pufendorf develop a form of natural-law think-ing that differs markedly from the older, Roman Catholic tradition (and is equally distinct from the modern natural-law approach of the likes of John Finnis).[6] Perhaps the chief distinctions were their distaste for casuistry and their desire to connect the principles of a natural law to the evidence of actual human practice.

Smith imbibed this approach to social philosophy at a young age and combined it with the parallel influence of empirical science as developed by Isaac Newton. The

Newtonian method of identifying simple, general rules from observation was a major influence on the Scottish Enlightenment, with thinkers such as Adam Ferguson and Henry Home, Lord Kames, applying the approach to the sociological explanation of political and legal institutions. The name given to this kind of theoretical social science was 'natural history'. As Duncan Forbes puts it, the Scottish natural historians start from the 'basic fact of human nature in society'[7] and develop generalizations from the observation of how people have actually lived together. This approach differs from much traditional natural-law thinking in that it is grounded in empirical observation and generalization rather than deduction from *a priori* first principles. The distinction here is between a natural-law theory that sees human nature as the cause of the generation of a set of commonly held moral beliefs, and one that derives moral principles from human nature.[8]

The other major influence on Smith's formative years was the writing of his close friend David Hume. Hume himself admired and was influenced by Hutcheson's philosophy and by the innovative use of the conceptual language of natural law as a framework for understanding the nature of moral life. However, Hume disagreed with much of the detail of Hutcheson's philosophy, in particular the identification of a specific moral sense that formed the basis of his moral psychology and his dependence on benevolence as the root virtue. In contrast, Hume set out to deploy the Newtonian method of experimental, or empirical, philosophy to moral questions. He believed that he could apply social-scientific method to provide an explanatory account of the generation of shared moral beliefs in a society.

Hume's project was intended not to provide a normative argument in favour of moral principles, nor was it to describe in detail the process of actual moral judgment. Instead, he wanted to demonstrate how our basic moral beliefs arise and how they operate to make social life possible. This project was to be undertaken through the development of a new theory of natural law. In this theory, the language of natural law would serve as a conceptual framework to provide an account of how humans come to regard their behaviour as restricted by moral rules or principles that they accept as normatively binding.

David Hume

In *A Treatise of Human Nature,* Hume sets out to provide a naturalized account of the origin of justice that he relates in the language of natural law. His conceptualized account of the origins of justice is based on the identification of a series of universal principles of human nature that come to interact with a set of universally experienced external circumstances. At the heart of this account lie three concepts: 'confin'd generosity',[9] scarcity of goods, and the human propensity to associate. The interaction of these circumstances lead human beings 'naturally' to develop a convention that comes to be known as justice. Justice is a result of a gradually evolved convention, whereby human beings come to restrict their behaviour toward others in order to secure their possession of external goods. The key feature to note here is that this process is unintentional. That is to say, we do not set out to create the institutions of justice and its coeval concept, property; rather, we come to realize the value of these conventions after they have been entered into and accepted as habitual. Once these conventions have arisen, human beings 'naturally' assign value to the institution and its guiding ideals, and this results in the emergence of a moral value attached to the observance of justice.

In Hume's account, the rules of justice come to be viewed as both 'natural' and of moral significance through a gradual process of being embedded in custom. He is careful to stress that the institution of justice is 'artificial' in the sense that it is made by men, and not 'natural' in the sense that it is not part of the pre-existing order of the natural world. However, the important distinction he wants to draw is between phenomena that are 'natural' in the sense of natural philosophy (physics) and phenomena that are necessary for all human social life and so 'natural' to man:

> I must here observe, that when I deny justice to be a natural virtue, I make use of the word, *natural,* only as opposed to *artificial*. In another sense of the word; as no principle of the human mind is more natural than a sense of justice; so no virtue is more natural than justice. Mankind is an inventive

species; and where an invention is obvious and absolutely necessary, it may as properly be said to be as natural as anything that proceeds immediately from original prin- ciples, without the intervention of thought or reflexion. Tho' the rules of justice be *artificial,* they are not *arbitrary.* Nor is the expression improper to call them *Laws of Nature,* if by natural we understand what is common to any species, or even if we confine it to mean what is inseparable from the species.[10]

What Hume has in mind here is the idea that certain facts about a universal human nature and certain facts about human social life lead necessarily or 'naturally' to the discovery of certain rules of conduct that form the basis of human moral life. As Haakonssen puts it, justice for Hume is 'a necessary by-product of men's natural responses to their situation in the present world'.[11] All societies will develop something like justice, and all societies will come to assign normative value to that concept. If this were not the case, human social life would be impossible.

To explain how this comes about, Hume refers to individuals realizing the 'utility' of such an institution. But we should be absolutely clear about what Hume, and later Smith, mean when they use this term. It is not a reference to some sort of hedonistic ethical principle of pursuing pleasure; instead it refers to the usefulness of justice in the pursuit of our other concerns. Realization of usefulness leads to repetition of the practice, and over time, we develop an emotional bond or commitment, what Hume calls a sym- pathy, with justice that leads us to value it on normative as well as practical grounds.

One other element of Hume's natural-law approach is vital for understanding Smith's thought: that Hume's theory is entirely secular. Unlike his predecessor Hutcheson and later Scottish thinkers, Hume does not set his account within a providentialist moral order. It is a philosophical recons- truction that purports to explain the origin of justice and our identification of it as a virtue in wholly sociological terms. God and religion haven't any active role in Hume's version of the natural law, and this sets his account apart from those where the normative force of natural law comes from divine sanction. We see this approach continued in Adam Smith, who tries to provide a natural history of moral development that does not necessarily depend upon divine sanction or providence but that can be attached to both in a perfectly consistent manner.

Adam Smith

Adam Smith was convinced by the methodological approach that Hume developed and agreed with his co-option of the language of natural law as a critical vocabulary through which to provide a naturalized account of human social institutions. However, in his *Theory of Moral Sentiments,* Smith voices his disquiet about the centrality of utility in Hume's account of justice. Utility, he writes, is 'plainly an afterthought'.[12] It is a philosopher's reconstruction that accounts for the generation of conventions concerning justice. Smith thought it an inaccurate depiction of moral psychology on the grounds that we do not submit to and value moral rules on the basis of a calculation of their usefulness. He believed that this was illustrated by the fact that what moral judgment primarily involves is a judgment about the propriety of the motivation behind an action. Moral judgment involves assessment of the character of the individual as well as the consequences of his actions. An accurate account of how justice and natural law come to be identified and assigned normative value thus could not be grounded on abstract considerations of usefulness.

This point provides Smith with the starting point for his own theory. He observes that it is a universal principle of human nature that we are sociable creatures. We have an emotional need to live with our fellows and be approved of by them. We are thus naturally interested in their reaction to our actions while at the same time we pass judgment on them in a like manner. Smith develops the technical notion of sympathy, or empathetic 'fellow-feeling' with 'any passion whatever',[13] to account for this process. Moral judgment is grounded in an act of sympathetic imagination. We assess the behaviour of others by imagining how we would react in their place. Drawing on the knowledge we acquire from watching the judgments that others make of our actions, and of each other's, we form a stock of moral knowledge that we come to regard as rules of appropriate behaviour.

It is at this point that Smith introduces his major innovation on the Humean notion of sympathy. For Hume sympathy is an emotional contagion where passions pass through a society by emulation, but for Smith it is an imaginative process involving reflection. We can imagine how others will react to our behaviour before we act and are thus able to anticipate approval or disapproval and control our actions in line with this. Smith then adds a further element: the approval process we develop internally as conscience means that we are able to judge and to assess our own conduct. Sympathy is thus extended beyond thoughtless contagion. To illustrate this, Smith distinguishes praise and praiseworthiness. Mere praise does not satisfy our internal judge, because he is aware that we may not deserve that praise. We are discomforted unless we find ourselves to be that which deserves praise, and we are ashamed when we fall short. The 'man within' thus takes on a life of his own as a judge of our own actions. The final feature of this process is the introduction of impartiality. Because we are partial to ourselves, we imagine the response of an impartial spectator who neither favours nor disapproves of us, and we seek his approval. If, on reflection, we feel that we have secured this, we are able to withstand the disapproval of actual spectators who may disapprove of our behaviour because of personal bias or incomplete knowledge.

Smith provides us with an account of the generation of shared beliefs about appropriate behaviour that we come to refer to as virtues. Justice is a specific and perhaps unique type of virtue for Smith. Part of its uniqueness is that it is absolutely essential for the existence of society, while the other part is its precision and openness to coercive enforcement.

In the *Lectures on Jurisprudence*, Smith is very clear that his topic is commutative justice and not distributive justice. Drawing on the jurisprudential distinction between perfect (commutative) and imperfect (distributive) rights that he inherits from Grotius and Pufendorf by way of Hutcheson, he draws a line between his natural jurisprudence and other virtues 'not properly belonging to Jurisprudence, but rather to a system of morals as they do not fall under the jurisdiction of the laws'.[14] This strictly 'negative' understanding of the proper use of the term justice restricts its application to cases of deliberate injury or, to be more accurate, to cases of resentment aroused by deliberate injury. Smith believed that such injuries could be easily identified by all individuals and that, as a result, the same sort of rules of restraint from injury would develop and be clearly enforceable in any society.

This approach fits well with the conceptual stress on property rights that characterizes the Protestant natural-law tradition. Injury to property is a useful test for the application of justice, because it both is easily identifiable and arouses resentment in the observer. This is compounded by the fact that justice and, in particular, stability of property are absolutely essential to the stability of society, as Smith famously puts it:

> The rules of justice may be compared to the rules of grammar; the rules of the other virtues, to the rules which critics lay down for the attainment of what is sublime and elegant in composition. The one, are precise, accurate, and indispensable. The other, are loose, vague, and indeterminate, and present us rather with a general idea of the perfection we ought to aim at, than afford us any certain and infallible directions for acquiring it.[15]

Smith concludes that justice may be coercively enforced, while the other virtues can only be exhorted through persuasion and social opinion.

For Smith, the habituated rules that are the product of this process of human moral judgment and reflection take the form of natural laws. They are a product of human nature interacting with other human natures in social circumstances. The danger he foresees, and to which he constantly reacts through his changes to the various editions of *The Theory of Moral Sentiments,* is that it leaves open the possibility of moral relativism. If different societies develop different customary rules and internalize these as conscience, each society will view the resulting beliefs as equally sanctioned by nature. One way in which Smith attempts to avoid the danger is through the idea of the impartial spectator. If human nature is universal and conscience is characterized by impartiality, an idealized impartial spectator should be capable of reflection on the moral rules of his own society in light of his imaginary consultation with his feelings about right conduct. This then provides Smith with a mechanism through which we, as moral creatures, can consider the validity of the claims made by various rules to moral status. Smith's response, however, merely shifts the problem into the background, because the impartial spectator depends on moral knowledge learned from experience and actual judgments—and these take place within particular societies. The problem is further complicated by the fact that actual spectators and their internalized impartial spectator are fallible and subject to epistemic restrictions on their ability to assess the motivations of others.

So Smith has not solved the problem, and it seems certain that he was aware he had not. However, he does attempt another solution, and this lies in the development of his natural jurisprudence. Justice is necessary for society to exist and therefore vitally important to mankind and a key focus of attention. Moreover injury is a precise and universally identifiable notion. The natural law is discovered when we begin to reflect on the customs and habits that have arisen amid a people concerning deliberate injury. These shared beliefs develop as an unintended consequence of specific acts of moral judgment that accrue over time and become the basis for generalizations about appropriate behaviour. This leaves open the possibility that the legal process of a society and its reflection on what it regards as natural law may provide the path out of the problem of relativism. Or put another way, our moral reflections and development of law are a search for the natural law.

Actual Law and Natural Law

In the *Lectures on Jurisprudence,* Smith considers the relationship between this reflectively identified natural law and a society's positive law. Student notes on these lectures reveal that Smith sought to teach the subject in a natural-law framework and provide a theory of law grounded in the empirical evidence of actual legal orders. He looks at how particular legal systems have responded to particular universally recurring problems of social life through time, and he then compares these legal codes to draw theorized generalizations about underlying universalities or similarities of their rules.

This analysis is undertaken against the backdrop of a moral order that is similarly understood in terms of natural law. Smith believes that particular legal orders are engaged in a constant process of attempting to enact the natural law to the best of their abilities. As he puts it, 'Every system of positive law may be regarded as a more or less imperfect attempt towards a system of natural jurisprudence, or towards an enumeration of the particular rules of justice'.[16] None of these systems is a perfect embodiment of all the details of natural law, but the philosopher can apply the comparative method to extract generalizations that will allow us to come closer to a theoretical identification of the basic framework of natural law.[17]

Notice the implication of this approach. There are underlying universalities of human nature, and there are recurring social problems experienced by all societies. Societies may respond to these problems in different ways, depending upon the particular circumstances in which they find themselves, but the philosopher or social scientist is able to compare these various approaches and identify similarities that form the basis of our understanding of the natural law.

The most celebrated example of this approach occurs in what has come to be known as Smith's 'four stages' theory.[18] The theory is an example of 'conjectural history' — that is, the use of historical evidence to produce generalized theoretical accounts of society and social change in an abstract sense. According to the four-stage account, the generation of property, law, and government takes place against the backdrop of changes in the dominant mode of economic production. Smith distinguishes four types of society — hunting, shepherding, agricultural, and commercial — and provides us with a generalized account of how property, law, and government would operate in each of these types.

This sort of social science can then be united with the moral philosophy that Smith has generated. How positive law and its institutions arise and the features to which they respond provide a further set of information that the informed impartial spectator can bring to bear on his imaginative consideration of the morality of a particular rule. Smith accepts the reality of differences in the instantiation of beliefs about law — he admits legal diversity, just as he accepted diversity in moral belief—but the universality of human nature and the ubiquity of certain features of social life provide the common ground for a universal moral and legal order that can be identified on a philosophical level.

Once law is understood, we can begin to see Smith's understanding of the relationship between a natural law and the legal order that holds in any given society. His view is that the most effective legal orders are common-law orders, because the common-law judge draws upon and makes precedent based on actual judgments of actual cases and is involved at the same time in a discovery process of searching for the natural law as it can be applied in a given set of circumstances. This search for the natural law favours common law over statute law for two main reasons.

The first is that common law is epistemically more efficient than statute law because it is more reactive to actual events and circumstances and draws on the accumulated knowledge of precedent while not being bound absolutely by it. In contrast, statute law is based on deliberate rational attempts to design a legal order in such a way that it will hold universally over time as a set of unchanging moral principles. On a superficial level, this might appear closer to what we mean when we use the term natural law, but Smith's point is that we do not know all of the details of the natural law, we are only beginning to approach it through moral reflection and legal development. Statute law erects a set of rules that are less reactive to changes of opinion about the natural law itself. While the natural law is universal and objective, it is only available to us in an imperfect sense in our positive law.

Smith's second reason is that statute law is grounded in the political order. He is very clear that he regards the generation of law, and its administration, as a distinct task from politics or the activities of the executive. He stresses the role of judge-made law in the early stages of political development: laws are 'posterior' to judges.[19] The problem is that in the early stages of social development, the judge and the chief are usually the same person. It is only later, when the division of labour has separated out the roles of judge and legislator from that of executive, that we are able to establish secure general rules that are freed from political expediency. The legislator deals with rules guided by general principles; 'that insidious and crafty animal, vulgarly called a statesman or politician'[20] deals in compromise and expediency.

If our system of positive law is to be understood as an attempt to reflect upon and come closer to the natural law, it is as well to keep that activity as far as possible from the expediency-based decisions of politics. This is as Smith would have it:

> When the judicial is united to the executive power, it is scarce possible that justice should not frequently be sacrificed to, what is vulgarly called, politics. The persons entrusted with the great interests of the state may, even without any corrupt views, sometimes imagine it necessary to sacrifice to those interests the rights of a private man. But upon the impartial administration of justice depends the liberty of every individual, the sense which he has of his own security.[21]

Smith has identified a psychological and an institutionalized version of the natural law. He is then able to provide an account of changing beliefs about law over time, which reflect our comparison of positive law to our opinions about natural law. Common law has the advantage, as evolving beliefs can be more easily accommodated in the process of reform by individual judgment than through a process of deliberate political reform. What Smith seems to be offering is a process of immanent criticism whereby we reflect on the moral and the legal order of our society in a constant search for refinement of its laws. This sort of critical jurisprudence and moral reflection drives a process where we seek to discover an objective natural law—or at least to have our beliefs and institutions come closer to realizing it in our intersubjective social institutions. It should be very clear then that Smith believed that our economic life exists within and is constrained by a moral order grounded in our beliefs about natural law. This is a process of moral and legal evolution toward an objective moral order that Smith thought 'might properly be called natural jurisprudence'.[22]

---

[1]   See Fonna Forman-Barzilai, *Adam Smith and the Circles of Sympathy* (Cambridge: Cambridge University Press, 2010).

2   Adam Smith, *The Theory of Moral Sentiments*, ed. D.D. Raphael and
     A.L. Macfie (Oxford: Clarendon Press, 1976): 210.
3   *Ibid*.: 209.
4   See Duncan Forbes, 'Natural law and the Scottish Enlightenment', in
     The Origins and Nature of the Scottish Enlightenment, ed. R.H.
     Campbell and Andrew S. Skinner (Edinburgh: John Donald, 1982):
     186–204; Knud Haakonssen, *The Science of a Legislator: The Natural
     Jurisprudence of David Hume and Adam Smith* (Cambridge: Cambridge
     University Press, 1981); Knud Haakonssen, *Natural Law and Moral
     Philosophy: From Grotius to the Scottish Enlightenment* (Cambridge:
     Cambridge University Press, 1996); Knud Haakonssen, 'Natural
     Jurisprudence and the Theory of Justice', in *The Cambridge
     Companion to the Scottish Enlightenment*, ed. Alexander Broadie
     (Cambridge: Cambridge University Press, 2003): 205–21.
5   See Gershom Carmichael, *Natural Rights on the Threshold of the
     Scottish Enlightenment*, ed. James Moore and Michael Silverthorne
     (Indianapolis, IN: Liberty Fund, 2002); Francis Hutcheson,
     *Philosophiae Moralis Institutio Compendiaria: With A Short Introduction
     to Moral Philosophy*, ed. Luigi Turco (Indianapolis, IN: Liberty Fund,
     2007).
6   For historical approaches to natural law in early modern thought,
     see Richard Tuck, *Natural Rights Theories: Their Origin and Develop-
     ment* (Cambridge: Cambridge University Press, 1979); T.J.
     Hochstrasser, *Natural Law Theories in the Early Enlightenment*
     (Cambridge: Cambridge University Press, 2000). A contemporary
     revival of the approach is found in John Finnis, *Natural Law and
     Natural Rights* (Oxford: Clarendon Press, 1980).
7   Forbes, 'Natural Law': 189.
8   See Haakonssen, *Science*: 37.
9   David Hume, *A Treatise of Human Nature*, 2nd ed., ed. L.A. Selby-
     Bigge, rev. P.H. Nidditch (Oxford: Clarendon Press, 1978): 495.
10   *Ibid*.: 484.
11   Haakonssen, *Science*: 38.
12   Smith, *Theory of Moral Sentiments*: 20.
13   *Ibid*.: 10.
14   Adam Smith, *Lectures on Jurisprudence*, ed. R.L. Meek, D.D. Raphael
     and P.G. Stein (Oxford: Clarendon Press, 1978): 9.
15   Smith, *Theory of Moral Sentiments*: 175–6.
16   *Ibid*.: 340.
17   For a discussion of this aspect of Smith's jurisprudence, see David
     Lieberman, 'Adam Smith on Justice, Rights, and Law', in *The
     Cambridge Companion to Adam Smith*, ed. Knud Haakonssen
     (Cambridge: Cambridge University Press, 2006): 214–45.
18   For a general discussion of this Scottish social theory, see
     Christopher J. Berry, *Social Theory of the Scottish Enlightenment*
     (Edinburgh: Edinburgh University Press, 1997). For a discussion
     relating the theory to the natural-law tradition, see Istvan Hont, 'The

Language of Sociability and Commerce: Samuel Pufendorf and the Theoretical Foundations of the "Four-stages Theory"', in *The Languages of Political Theory in Early-Modern Europe*, ed. Anthony Pagden (Cambridge: Cambridge University Press, 1987): 253–76.

19   Smith, *Lectures on Jurisprudence*: 314.

20   Adam Smith, *An Inquiry into the Nature and Causes of the Wealth of Nations*, ed. R.H. Campbell, Andrew S. Skinner and W.B. Todd (Oxford: Clarendon Press, 1976): 468.

21   *Ibid.*: 722–3. See also Adam Smith, *Lectures on Rhetoric and Belles Lettres*, ed. J.C. Bryce (Oxford: Clarendon Press, 1983): 176; Smith, *Lectures on Jurisprudence*: 271, 313.

22   Smith, *Theory of Moral Sentiments*: 341.

Arthur Waldron

China, Natural Law, and Economics
The Discourses on Salt and Iron

Tian ze (天則)[1] or 'rule of heaven' is probably the closest classical Chinese equivalent to the Western concept of natural law. The first character, *Tian,* represents the sky or the sky deity or the highest authority, while *ze* consists of two components: The graph on the left, 貝, originally represented a bronze cauldron (although it evolved into a cowrie shell), while the two vertical lines on the right represent the knife, 刀, with which, ceremonially, 'rules' or 'laws' would be incised into the metal (the character can also mean 'pattern'). Other phrases having similar import include *chang ze* (常則), or 'regular pattern', which refers to 'the number of degrees passed through by constellations in a given time, their risings and settings, etc.'[2] Furthermore, a connection is repeatedly asserted between these heavenly rules and human law, for example, by Lu Zhi (陸 贄) (754–805): 'When laws are to be proclaimed they should always be verified / according to the rules of Heaven.'[3] For American historian of China Derk Bodde (1909–2003), these and other examples are sufficient evidence of concepts of natural law and of laws of nature.

Against Bodde's thesis, Joseph Needham (1900–1995), the English historian of Chinese science and a Christian, argued that although the Chinese tradition contained an idea of natural law applied to human affairs, the concept of 'laws of nature' such as those discovered by Isaac Newton (1642–1727) was missing. The reason, he suspected from the late 1930s on as he developed and wrote his life work, *Science and Civilisation in China*,[4] was that China lacked the idea of a serious creator-deity, an author of nature whose laws of the universe were present for man to decipher. This fact, along with the existence of 'bureaucratic feudalism', explains why China, though technically advanced, never developed comprehensive scientific theory comparable to that in the West.[5]

Not science, however, but economics is our concern here. Remarkably, China developed economic terms and concepts millennia before the West, and in a way that strongly suggests a form of natural-law thinking.[6] On this question, near unanimity exists not only that China had such a concept but also that it was far more important, relatively speaking, than the rather weak Chinese counterparts to Western positive law. These arguments are already present in the canonical philosophical works of China, dating from as far back as the fifth century BC. They cover a wide range of human behaviours and continue to be a recurrent focus of thought and dispute.

Here our chief evidence will be the *Yantielun* (鹽鐵論), or *Discourses on Salt and Iron*, written by the Han (漢) dynasty (206 BC–AD 220) scholar Huan Kuan (桓寬) in the first century BC, perhaps the most important classic of economic thought in the entire Chinese tradition. Huan gives a dramatized rendering, written many years after the fact, of a court debate in 81 BC that pitted the ideas of the 'Modernists', who wanted to use monopolies, price regulation, and so forth to increase the power of the state for war, and the 'Reformists' (the terms are Michael Loewe's),[7] who wished to restore a more humane system in which society and enterprise were permitted to develop themselves spontaneously, as envisioned in the classics. The debate has been going on in China for more than two millennia — during the Great Proletarian Cultural Revolution, our text was used in the violent *pilinpikong* (批林批孔) campaign to 'criticize Lin Biao

(林彪) (1907–1921), and criticize Confucius' — and the issues are not resolved today.

The *Discourses* brings together in debate two distinct strands in early Chinese economic thought. The basic question for Chinese philosophy was always how social, political, and economic order came into being. The school of thought named for Confucius (孔子) (ca. 551–479 BC) maintained that such order was possible only if human beings conformed themselves to the ways of heaven, which could be known by introspection, meditation, and 'the investigation of things' (格物). Among his followers, Mencius (猛子) (ca. 372–279 BC) presented with particular explicitness the sorts of administrative measures that would permit an economy to flourish on its own in the manner of self-actualization, or achievement of a result not through positive means but through inaction, *wuwei* (無為). This approach was rejected by contemporaries such as Shang Yang (商鞅) (ca. 390–338 BC), author of the treatise that bears his name and a follower of Guanzi (管子), or Guan Zhong (管仲), (725–645 BC) — probably not the author of the much-later text that bears his name — who stressed the need, if the kingdom was to be strong, for discipline of the people and the structuring of the economy by the state using *fa* (法). This term is usually translated as 'law' and has given to this group the name 'legalists'.

During the period of independent states, before the entire Chinese cultural realm was conquered by the kingdom of Qin (秦) (221–206 BC), these schools of thought contended in the various scattered courts. But with unification came the need for uniformity. The Qin adopted harsh legalist methods that, according to traditional history, brought revolts and its overthrow. The succeeding Han (漢) dynasty (206 BC–AD 220) brought the question to its crisis, however, through the ambitious military campaigns of Han Wudi (漢武帝), 'the martial emperor', (ruled 141–87 BC) against the horse nomads called Xiongnu (匈奴) and others. Wudi paid for his campaigns in legalist fashion, imposing monopolies, controlling prices, and so forth, but by the end of his rule not only had his military position collapsed but also—and this was the occasion for the *Discourses*—the kingdom was utterly bankrupt. Was the basic problem a failure to conform human policies to *tianze* (天則), or natural laws?

The *Discourses*

The sixty chapters of the *Discourses on Salt and Iron* have existed in various Chinese editions, copiously annotated, since ancient times.[8] Although arguably the key text for the whole of Chinese economic history, as well as one of profound relevance to numerous other issues, the *Discourses* never have received the sort of sustained attention from many scholars that they deserve. The academic literature dealing with them is little more than what is found in the notes of this article.

No reader can fail to be impressed by the numerous parallels between the issues discussed in the text and the problems facing China's economy and society today. But for Chinese of a certain age, the text is known if at all because of the use made of it in the 1972 *pilinpikong* (批林批孔) campaign aimed ultimately at Prime Minister Zhou Enlai (周恩來) (1898–1976), then already ill with cancer. Mao Zedong (毛澤東) (1893–1976) loosely identified himself with the legalists or statists, or 'modernists' in Loewe's terms. He accused his former military commander, who had perished in a plane crash as he attempted to flee to the USSR after trying to kill the chairman in the previous year, of having been a secret Confucianist or humanist or Reformist—which was absurd. The *Discourses* provided an ideal script, however. They were invoked by the left-wing Maoist writing group, having a series of pen names—Liang Xiao (梁 效), Luo Siding (羅 思 鼎), and Tang Xiaowen (唐曉文)—and were widely studied.[9] But this is a digression, albeit an important one, given the relevance of the issues to contemporary China.

The main lines of the argument in the *Discourses* are clear enough. The details, however, are not: scholars are only beginning to explore how exactly the state institutions at issue functioned, the precise meanings of various passages, and so forth. What follows, therefore, does not pretend to deal with the philological and historical complexities of the text. The purpose is to demonstrate that one set of pro-tagonists assumes an implicit natural-law argument, while their opponents believe that without positive human law, nature and economy can only be chaotic.

The debate was between advocates of what is translated as 'the school of law' or 'legalism', *fajia* (法家)—although as will become clear, the word 'law' is a poor English trans-lation of their views—and those of the school of the Confucians, or *rujia* (儒家). Michael Loewe (b. 1922), former University Lecturer in Chinese Studies at the University of Cambridge, puts the issues into modern English as successfully as anyone has in his *Crisis and Conflict in Han China 104 BC to AD 9*; he renders the legalists as 'Modernists' and the Confucians as 'Reformers':

> The Modernists were concerned with directing the efforts of statesmen to the problems of the contemporary world; the Reformists wished to eliminate the political and social abuses of the day by a return to conditions which they believed to have existed in the remote past. The Modernists derived their tradition from [Qin] and its unification of the world under a single rule, and the occult forces which they worshipped had been served by the kings and then the emperors of [Qin]. The Reformists harked back to a tradition which they traced to the kings and ethical ideas of [Zhou]; and they worshipped Heaven as kings of Zhou had done before them.
>
> The Modernists tried to shape imperial policies so that they could control human endeavour, utilise human strength and exploit natural resources in order to enrich and streng-then the state. The Reformists found it repugnant to exercise more controls on the population than was absolutely necessary, and in place of the obedience to official orders which the Modernists demanded, the Reformists looked to the people of China to follow the example and moral lead given by the Emperor. The Modernists saw useful purposes being served by lavish expenditure designed to display the strength, wealth and dignity of the throne. The Reformists preferred to eliminate unnecessary extravagance in the interests of devoting public resources to the benefit of the people of China.[10]

Such were the differences in the general approaches of the Modernists and the Reformists. They also disagreed about policy, in particular about the foreign policy of Han Wudi (漢武帝). This emperor sought expansion of his realms or, to put the most favourable interpretation upon it, he sought to guarantee security by conquering the Xiongnu (匈奴) nomads to the north and west. The Xiongnu were unlike the 'barbarians' described in the classics who, in theory and often in practice, were attracted by Chinese ways of life to the extent of Sinifying themselves. In such things, these true Inner Asian horse nomads had no interest; they raided and conquered, quite indifferent to the achievements of China. In Chinese they came to be designated by the term *hu* (胡), whose character, significantly, does not occur in any of the foundational classics of Chinese civilization. (They came into being very roughly ca. 500 BC; the *hu* turned up a bit more than two hundred years later.) Those classics had taught that all barbarians could be acculturated.

The *hu* brought a challenge that the Chinese never solved: how to deal with groups who were unwilling to defer to them (the Chinese viewed themselves as the capstone of the human hierarchy and refused horizontal dealings) and who were also militarily more powerful. The problem was still alive nearly two millennia after the events described here, in questions of how to deal with the Mongols in the Ming dynasty (AD 1368–1644) and a variety of Europeans in the Qing (AD 1644–1912). Arguably it is not completely resolved even today.[11]

After 139 BC, wrote Loewe, 'Han took the initiative, and the numerous campaigns fought against the [Xiongnu] culminated in the Han victories of 119'. These victories

> were followed by the penetration of Chinese officials and soldiers in the south, south-east, and south-west and into the Korean peninsula (112–108); and diplomatic ventures in the northwest were followed by military expeditions (from 104) which were intended to complete the expulsion of the Xiongnu or to provide a line of communication with Central Asia… In these ventures it is to be observed that Han statesmen were capable of taking strategic considerations into mind and trying to avoid dissipation of their resources. Unfortunately the tactical implementation of these plans did

not always avoid such errors, with the result that from 99 onwards Han resources had been spent, and we hear of Han reverses on the field and of large scale military losses. Sustained efforts of this sort cost the Han treasury large sums.[12]

To finance these military campaigns, the Han instituted extensive state control of the economy. Both salt manufacture and the iron industry already had developed in China at this time.[13] To quote Loewe again, 'State monopolies for salt and iron were introduced in ca. 119 BC; within the next five years attempts were made to regulate the transport of staple goods and to standardise prices; and from 112 the State eventually established a firm control over the minting of coins to the government's specification'.[14] By 81 BC, with the military campaigns lost and the economy in ruins, the debate with which we are concerned got under way.

Modernists and Reformists

Much of what ensued will seem uncannily familiar to the modern reader, who may be tempted to assimilate this argument of two thousand years ago into contemporary debates between advocates of free markets and economic planning. That would be misleading. A full reading of the text discloses that the opposition is more like that between physiocrats and mercantilists in the eighteenth century. The Reformists stress agriculture as the basis of all genuine wealth, and the welfare of the ordinary people as the true strength of the state. The Modernists view the state as the indispensable actor both for creating any social order at all and for its own strength, which they understand in the end as being to the benefit of the people. My quotation is selective, however, concentrating on points that may have bearing on natural law. The points I cover do not do justice to the full breadth of the argument or to its complexity.

The initial point by the Reformists is that the system of government control of the economy has undermined the health of the state. As the *Discourses* puts it:

> With the system of salt and iron monopolies, the liquor excise, and equable marketing[15] established... the Government has entered into financial competition with the people... As a result, few among our people take up the

fundamental pursuits of life, while many flock to the non-essential. Now sturdy natural qualities decay as artificiality thrives, and rural values decline when industrialism flourishes. When industrialism is cultivated, the people become frivolous; when the values of rural life are developed, the people are simple and unsophisticated. The people being unsophisticated, wealth will abound; when the people are extravagant, cold and hunger will follow.[16]

The grand secretary Sang Honyang (桑弘羊) (152–80 BC) responds that, in effect, prosperity always has been a result of positive government policy. The Commonwealth's founders 'made open the ways for both fundamental and branch industries and facilitated equitable distribution of goods', he says.

Markets and courts were provided to harmonize various demands; there people of all classes gathered together and all goods collected, so that farmer, merchant, and worker could each obtain what he desired; the exchange completed, everyone went back to his occupation. Facilitate exchange so that the people will be unflagging in industry says the Book of Changes. Thus without artisans, the farmers will be deprived of the use of implements; without merchants, all prized commodities will be cut off. The former would lead to stoppage of grain production, the latter to exhaustion of wealth. It is clear that the salt and iron monopoly and equable marketing are really intended for the circulation of amassed wealth and the regulation of the consumption to the urgency of the need. It is inexpedient to abolish them.[17]

Both parties profess to be concerned with the well-being of the farmers. This has of course been a theme of Chinese politics for a century: the Communist seizure of power in 1949 was widely (but incorrectly) thought to have been a rural uprising, while the policies of the new government were (equally incorrectly) thought to have benefited the rural poor. In fact, the imbalance between rural and urban incomes in China today is at least a factor of three.

The Reformists are also concerned with inattention to agriculture, a result as they see it of concentration of power in the state. Given these conditions, rulers and officials will become corrupt: 'When the princes take delight in profit, the ministers become mean; when ministers become mean, the minor officials become greedy; when the minor officials become greedy, the people become thieves.'[18]

The Modernists make a stout defence of their policies as benefiting all and necessary to the well-being of the country-side. The Reformists dismiss them. (The 'Profit-and-Loss System' mentioned refers to the system by which the state evened markets by buying when prices were low and selling when high):[19]

> Far-sighted and far-reaching in intent is your policy but contiguous with profit for powerful families. The aim of your prohibitory laws is profound indeed but manifestly leading you into the path of wild extravagance. Since the establishment of the Profit-and-Loss System and the initiation of the Three Enterprises, the privileged families throng the streets like drifting clouds, the hubs of their chariots knocking against one another on the road. Violating all public laws they promote but their own interests; sitting astride mountains and marshes and monopolizing all offices and markets, they present a far greater problem than the feudal possessors of fisheries and salt-beds. They hold the state authority... The result is that we see the farmer abandoning his plough and toiling no more; the people becoming vagabonds, or growing idle.[20]

The Modernists argue that the supply of goods to the state (for palace construction, the waging of wars, and so forth) was unpredictable under the freer regime that the Reformists advocate. In the past, they argue, the princes and others sent their products as tribute, but the transportation 'was vexatious and disorganized' and the products sent usually 'of distressingly bad quality' that often did not even pay the costs of transportation.

> Therefore Transportation Officers have been provided in every province to assist in the delivery and transportation and for the speeding of the tribute from distant parts. So the system came to be known as equable marketing. A receiving bureau has been established in the capital to monopolize all the commodities, buying when prices are low, and selling when prices are high, with the result that the Government suffers no loss and the merchants cannot speculate for profit. With the balancing standard people are safeguarded from unemployment; with the equable marketing people have evenly distributed labor. Both these measures are intended to equilibrate all goods and convenience the people, and not

to open the way to profit and provide a ladder for popular misdemeanor.[21]

The Modernists illustrate this with an adage: the 'prince's kitchen stuffed with rotting meat... while people hunger in the provinces; the prince's stable full of sleek horses, while starvelings walk the highways.'[22] They also illustrate it with a parallel to medicine:

> [Pian Qiao (扁 鵲) (ca. 6 BC)] diagnosed the cause of a disease by merely feeling the pulse of the patient. Where the positive fluid was over-developed, he would lessen it to harmonize with the negative. When the cold fluid was predominant, he would subdue it to harmonize the positive. Consequently the vital fluid and the pulse were harmonized and balanced, and evil influences were unable to remain. The inferior physician does not know the lines of artery and vein, or the difference between the blood and the vital fluid. He stabs in his needle blindly without any effect on the disease and only injures the skin and flesh. Now [the government] desires to subtract from the superabundant to add to the needy. And yet the rich grow richer and the poor grow poorer. Severe laws and penalties are intended to curb the tyrannical and suppress malefactors. Yet the wicked still persist. Possibly these measures differ from the way [Pian Qiao] used his acupuncture and probing and hence the multitude have not felt their salutary effect.[23]

Here we find the embryo of the still-debated concept of 'general equilibrium' in economics, the situation in which supply and demand for all goods are in balance. This is theoretically possible between two goods, but what happens when demands for a multiplicity of goods crisscross is still unclear. Many Chinese believed that such an equilibrium could only be brought about by government — this, two thousand years before input-output theories and attempts at planning. The ideal for the Modernists was a completely state-owned and administered economy in which every transaction would be managed so as to maintain complete balance. The Reformists saw equilibrium as self-actualizing and inherent in the structure of nature.

Another economic concept clearly present in the *Discourses* is that of comparative advantage, which the Reformists stress:

> The Ancients in levying upon and taxing the people would look for what the latter were skilled in, and not look for those things at which they were not adept. Thus the farmers contributed the fruits of their labor, the weaving women, their products. Now the Government leaves alone what the people have and exacts what they have not, with the result that the people sell their products at a cheap price to satisfy demands from above... We have not yet seen that your marketing is 'equable'.[24]

They make the same point in relation to the differing quality of soil and the different ways of cultivating them:

> The use of large or small, the suitability of straight or curved ploughs are different according to districts and customs. Each has its convenient use. But when the magistrates establish monopolies and standardize, then iron implements lose their suitability, and the farming population loses their convenient use. When the tools are not suited to their use, the farmer is exhausted in the fields.[25]

When natural equilibrating and adjusting processes are disturbed, the Reformists argue, the result is what today would be called 'black markets':

> The government officers swarm out to close the door, gain control of the market and corner all commodities. With commodities cornered, prices soar; with prices rising, the merchants make private deals by way of speculation. Thus the officers are lenient to the cunning capitalists, and the merchants store up goods and accumulate commodities waiting for a time of need. Nimble traders and unscrupulous officials buy in cheap to get high returns. We have not yet seen that your system is 'balanced'.[26]

Likewise, they are concerned about government control of money:

> In former times there were many currencies, wealth circulated and the people were happy. But afterwards, as the old currency was gradually replaced by the white metal of the tortoise and the dragon issue, they became wary of the new. As coinage changed frequently, the questionings of the people increased. Then all the coinage in the empire was demonetised, and the authority to reissue new was lodged with the three officers of the [Shuiheng (水 衡), the office that eventually took control of the monopolies]. Recently it seems a profit has been made and the coins are not up to standard;

they are thin or thick, light or heavy. The farmers are not experienced in comparing the relative trustworthiness of such tokens. They suspect the new issue, not knowing the false from the true. The dealers and shopkeepers for the bad barter the good... If there were proper laws about coining bad money, the presence of privately made coins with official issues would neither aid not harm the government. But if money is discriminated against, goods will stagnate.[27]

The Modernists argue that the state should own common goods and resources: 'The profit of the mountains and sea and the produce of the broad marshes are the stored up wealth of the Empire and by rights belong to the privy coffers of the Crown.'[28] The Reformists disagree: 'Let the Prince on the one hand, for the sake of the people's needs, not restrict the use of the seas and the marshes, and on the other, for the sake of their benefit, not shut down on the privately made coinage',[29] they argue at one point—and a little later:

To give the people free rein to strive after power and profit and to end the salt and iron monopoly would be to give the advantage to the overbearing and the aggressive in the pursuit of their covetous practices. All the evil-minded would come together, cliques would become parties—for the aggressive if not constantly curbed are ungovernable—and combinations of disorderly persons would take form.[30]

A difficult question to judge is exactly what the Reformists thought of commerce and heavy industry. Clearly they considered them secondary to agriculture. Some passages make clear, however, that they see as fundamentally innocuous the existence, for example, of iron works and believe in private ownership and free movement and hiring of labour. 'The business of the workmen and the merchants, the duties of the iron smelters—what evil could grow out of these?' they ask.[31] They answer:

Because the places where salt is crystallized and iron smelted are in most cases in mountains and on rivers near to iron and coal, their operation is all remote and their working is laborious. The shifts of the laborers are assembled in the demesnes without any investigation of their liability [that is, without regard to legal obligations to work]. Utilizing conscripted labor, the county and city magistrates sometimes cheapen the equalized price and make per capita levies [through forced sales]. People of good families are forced in their turn to work on the roads. The transport of salt and iron cause trouble and expense; cities are in doubt as to their population; the people suffer bitterly. As I see it, a single magistrate damages a thousand hamlets.[32]

In the end, the Modernists' argument comes down to military and social necessity: 'The Sage Ruler gives much thought to the fact that the Middle Kingdom is not yet tranquilized and the northern frontier not yet pacified.'[33] To which the Reformists respond in classic, pacifistic Confucian fashion:

If one desired to find the Way to pacify the people and enrich the country, one would find it in a return to the fundamental; for when the fundamental is established the Way comes of itself. Follow the principles of Heaven and utilize the wealth of the Earth, and you will accomplish deeds without laborious effort.[34]

The Reformists, the Modernists, and Natural Law

Most specialists would agree that a variety of natural-law thought lies behind the arguments of the Reformists in the debate summarized above. They believed that the best government was the least government, because left to itself, human society would order itself spontaneously. *Wuwei* (無為) or 'inaction' was better than action, and *ziran* (自燃), often mistranslated as 'nature' but meaning properly 'of itself becoming thus', was a powerful force. ('Natural law' is often translated into Chinese as 自燃法.) Joseph Needham and Derk Bodde, among the most distinguished Sinologues of the last generation, agreed that a concept of human self-ordering was basic to Chinese thought. More recently, Professor Karen Turner has insisted on the presence of natural law in texts related to those we are discussing.[35]

Note also that the Modernists, or the Legalists, about whom we are saying little, seem to have believed that both nature and human nature were chaotic, therefore requiring positive ordering (in the human case) by often brutal means. It is often said that China fears disorder or chaos, *luan* (亂), which explains everything from the lack of freedom in contemporary China to the Tiananmen Square Massacre. Not so:

the mainstream of Chinese thought, both Daoist and Confucianist, trusts both nature to abide by her laws and humankind without government to live in harmony, provided only that virtue is present.

We can trace with certainty the fundamental confidence in self-actualizing economic order found in the *Discourses* at least to Mencius. It is found in a well-known passage:

孟子曰：'尊賢使能，俊傑在位，則天下之士皆悅而願立於其朝矣。市廛而不征，法而不廛，則天下之商皆悅而願藏於其市矣。關譏而不征，則天下之旅皆悅而願出於其路矣。耕者助而不稅，則天下之農皆悅而願耕於其野矣。廛無夫里之布，則天下之民皆悅而願為之氓矣。信能行此五者，則鄰國之民仰之若父母矣。率其子弟，攻其父母，自生民以來，未有能濟者也。如此，則無敵於天下。無敵於天下者，天吏也。然而不王者，未之有也。

If a ruler give honour to men of talents and virtue and employ the able, so that offices shall all be filled by individuals of distinction and mark — then all the scholars of the kingdom will be pleased, and wish to stand in his court. If, in the market-place of his capital, he levy a ground-rent on the shops but do not tax the goods, or enforce the proper regulations without levying a ground-rent — then all the traders of the kingdom will be pleased, and wish to store their goods in his market-place. If, at his frontier-passes, there be an inspection of persons, but no taxes charged on goods or other articles, then all the travelers of the kingdom will be pleased, and wish to make their tours on his roads. If he require that the husbandmen give their mutual aid to cultivate the public field, and exact no other taxes from them — then all the husbandmen of the kingdom will be pleased, and wish to plough in his fields. If from the occupiers of the shops in his market-place he do not exact the fine of the individual idler, or of the hamlet's quota of cloth, then all the people of the kingdom will be pleased, and wish to come and be his people.

If a ruler can truly practise these five things, then the people in the neighbouring kingdoms will look up to him as a parent. From the first birth of mankind till now, never has anyone led children to attack their parent, and succeeded in his design. Thus, such a ruler will not have an enemy in all the kingdom, and he who has no enemy in the kingdom is the minister of Heaven. Never has there been a ruler in such a case who did not attain to the royal dignity.[36]

Here we find a remarkably forthright statement, in its economic prescriptions, of concepts that were not made explicit in Western thought for another two thousand years. Economic matters such as ground rents and transit taxes, however, are of relatively little concern to Mencius. This is the only place where he mentions them. Nor are they even the primary concern of the *Discourses*, which are fundamentally a debate over what constitutes a moral relationship between the state and the people. The contemporary-sounding arguments — against state ownership and monopoly, in favour of free trade and low taxes, and so forth — that we find here are simply applications of broader principles. It is by looking at these principles that we can assess the status of natural law in ancient Chinese thought.

The idea of self-ordering in economics is a subset of a general idea of self-ordering that we have already mentioned. It pervades the Confucian classics and the writings of all that follow, to the present.

We find it most famously in a utopian passage from the *Book of Rites*, or *Li Ji* (禮記), which is among the most widely quoted of anything in Chinese:

> 大道之行也，天下為公；選賢與能講信修睦。故人不獨親其親，不獨子其子；使老有所終，壯有所用，幼有所長，矜、寡、孤、獨、廢疾者皆有所養。男有分，女有歸。貨惡其棄於地也，不必藏於己；力惡其不出於身也，不必為己。是故謀閉而不興，盜竊亂賊而不作；故外戶而不閉。是謂大同。

> When the Great Principle prevails, the world is a Commonwealth in which rulers are selected according to their wisdom and ability. Mutual confidence is promoted and good neighborliness cultivated. Hence, men do not regard as parents only their own parents, nor do they treat as children only their own children. Provision is secured for the aged till death, employment for the able-bodied, and the mean of growing up for the young. Helpless widows and widowers, orphans and the lonely, as well as the sick and the disabled, are well cared for. Men have their respective occupations and women their homes. They do not like to see wealth lying idle, yet they do not keep it for their own gratification. They

despise indolence, yet they do not use their energies for their own benefit. In this way, selfish scheming is repressed, and robbers, thieves and other lawless men no longer exist, and there is no need for people to shut their gates. This is called the Great Harmony.[37]

In the *Great Learning*, or *Daxue* (大學), we find one of the most eloquent of the ancient statements of how, given virtue, human society will constitute itself:

大學之道：在明明德，在親民，在止於至善。知止而后有定，定而后能靜，靜而后能安，安而后能慮，慮而后能得。物有本末，事有終始，知所先後，則近道矣。

古之欲明明德於天下者，先治其國；欲治其國者，先齊其家；欲齊其家者，先脩其身；欲脩其身者，先正其心；欲正其心者，先誠其意；欲誠其意者，先致其知；致知在格物。物格而后知至，知至而后意誠，意誠而后心正，心正而后身脩，身脩而后家齊，家齊而后國治，國治而后天下平。天。子以至於庶人，壹是皆以脩身為本。其本亂而末治者否矣；其所厚者薄，而其所薄者厚，未之有也

What the Great Learning teaches, is to illustrate illustrious virtue; to renovate the people; and to rest in the highest excellence.

The point where to rest being known, the object of pursuit is then determined; and, that being determined, a calm unperturbedness may be attained to. To that calmness there will succeed a tranquil repose. In that repose there may be careful deliberation, and that deliberation will be followed by the attainment of the desired end.

Things have their root and their branches. Affairs have their end and their beginning. To know what is first and what is last will lead near to what is taught in the Great Learning.

The ancients, who wished to illustrate illustrious virtue throughout the kingdom, first ordered well their own states. Wishing to order well their states, they first regulated their families. Wishing to regulate their families, they first cultivated their persons. Wishing to cultivate their persons, they first rectified their hearts. Wishing to rectify their hearts, they first sought to be sincere in their thoughts. Wishing to be sincere in their thoughts, they first extended to the utmost their knowledge. Such extension of knowledge lay in the investigation of things.

Things being investigated, knowledge became complete. Their knowledge being complete, their thoughts were sincere. Their thoughts being sincere, their hearts were then rectified. Their hearts being rectified, their persons were cultivated. Their persons being cultivated, their families were regulated. Their families being regulated, their states were rightly governed. Their states being rightly governed, the whole kingdom was made tranquil and happy.

From the Son of Heaven down to the mass of the people, all must consider the cultivation of the person the root of everything besides.

It cannot be, when the root is neglected, that what should spring from it will be well ordered. It never has been the case that what was of great importance has been slightly cared for, and, at the same time, that what was of slight importance has been greatly cared for.[38]

Do not miss what this passage says: summed up, if one wishes to have all under heaven well-ordered and at peace, one need only rectify his heart (正 其 心).

So sublimely smooth does the whole process seem that we are jarred near the end by the phrase:

天子以至於庶人，壹是皆以脩身為本。其本亂而末治者否矣:

'From the Son of Heaven down to the mass of the people, all must consider the cultivation of the person the root of everything besides.'

Who is the *tianzi* (天子), and where has he come from? This is the first mention in the text, and it appears unintroduced. The meaning is the 'Son of Heaven', which is to say, the Chinese emperor. According to the classic, however, his task is properly limited to the cultivation of virtue. For with virtue, things become harmonious of themselves. Thus the *Shujing* (書經), or *Classic of History*, describes how the King of Zhou (ruled 1046–1043 BC) restored order after peacefully displacing the Shang (1766–1050 BC):

列爵惟五，分土惟三。建官惟賢，位事惟能。重民五教，惟食

、喪、祭。惇信明義，崇德報功。垂拱而天下治。

He arranged the nobles in five orders, assigning the territories to them according to a threefold scale. He gave offices only to the worthy, and employments only to the able. He attached great importance to the people's being taught the duties of the five relations of society, and to measures for ensuring a sufficient supply of food, attention to the rites of mourning, and to sacrifices. He showed the reality of his truthfulness, and proved clearly his righteousness. He honoured virtue, and rewarded merit. Then he had only to let his robes fall down, and fold his hands, and the kingdom was orderly ruled.[39]

The Concept of Nature and Natural Law

Not only then does traditional Chinese thought, both economic thought particularly and statecraft in general, rest intellectually on a concept of natural law, but that concept is strong; the inherent ordering powers of the universe and of morality properly diffused among mankind are so strong as to trump, in the honest opinion of Confucian literati, both the police power of the state and even its military power. Numerous texts could be adduced. (Whether this very strong confidence in natural law is justified is of course another question. This author vividly remembers his late colleague, the great Princeton sinologist Frederick W. Mote [1922–2005] attempting to follow Confucian methods of virtue and inaction in university affairs. He had no success. The question arises of why he should have expected otherwise.)

Scholars have disentangled rather satisfactorily the various elements that are thought to interact in Chinese natural-law thought, described here by Wolfgang Bauer:

> The concept of nature is very much older than [the highly specific expression for 'freedom': *ziyou* (自由), literally 'self-initiating', narrower than and distinct to the more general notion of freedom found in the West even at that time] and yet it is connected with it in a very conspicuous matter. The old concept of [*xing* (性)], which we encountered while considering the ideas of 'life' in China, had designated only the nature of a creature, a tree, an animal, a human being or a group such as humanity, but not nature in its totality. To the extent people were aware of it at all, they, and especially the [Daoists] called it 'Dao' [道, 'Way']. But this made it impossible to contrast nature and civilization [since Dao included everything, even civilization].[40]

In parts of the West, free will has been seen as an origin of evil; free will for everyone, carried to its utmost, no matter with what good intention, would lead to chaos. Thus nearly every Western utopia is in one way or another authoritarian, from Plato's *Republic* to Hugh Lofting's (1886–1947) World War I-inspired *Doctor Dolittle in the Moon*,[41] which describes a perfect society there, under the beneficent dictatorship of the Man in the Moon.

Note therefore that for the Confucian philosophers of China, the freeing of the will was simultaneously a process of self-conforming to the way. Thus Confucius summed up the stages of his life:

子曰：「吾十有 (1) 五而志於學，三十而立，四十而不惑 (2)

，五十而知天命

(3) ，六十而耳順，七十而從心所欲，不逾矩。

The Master said: When I was fifteen I set my heart on learning. At thirty I took my stand. At forty I was without confusion. At fifty I knew the command of Tian. At sixty I heard it with a compliant ear. At seventy I follow the desires of my heart and do not overstep the bounds.[42]

In other words, to learn and to develop is to require less and less law and restriction and naturally become more conforming to the natural order — very unlike the Western ideas of Prometheus, Satan, Adam, and others, who affirm their independence and autonomy precisely by overstepping their bounds. But how could such a situation exist? Only if the universe were governed by powerful laws? And how could the universe have such a character?

Natural-Law Thought Today

Natural-law thought is by no means mainstream today, in either the West or in China. The philosophical study of ethics is probably the most fragmented and least satisfactory aspect of that discipline today, relying as it does chiefly on the elaboration of apodictic statements by individual authorities as to what is good, thus begging the fundamental question.[43] In China today, not even positive, human law exists: administration is simply arbitrary. As for individuals, they are caught in a widely recognized post-Marxist moral vacuum.[44]

As for the West, Roger Scruton puts it this way:

> Locke [1632–1704] had a less bleak vision of the state of nature than Hobbes [1588–1679]. Even in a state of nature, he argued, there is a law which all people recognise, and which they would uphold if their interests did not conflict with it. This law is implanted in us by reason (which is in turn the medium through which God's will is manifest to us). This 'law of nature' generates the 'natural rights' which are commonly recognised by all rational beings, whatever the particular political constitution which might have been imposed upon them. In subscribing to the existence of these 'rights' Locke showed the influence of the ecclesiastical philosopher Richard Hooker (1553–1600), who in his turn had reworked the mediaeval idea of 'natural law' in order to endow the Church with an authority which could transcend, regulate, and also take part in the practice of government. The theory of 'natural rights' — variously stated and defended — still has its following. It is characterised by its 'international' character'; it specifies rights which are supposed to be independent of, and antecedent to, the rights generated by any particular political arrangement.[45]

The player without which this argument becomes difficult is God, Who is at the basis, by most accounts, of natural law. According to Thomas Aquinas (1225–1274), the natural law is 'nothing else than the rational creature's participation in the eternal law... The eternal law is God's wisdom, inasmuch as it is the directive norm of all movement and action'.[46] Lack of belief in God has proved a substantial if not absolutely insurmountable obstacle to the acceptance of natural-law concepts in the West. What of China, where, proverbially, no idea of a creator-god has ever existed?

Joseph Needham explains the differences:

> One of the oldest notions of western civilisation was that just as earthly imperial lawgivers enacted codes of positive law, to be obeyed by men, so also the celestial and supreme rational creator deity had laid down a series of laws that must be obeyed by minerals, crystals, plants, animals and the stars in their courses.[47]

Needham believed that the Chinese approach was completely different:

> The development of the concept of precisely formulated abstract laws capable, because of the rationality of an Author

of Nature, of being deciphered and restated, did not... occur. The Chinese world-view depended upon a totally different line of thought. The harmonious cooperation of beings arose, not from the orders of a superior authority external to themselves, but rather from the fact that they were all parts in a hierarchy of wholes forming a cosmic pattern, and what they obeyed were the internal dictates of their own natures.[48]

Needham stressed these points because he believed they bore on his particular concern: Chinese science, although rich in innovation and practical discovery, never developed nor sought the sort of bold and simplifying insights of, for example, an Isaac Newton (1643–1727). But clearly these points also have implications not just for laws of nature but also for the theory of natural law. Chinese civilization, he wrote, 'did not have any well-developed theology of a creator deity... Chinese thinkers thought rather in terms of an impersonal force (*Tian*), meaning "heaven" or "the heavens," indeed here better translated as "the cosmic order"'. Similarly, the Tao (or *Tiandao*) was the 'order of Nature'. Mankind had a place in this, as part of a triad also consisting of heaven and earth. 'Thus, for the Chinese the natural world was... something much more like the greatest of all living organisms, the governing principles of which had to be understood so that life could be lived in harmony with it.'[49]

But surely we need to understand what those rules are and why, in particular, they are not contradictory? If knowing is by introspection, then why does introspection lead to identical and harmonious results? This does not explain why there isn't any science in any logical way. It simply says that Chinese intellectuals chose not to investigate these laws, perhaps because individual religion was not at stake. Religion is often seen as an enemy of science. Needham seems to argue that belief in a personal god is close to a prerequisite for science.

This point is not easily reconciled with his sociology of knowledge, which was taken almost directly from Engels. He deals with this objection:

Before any theory of evolution had arisen, there were only two possible answers—either that someone in His wisdom had made the creatures that way, or if, as in China, there was no known creator, then because the materials composing each body were different or because their proportions varied. But why should they vary? Thinkers in China could scarcely avoid trying to discover what it was that apparently influenced the proportionate mixtures in different bodies. But in attempting to answer this question, it was necessary to enquire how exactly such influencing was done. In modern parlance, where Heaven and Earth meet, what happens at the interface?[50]

In the West, he argues,

This problem of interface was dealt with for a time by the linguistic device of personification. If the Creator wishes something to be done, he sends a message... In China, on the other hand, as there was no Creator there could be no messenger. Activity at the interface was therefore explained in terms of Wu Hsing 五行 of Five Avenues or passageways up and down between Heaven and Earth, the five ways in which Heaven influences things on Earth, by descending and soaking (water), by ascending and burning (fire), by submitting to cutting and accepting form (wood), by moulding or remoulding (metal) or by growth and the production of vegetation (earth).[51]

So for Needham, without a personal creator-deity, China cannot have any laws of nature. As for natural law governing human society, he and Bodde agree that the concept of *li* (禮), or ritual propriety, comes close to supplying it.

Li (禮), 'propriety', is difficult to sustain as a final moral category. It refers to acting in accordance with the laws of the way, *Dao* (道), which are objective and real, although Chinese discussion often treats them as if they were unexplainably immanent rather than having originated somewhere. Viewed this way, the argument about *li* is rather like the argument about conscience: you do the right because you know it is right. But how do you know? And how is it that everyone who properly examines his or her own conscience will come to congruent understandings that, cumulated, lead to utopia, as is quite clearly assumed in the passages cited above?

The possibility of an external source for natural law is not in fact excluded in China by the putative lack of a creation myth or creator-deity, the assertion of which has, since at least the nineteenth century, been a perennial error in discussions of China. In fact, not only does China have several creation myths, but those myths are at least as explicitly about a god and the bringing of the universe into being *ex nihilo* as any found in the West.[52] Nor is it fair to say that the Chinese gods somehow lack the personal or creative attributes possessed by those of other religions that permit them to create a law-abiding universe. We have two candidates for supreme god in China: namely *Shangdi* (上帝), 'Lord on High', probably the more ancient, and *Tian* (天), 'Heaven'.

The concept of *Tian* is one of the most difficult in traditional Chinese philosophy. Historically some believe it to be the Chinese version of a Eurasian sky god called *Tenggri*. Whether the character is found in oracle bones, or it is an introduction of the Zhou dynasty, is much debated and an important issue. Whatever one thinks about that, however, *Tian* does not behave like most other gods: unlike those of the Greeks and the Romans, he intervenes only rarely in human affairs; unlike Yawheh or Ba'al, he does not walk upon the wings of the clouds, intervening in battle on behalf of his favoured people; and so forth. Indeed, in China, *Tian* does much less than *Tenggri* does two thousand years later for the Mongols.

Tian is not conceived of as having consciousness or thinking, which is baffling, given that *Tian* does intervene in history from time to time. *Tian*'s actions take the form of orders (命), which affirm or remove legitimacy, bring seasonal rain or drought, and govern human life and its vicissitudes. The character 命 is regularly translated as 'fate' or 'lot' — and it is inscrutable, like the threads of life woven by the Western fates beyond the power even of Zeus. Most commonly, *Tian* is associated with the phrase that brings it together with a second character, the 'mandate of heaven' or licence to rule (天命), granted a person or a house on the proviso of accordance with the way, and subject to removal failing that.

Nevertheless, *Tian* is sometimes personified. Dong Zhongshu (董仲舒) (179–104 BC) 'attributed personality to

Heaven and conceived of it as giving commands to men [but] he did not, as Needham makes clear, go to the length of saying that it likewise commands non-human things—for example, the stars—to behave in the way they do'.[53] We find the phrase *Laotianye* (老天爺), 'old grand-father Heaven', in novels of the Qing (1644–1912). This is certainly personal. The idea of a personal god, even a creator-deity, may therefore be present in the Chinese tradition. What is certainly not present, however, is the sort of prolonged and exacting elite philosophical discussion of the problems of creation and the status of morality that is found in the West. The tradition may not, therefore, be sufficient to support a fully articulated concept of natural law comparable to that found in the West.

Conclusion

In conclusion, then, we can say that Chinese and Western discussions of natural law are structurally rather similar. Certainly the alterity that is so often incorrectly imputed to things Chinese is as absent in this case as in most others. Furthermore, when we speak of a lack of prolonged and elite philosophical discussion—for example, of issues associated with morality—this is best understood as not specifically involving lack of morals but rather a general absence of genuine parallels in the Chinese world to the academic philosophy and the philosophically grounded religion of the West—a much contested point, but I believe clear enough.

---

[1] To the extent possible, I have used the pinyin romanization that is now standard in China. Where quoted authors have used the earlier Wade-Giles or other systems, I have simply substituted the pinyin in brackets for their original rendering. Standard characters are used throughout, except when rendering titles of books published in China since 1949 and the names of their authors, which are given in simplified characters.

[2] Derk Bodde, 'Evidence for "Laws of Nature" in Chinese Thought', *Harvard Journal of Asiatic Studies*, 20 (December 1957): 709–27, 711.

[3] *Ibid.*: 714. See also Derk Bodde, 'Chinese "Laws of Nature": A Reconsideration', *Harvard Journal of Asiatic Studies*, 39 (June 1979): 139–55; Derk Bodde, 'The Attitude Toward Science and Scientific Method in Ancient China', *Tien Hsia Monthly*, 2 (February 1936): 139–60.

4   Joseph Needham, *Science and Civilisation in China* (Cambridge: Cambridge University Press, 1954).

5   *Ibid.*: VII, 2.

6   For contemporary Chinese economics, see Paul B. Trescott, *Jingji Xue: History of the Introduction of Western Economic Ideas into China, 1850–1950* (Hong Kong: Chinese University Press, 2006).

7   See Michael Loewe, *Crisis and Conflict in Han China: 104 BC to AD 9* (London: Allen & Unwin, 1974).

8   The Chinese version of the text used here, 盐铁论电子图书, is from the Chinese Internet and provided by my colleague Danqing Yu. For a complete translation into Russian, see Ju. L. Kroll (trans.), *Huan Kuan: Spor o Soli y Zheleze (Yan Te Lun)*, vol. 1 (St. Petersburg: Russian Academy of Sciences, Institute of Oriental Studies, St. Petersburg Branch, 1997) and vol. 2 (Moscow: Russian Academy of Sciences, Institute of Oriental Studies, 2001). For a review, see Derk Bodde, untitled review, *Journal of the American Oriental Society*, 122 (July–September 2002): 652–53. For a partial translation of chapters 1–19, see Esson M. Gale (trans.), *Discourses on Salt and Iron: A Debate on Commerce and Industry in Ancient China* (Leiden: Brill, 1931). For chapters 20–28, see Esson M. Gale, Peter A. Boodberg and T.C. Lin (trans.), (title not available), *Journal of the North China Branch of the Royal Asiatic Society*, 65 (1934): 73–110. See also Esson M. Gale, *Salt for the Dragon: A Personal History of China from the Last of the Emperors to World War II* (East Lansing: Michigan State College Press, 1953).

9   In 1973 Luo Siding published an essay in 红旗杂志 (November 1, title not available) and another, 汉代的 一场 儒法 大 论战 - - 读 盐铁论 in 札记 学习与批判, No. 4 (December 16). See a thesis by 王宝国盐铁论的经济伦理思想及其历史影响中国优秀波硕士论文数据库硕士 (2005, issue 5). See also Zhu Zhongbo and Wang Ning, 'Discourses on Salt and Iron and China's Ancient Strategic Culture', *Chinese Journal of International Politics*, 2 (2008): 263–86.

10   Loewe, *Crisis and Conflict*: 11–12.

11   See Arthur Waldron, *The Great Wall of China: From History to Myth* (Cambridge: Cambridge University Press, 1990): 32.

12   Loewe, *Crisis and Conflict*: 63.

13   For iron, see Donald B. Wagner, *The State and the Iron Industry in Han China* (Copenhagen: Nordic Institute of Asian Studies, 2001).

14   Loewe, *Crisis and Conflict*: 62.

15   Equable marketing, *junshu* (均輸), has also been rendered as 'equalized transportation' and 'adjusted taxation'. No one knows exactly what it was (see Gale, *Discourses*: 2 [note3]). A special office, or *guanfu* (官府), was established within the treasury, *danong* (大農),

literally 'great [office] of agriculture', to administer the monopolies (see Gale, *Discourses*: 2 [note 1]).

16   Gale, *Discourses*: 2-3.
17   *Ibid.*: 6.
18   *Ibid.*: 9.
19   See *ibid.*: 10 (note 4).
20   *Ibid.*: 56.
21   *Ibid.*: 9-10.
22   *Ibid.*: 82.
23   *Ibid.*: 88.
24   *Ibid.*: 10.
25   *Ibid.*: 33.
26   *Ibid.*: 10-11.
27   *Ibid.*: 29.
28   *Ibid.*: 34.
29   *Ibid.*: 29.
30   *Ibid.*: 31.
31   *Ibid.*
32   *Ibid.*: 33.
33   *Ibid.*: 76.
34   *Ibid.*: 77.
35   See Karen Turner, 'The Theory of Law in the Ching-fa', in *Early China*, 14 (Berkeley, CA: Society for the Study of Early China, 1989): 55-76. See more generally R.P. Peerenboom, *Law and Morality in Ancient China: The Silk Manuscripts of Huang-Lao* (Albany, NY: State University of New York Press, 1993): 19-26, 300. On wuwei, see Edward Slingerland, *Effortless Action: Wu-weias Conceptual Metaphor and Spiritual Ideal in Early China* (Oxford: Oxford University Press, 2007).
36   James Legge (trans.), *The Chinese Classics*, 2: iv, reprint ed. (Taipei: Wen-shih-che, 1971): 199.
37   禮記進駐盡意 (ed.), 王運五 (Taipei: Shangwu, 1972): 289-313. For Legge's translation, see http://www.sacred-texts.com/cfu/liki/liki 07.htm.
38   Legge, *Chinese Classics*, 1: 356-59.
39   Legge, *Chinese Classics*, 3: 316.
40   Wolfgang Bauer, *China and the Search for Happiness: Recurring Themes in Four Thousand Years of Chinese Cultural History*, trans. Michael Shaw (New York: Seabury, 1976): 141.
41   See Hugh Lofting, *Doctor Dolittle in the Moon* (Philadelphia and New York: Lippincott, 1928). Like Sir Arthur Conan Doyle (1859-1930) with Sherlock Holmes, Lofting was trying to get rid of his overly popular character by sending him to the moon. But public outcry soon led to his return, via an enormous moth. The book is fascinating as an illustration of the inability of utopian thinkers, even those writing for children, to escape the necessity of a benign despot.

42 Legge, *Chinese Classics*, 1: 146–7.
43 I owe this observation to Professor Patrick Burke of Temple University.
44 See, for example, *China Rights Forum 1: Rule of Law?* (2009), http://www.hrichina.org/crf/issue/2009.01.
45 Roger Scruton, *A Short History of Modern Philosophy: From Descartes to Wittgenstein* (London: Routledge, 1995): 198.
46 As quoted in *The Catholic Encyclopedia* (New York: Encyclopedia Press, 1913): 76–7.
47 Needham, *Science and Civilisation*: II, 518.
48 *Ibid.*, II: 582.
49 *Ibid.*, VII: 91.
50 *Ibid.*, VII: 131.
51 *Ibid.*, VII: 129.
52 Paul R. Goldin, 'The Myth That China Has No Creation Myth', *Monumenta Serica*, 56 (2008): 1–22.
53 *Cf.* Needham, *Science and Civilisation*: 548, 722.

Benn Steil

Globalism and Natural Law
A brief History[1]

The further backward you look, the further forward you can see.
Winston Churchill

Globalism — broadly speaking, the view that increasing economic and cultural interconnections across the globe are a positive development, to be advanced rather than resisted — has a much older and historically esteemed pedigree than is widely recognized. In the context of the contemporary debate over the legitimacy of globalization, particularly as it relates to the sovereign powers of states vis-à-vis individuals, the historical development of Western law has been very much consistent with globalist thought — in particular, the notion that individuals have certain natural universal rights that transcend the will of rulers.

The Philosophy of Globalism

There is… a broader need to wrench globalization from all the dry talk of markets penetrated, currencies depreciated, and GDPs accelerated and to place the process in its proper political context: as an extension of the idea of liberty and as a chance to renew the fundamental rights of the individual… The first principle [of liberalism] is that rights belong to individuals rather than to governments or to social groups. The second is that the essence of freedom lies in individual choice. (John Micklethwait and Adrian Wooldridge[2])

As with John Micklethwait and Adrian Wooldridge, authors of *A Future Perfect: The Challenge and Hidden Promise of Globalization*, Martin Wolf identifies his convictions as being those of the 'classical liberal'. He ends his book *Why Globalization Works* not with 'dry talk' on economics, but with a defence of the Popperian liberal open society.[3] In a similar critical analysis of globalization, Deepak Lal calls for a revival of 'classical liberalism in the twenty-first century'.[4] Tom Friedman begins his most recent best seller explaining optimistically that 'what the flattening of the world means is that we are now connecting all the knowledge centers on the planet together into a single global network, which—if politics and terrorism do not get in the way—could usher in an amazing era of prosperity, innovation, and collaboration, by companies, communities, and individuals'.[5] In his earlier globalization treatise, he even strays into what might be termed a classical liberal 'theology' of global cyberspace: 'God celebrates a universe of such human freedom, because he knows that the only way He is truly manifest in the world is not if He intervenes, but if we all choose sanctity and morality in an environment where we are free to choose anything.'[6] In other words, globalization may or may not turn out well, but the only way to approach it morally is to allow individuals to seek each other out on their own terms.

Writers of the most prominent pro-globalization screeds do not simply applaud commerce. Rather, they celebrate technological and political forces advancing and deepening interaction among people across national boundaries for their consistency with, and advancement of, older ideas about human nature and society of which they approve. Generally speaking, these are the ideas of eighteenth- and nineteenth-century Scottish and English cosmopolitan liberals such as Adam Smith and John Stuart Mill.[7] I would argue, however, that the idealistic roots of globalism actually go much deeper in history and that much of what seems new and radical about the changing relationship between states and societies actually reflects a movement *back* to the way in which concepts such as law and sovereignty were widely understood in the West from the time of the deaths of Aristotle and Alexander to at least the late nineteenth century. What is truly new in Friedman's flat world is the technological change in communications and transport encouraging a revival of the world's oldest systematic body of cosmo-politan political thought.

Stoicism and the Rise of Natural Law

CREON: Now, tell me thou—not in many words, but briefly—knewest thou that an edict had forbidden this?
ANTIGONE: I knew it: could I help it? It was public.
CREON: And thou didst indeed dare to transgress that law?
ANTIGONE: Yes; for it was not Zeus that had published me that edict; not such are the laws set among men by the justice who dwells with the gods below; nor deemed I that thy decrees were of such force, that a mortal could override the unwritten and unfailing statutes of heaven. For their life is not of today or yesterday, but from all time, and no man knows when they were first put forth.

(Sophocles, *Antigone*, 442 BC[8])

Whereas it is today commonplace to think of law as nothing more than the will of a legislator, such thought has been mightily resisted by great thinkers each time it has emerged throughout history. This resistance is perhaps nowhere more eloquently displayed than by Sophocles' female heroine Antigone, who refuses to obey her king's edict against burying her brother, asserting that such an edict, which is contrary to morality and custom, cannot possibly be law and therefore cannot be obeyed.

In the Western tradition, 'good law'—law worthy of the name, worthy of obedience—has always been law that was eternal, in the sense that it was rooted in human nature, or a divine design for mankind. The earliest coherent formal philosophy of law so understood can be traced back to ancient Hellenistic society. Widely known as 'natural law', this philosophy is embedded in the ideas that inspired the American Declaration of Independence and Constitution. But it is also a philosophy that is indelibly linked with the development of commerce and trade over millennia.

Two great bodies of thought are commonly held to lie behind the development of Western civilization, one deriving from classical Greece and the other from Christian-ity. Phillip Cary likens their roles to the left and right legs of the human body.[9] The right, stronger leg represents the conservative moral tradition deriving from Judeo-Christian thinking. The left leg represents the ever-questioning, ever-critical older secular tradition deriving from Socrates, Plato, and Aristotle in fifth- and fourth-century BC Athens.[10] Globalization can be said to have an important foundational philosophy, but it is not to be found in either the classical Greek or Christian traditions. Commerce and the pursuit of wealth—the driving forces behind globalization, even in its cultural manifestations—have no place in the portrait of the good society represented by either. The philosophy underlying the intellectual passion in pro-globalization thought is to be traced back to the historical period between the decline of classicism, with the death of Aristotle in 322 BC, and the emergence of Christianity. This interregnum is the high era of Stoicist thought, which, while its founding fathers, in particular Zeno and Chrysippus, have lacked the cachet of Socrates or Jesus, has been critical in the development of Western legal philosophy and tradition.

The fundamental changes taking place in Greek social and political relations in the course of the late fourth and third centuries BC bear an important parallel with those taking place in global social and political relations today. The notion of man as a fundamentally political animal, a component of a self-governing city-state, the *polis*, steadily lost meaning after the death of Aristotle. Alexander the Great, who died a year before Aristotle, had ushered in a new era of much larger political units and distant rulers. Roman legions destroyed the distinction between Greek and barbarian, and broke down local and tribal loyalties. Political life could no longer be conducted on an intimate scale, and Greek thinkers struggled to redefine the understanding of man as an individual—one who was now more conscious of his isolated role in the universe and simultaneously of his need to relate to many distant others whose values and motivations he did not know. Whereas the intimacy of the *polis* is today virtually unknown, it is the *relative* intimacy of the nation-state which is being challenged for our attention by foreigners with whom we trade, share, correspond, and mingle with ever-greater frequency and intensity.

Stoicism emerged from the flux of the early Hellenistic Age. It elevated reason as the only way to comprehend the order of the universe, an order which no longer seemed apparent in social and political life. At the base of Stoic moral theory was the vision of the individual as a world citizen — an early Davos man. It posited the value of each person and simultaneously the importance of a common human nature, so that all were bound to respect the intrinsic worth of others. For most contemporary Westerners, such an outlook is so ingrained as perhaps to seem banal, but it was not an integral part of the ethics of Aristotle's world, where the significance of an individual derived from his specific function and status as a citizen of the *polis*.[11] But function and status are absent when the individual relates to the wider world, and so he must claim an *inherent* right if he wishes respect as an autonomous being from those residing outside the moral intimacy of the *polis*. Such a claim requires reciprocality and therefore lends ethical meaning to the idea of universality.

As a moral philosophy, Stoicism is exceptionally well suited to a social and political space in which agreement on common ends cannot be assumed, and therefore locates ethics wholly in the *means* through which people interact rather than the ends they seek. This is where the Stoic doctrine of natural law becomes critically important, particularly in a globalizing world. Men can have their own purposes, but their fundamental moral equality, whether 'Greek' or 'barbarian', is manifested in all being subject to the highest possible authority, the law of nature, which is the product of universal reason and above the multiplicity of local customs. In the striking words of Stoicism's most influential thinker, Chrysippus of Stoa (280–206 BC):

> Law is the ruler over all the acts both of gods and men. It must be the director, the governor and the guide in respect to what is honorable and base and hence the standard of what is just and unjust. For all beings that are social by nature the law directs what must be done and forbids what must not be done.[12]

The parallels between the thinking of Chrysippus and the Dutch father of modern international law, Hugo Grotius, nearly nineteen hundred years later is remarkable. When American politicians today invoke the notion that theirs is 'a nation of laws and not of men', they are reprising thought that is distinctly Stoicist.

Stoic philosophy became part of normal life in the Hellenistic world. Arbitration developed into the accepted practice for adjudicating disputes across cities and kingdoms, which necessarily involved a comparison of customs and an appeal to a common standard of equity. The idea of natural law thus emerged as far more than a body of philosophical utopian principle; it emerged as a critical, practical means to promote harmony among civilizations, based on establishing common justice rather than common ends. Importantly, international private commercial arbitration, having all but disappeared during the age of the nation-state ideology of the nineteenth century,[13] saw a massive revival during the 1980s; *The Economist* in 1993 declaring arbitration 'the Big Idea set to dominate legal-reform agendas into the next century'.[14] The social and commercial forces that led to the emergence of international arbitration in the Hellenistic world are identical to those that are driving its conspicuous revival today.

It was the accomplishment of Panaetius of Rhodes (ca. 180–109 BC) to restate Stoicism as a less austere philosophy of humanitarianism, one that was attractive to the Roman aristocratic class, which coveted the learning of Greece but knew little of philosophy. Stoicism appealed to the native Roman virtues of self-control, devotion to duty, and public spiritedness, and it lent some universalist idealism to the gory business of imperial conquest. Stoic legal thinking also lent itself perfectly to the task of accommodating the proliferation of foreign traders in Rome, which required a new body of law based on what private business convention regarded as fair dealing, rather than one based on local custom and ceremony. Lawyers referred to this emerging body of law as *ius gentium* – the law of nations, or that law which natural reason establishes for all men.

Consistent with the commercial imperative behind its germination in republican Rome, *ius gentium* has been invoked throughout the ages in the context of trade. The famous sixteenth-century Dominican theologian and international jurist Francisco de Vitoria (1480–1546), for example, justified Spanish trading rights in the Americas on the basis of the law of nations: 'It is an apparent rule of the *ius gentium* that foreigners may carry on trade, provided they do no hurt to citizens... neither may the native princes hinder their subjects from carrying on trade with the Spanish; nor, on the other hand, may the princes of Spain prevent commerce with the natives.'[15] The great Spanish philosopher and theologian Francisco Suárez (1548–1617) argued that 'it has been established by the *ius gentium* that commercial intercourse shall be free, and it would be a violation of that system of law if such intercourse were prohibited without reasonable cause'.[16] The period's greatest natural-law thinker, Hugo Grotius (1583–1645), saw morality, law, and trade as indelibly intertwined. 'Under the law of nations,' he argued, 'the following principle was established: that all men should be privileged to trade freely with one another.' This 'freedom of trade is based on a primitive right of nations which has a natural and permanent cause; and that right cannot be destroyed, or at all events it may not be destroyed except by the consent of all nations'. Rulers could not prevent subjects from trading with subjects of other states, as the 'right to engage in commerce pertains equally to all peoples'. This was self-evident in that 'God has not willed that nature shall supply every region with all the necessities of life; and furthermore, He has granted pre-eminence in different arts to different nations'.[17] It is not surprising that thinkers living in sixteenth- and seventeenth-century maritime powers like Spain and the Netherlands should see free trade as a dictate of natural law, much as thinkers in cosmopolitan republican Rome saw commerce generally in this light.

Free trade is not, of course, an idea etched in the eternal fabric of the cosmos. Such historical thought is important, however, as it highlights the fact that today's trade mythology—that autarky is the natural state of affairs, and that people should not buy from foreigners except with dispensation from the state—is hardly one with a compelling pedigree.

The Romans distinguished *ius gentium* from *ius civile*, or the civil law peculiar to one state or people. Drawing such a distinction naturally led to the *ius gentium* being seen as higher law, which must through reason, the common faculty of humanity, be perceived as valid and just for all peoples. Although *ius gentium* had no particular philosophical meaning, it came naturally to fuse with the Stoic idea of natural law, translated into Latin as *ius naturale*, which lent the former an association with substantial justice, above and beyond mere ratification of observed practice.[18] The latter had a revolutionary impact in bringing enlightened criticism to bear on custom and ceremony and in promoting the notion of all being equal before the law.[19]

Stoicism's conception of natural law became the foundation of Roman jurisprudence, as it developed from the first century BC onward. It also came to provide a new political theory of the state which was radically different from that of the classical Greek tradition. The idea of legalism — the state itself being a *product* of law, circumscribed by it, and separate from questions of the content of ethical good — was fundamentally a Roman one, and one which has profoundly influenced Western political thought right up to the present. This idea, as we will discuss, is also directly challenged by the Romantic and anti-Enlightenment thought of Rousseau and Hegel, in particular, as well as contemporary anti-globalist thinkers, who aim to elevate the moral status of the nation-state and to reclaim what is seen as its lost authority to impose law on commerce.

It is first and foremost to the great Roman statesman, lawyer, scholar, and writer Cicero (106–43 BC) that we owe the transformation of Stoicism from philosophical ideal to political blueprint. Cicero is the earliest influential expositor of the notion that men should be governed by the rule of law: 'For as the laws govern the magistrate, so the magistrate governs the people, and it can truly be said that the magistrate is a speaking law, and the law a silent magistrate.'[20] The philosophical ideas expounded by the Stoics and Romanized by Cicero underpinned the development of Roman jurisprudence, the great compilation of which was brought to publication as the *Digest* by the Emperor Justinian in 533 AD. Whereas the *Digest*'s authors were lawyers and not philosophers, their body of thought owed everything to the Stoical philosophy of law and was unaffected by the growth of the Christian communities. (Christian influence in the development of law after Constantine is typically seen in pragmatic efforts to establish the legal position of the Church and assist in advancing its policies.) Great Christian scholastic thinkers came, however, to adopt natural-law thinking and were to argue on that basis that rulers could not 'make' law. The most important scholastic theologian, Thomas Aquinas (1224–1274) saw natural law as part of a hierarchy of laws, beneath the 'eternal law' by which God creates living beings and imprints them with a divine purpose, but, in its linking of human reason with God's creative will, standing morally above the civil laws of states, which are circumstantial and valid only in so far as they are consistent with natural law. Thus, according to Aquinas, 'we can only accept the saying that *the ruler's will is law*, on the proviso that the ruler's will is ruled by reason; otherwise a ruler's will is more like law-lessness'.[21]

Whereas the Napoleonic practice of codifying national law based on the Roman inheritance is today dominant in continental Europe and Latin America, Roman law itself shares with uncodified English common law a genesis wholly outside the realm of political legislation. The modern notion that law is nothing more than the expression of will of an authorized legislative body is of recent historical origin, having established itself in the popular consciousness over the course of the nineteenth century. This notion underlies much of the shock and awe visible in the anti-globalization movement today over the spread of transnational private commerce and financial contracting, which is commonly but confusingly often labelled 'antidemocratic' specifically because it is not 'authorized' by a competent law-making body. This is in spite of the fact that it is in 'the practices of the ports and fairs that we must chiefly seek the steps in the evolution of law which ultimately made an open society possible'.[22]

It is in a very tangible sense that law first took on great importance in allowing societies to expand because of the commercial need to accommodate outsiders. In the common-law tradition, it is precisely the spread of new interactions among people that is held to form the basis of the establishment of reasonable expectations, which is then extrapolated by judges to determine what the law 'must be'.

It is startling to note that Chrysippus and Cicero, in their conviction that a man must be treated as an end and never a means, are much closer to Kant and Hume than to Aristotle and Plato: 'Society is made for man, not man for society…

The individual is both logically and ethically prior', according to George Sabine, summarizing the moral basis of natural law.[23] Many contemporary anti-globalists, John Gray perhaps being the most philosophically literate among them, clearly find a common-law model for globalization repugnant precisely in so far as it leaves the emergent spontaneous social order, rather than a legislated general will, in the driver's seat.[24]

Though Christian writers through the late Middle Ages never denied or even doubted the existence of a fundamental, natural law, intrinsically just and therefore binding on all peoples, Christian doctrine did not provide stable ground for maintaining its validity. With the violent schism that emerged in the sixteenth century between Catholics and Protestants, neither the authority of the church nor appeals to Scripture could provide any basis for law inherently binding on both. Protestants in particular came, with justification, to fear that scholastic natural law would be used to undermine the legitimacy of Protestant rulers on the basis that their laws were inconsistent with Catholic theology and metaphysics, and the rulers themselves therefore heretics.[25]

Law so grounded was even less compelling as a basis for governing relations between Christian and non-Christian rulers. In detranscendentalizing and rejustifying natural law and positioning it as the foundation of international law, or law regulating relations between sovereign states, its greatest Renaissance expositor, Hugo Grotius, therefore appealed back beyond Christianity to the Stoic notion of law: law was valid because it sustained 'the social order', an order that, as man has 'an impelling desire for society', is an inherent and necessary good. In stark contrast, however, to modern invocations of 'social justice' as a marker for any particular distribution of wealth adjudged beauteous by the beholder, Grotius's notion of the just social order was that order which emerged *spontaneously* from the application of essential principles of just, voluntary interaction among people:

> To this sphere of law belong the abstaining from that which is another's, the restoration to another of anything of his which we may have, together with any gain which we may have received from it; the obligation to fulfil promises, the

making good of a loss incurred through our fault, and the inflicting of penalties upon men according to their deserts.[26]

Although this post-scholastic idea of natural law still had religious overtones, Grotius actually placed such law above and beyond God. Natural law would be valid 'even if we were to suppose... that God does not exist or is not concerned with human affairs'. And 'Just as even God... cannot cause that two times two should not make four, so He cannot cause that which is intrinsically evil be not evil.'[27] As man is intrinsically a social animal, an observation Grotius traced back to the Stoics, natural law was to be identified with the maintenance of the social order. It is a 'dictate of right reason', to be discovered, as it could in no sense be 'invented' by anyone. As God, should he exist (which Grotius passionately believed he did), cannot make true a proposition that is logically false, religious sanction can neither make edicts into natural law nor negate it.

The development of natural-law thinking in the seventeenth century was, as in the sixteenth century, fundamentally shaped by major contemporary political and social movements. In particular, there was a widely and deeply felt desire among philosophers to accommodate, first, moral principle; second, the political need to found an intellectual basis for justifying sovereign powers in the coalescing nation-states; and third, the practical imperative of stopping religious wars. In the English context, Richard Cumberland (1631–1718) attempted the accommodation by asserting that it was impossible to have metaphysical insight into God's willing of natural law, thereby undercutting the absolute authority of the priests, while asserting that human reason could only allow acquisition of 'probable' knowledge of its essence, thereby undercutting claims of absolute moral authority by a Hobbesian sovereign to impose all law.[28] The moral balance between the spheres of church and state was therefore perilously fragile in this thinking, but its maintenance was nonetheless essential to limit the social dangers of either the church or the state attempting to crush dissent.

David Hume (1711–1776) argued for an understanding of the laws of nations based on utility, rather than any principles of justice that could be derived either from so-called natural theology or sentiments intrinsic to human nature.

Governments come to interact with each other according to certain principles, because they find it in their interest to do so. But this conception of the laws of nations shared with Grotius's conception of natural law among nations the notion that it was the contribution to the maintenance of a certain *social order* that defined the content of such laws. In Hume's thought, this content became apparent only after the rise of commerce between nations, as it was only then that principles of just conduct became useful. He noted that when nations go to war, these laws are routinely violated, as the order and therefore principles undergirding them are no longer useful, and violations therefore no longer excite any sentiment of opprobrium. The implication is clearly that it is *commerce itself* that gives rise to notions of justice between peoples and that attempts to establish enduring principles of just interaction prior to the emergence of mutual commercial interest are wholly inconsistent with human nature as observed over millennia. To the extent, then, that we wish to inculcate enduring international law, commercial ties among people must be permitted to develop.

The first half of the twentieth century marked a dramatic turning away from Stoic ideas of universality. Enlightenment thinking had undermined natural law as a moral system, replacing that system with a utilitarian logic that rendered departures from behaviour consistent with natural law mere symptoms of a change in the incentives of international actors, rather than censorable departures from Stoic 'right reason'. This moral vacuum in political philosophy left considerable intellectual *lebensraum* to Romantic nationalist thinkers like Hegel, a virulent critic of natural law, who shifted the unit of moral analysis from the individual to the state and, in so doing, altered the basis for evaluating ethical action. The nation-state became the guiding principle of the historical development of civilization, with each nation-state having a unique telos toward which it tended according to historical 'necessity'. However confused was Hegel's notion of the dialectic as a logical law underlying history, the ideal-ized state at its apex proved a potent vehicle for twentieth-century reactionary nationalism. It took two world wars for Western Europe to turn its back on this dark development.

From Natural Law to Global Commercial Law

Between contracting parties there is a closer society than the common society of mankind. (Hugo Grotius[29])

Throughout recorded history new forms of trading have disturbed the established political order. Through all the groupings and regroupings of peoples, the shifts in power and the development of political ideas, the trader has woven and rewoven his web of international economic integration. (J.B. Condliffe[30])

Stoicism, in the words of a classic 1937 text on political theory, 'had boldly undertaken to reinterpret political ideas to fit the Great State'[31]—at that time, essentially the whole Mediterranean world. Pro-globalists today are making similar (if as of yet inchoate) attempts to refashion political ideas to fit the modern Great State. James Bennett's *The Anglosphere Challenge* is the most direct in seeing the growth of cross-border forms of organic law as being fundamental to generating international 'harmony without homogeniz-ation'.[32] He sees the English-speaking world as being the most natural laboratory in which such a process would develop, owing to a shared heritage of ever-evolving, non-statute-based common law. Indeed, the tradition of English common law shares much with the natural-law notion of legitimate law being 'discovered' by judges rather than 'created' by rulers. Historically, the most influential state-ment of the primacy of common law over legislation is the decision of the chief justice of England's Common Court of Pleas, Sir Edward Coke, in *Dr. Bonham's Case* of 1610:

In many cases, the common law will controul Acts of Parliament, and sometimes adjudge them to be utterly void; for when an Act of Parliament is against common right and reason, or repugnant, or impossible to be performed, the common law will controul it, and adjudge such Act to be void.[33]

In the common-law tradition, life comes first, and law follows in train according to the expectations established by repeated social interactions. Former French foreign minister Hubert Védrine sees common law as one of globalization's essential principles; these are 'principles that', in his view, 'correspond neither to the French tradition nor to French culture'. Védrine sees globalization, not surprisingly, as inconsistent with a French identity 'built upon a strong central state [that] was painstakingly built by jurists'.[34] It is indeed difficult to reconcile a state so characterized to the spread of organic forms of law.

Even outside the realm of common-law systems, commercial practice has throughout history driven the codification of systems of law, and not vice versa. 'The merchants who began the process of transforming European feudal society into the commercial, democratic, international trading world of our day', argued historian J.B. Condliffe, 'were merchant adventurers in the crudest sense. Unless we realise this fact, we cannot understand the continuous struggles between them and the church in its efforts to apply the doctrines of Canon law.'[35]

The Rise of the 'Lex Mercatoria'

Contract law has long and largely been driven by the shared needs of international traders.[36] The hugely important *Lex Mercatoria*, or the international 'laws merchant', which developed privately and spontaneously to govern commercial transactions, dates from the twelfth century, before the consolidation of states.

In Europe's pre-national stage, the *Lex Mercatoria* consisted of a 'body of truly international customary rules governing the cosmopolitan community of international merchants'[37] on the high seas and at commercial fairs.[38] Its emergence corresponded with a rapid expansion of European agricultural production, the accompanying dramatic increase in city size, and the consequent rise of a new class of professional merchants that marked the eleventh and twelfth centuries. Europe's urban population grew roughly tenfold from 1050 to 1200; its general population perhaps doubled, and its merchant class grew from a few thousand to several hundreds of thousands. 'Outsourcing' was already emergent nearly a millennium before Lou Dobbs declared it treason. English merchants bought wool from local manors and, instead of processing it locally, sold it on to Flemish merchants. They in turn distributed it to Flemish spinners and weavers to be worked into cloth, which was then re-imported back into England to be sold at international fairs.

All aspects of the commerce, from transport to insurance to financing to sale, were governed by the transnational *Lex Mercatoria*.[39]

Merchant law, as it evolved, was based on the customs of maritime port cities and inland fairs and markets. It came to be codified in a number of different forms. The Amalfitan Table of 1095, a collection of maritime laws, was an example of merchant custom becoming written legislation. Adopted by the Republic of Amalfi on the Italian coast, its authority spread throughout all the city republics of Italy. A compilation of maritime judgments by the court of Oléron, an island off the French Atlantic coast, became a form of judge-made common law. It was adopted by seaport towns of the Atlantic Ocean and North Sea, including those of England, around 1150. Norms of merchant practice also evolved into written commercial instruments of standardized character, disputes over which came to be adjudicated in specialized mercantile courts presided over by elected representatives of the merchants themselves.[40]

The importance of the *Lex Mercatoria* as transnational law was reflected in the fact that by the late eleventh century, transnational trade (generally conducted at large international fairs held at regular intervals throughout Europe, or more regularly in the leading market towns and cities) predominated over local trade across much of Europe. Its universal character is stressed in much early writing on it. The chancellor of England wrote in 1473, for example, that foreign merchants who brought suits before him would have them determined 'by the law of nature in chancery... which is called by some the law merchant, which is the law universal of the world'. Gerard Malynes, author of the first English book on the *Lex Mercatoria*, wrote in 1622, 'I have entitled the book according to the ancient name of Lex Mercatoria... because it is customary law approved by the authority of all kingdoms and commonweals, and not a law established by the sovereignty of any prince'. Its enduring nature is attested to by Lord Blackstone writing in the mid-eighteenth century:

> The affairs of commerce are regulated by the law of their own called the Law Merchant or Lex Mercatoria, which all nations agree in and take notice of, and it is particularly held

to be part of the law of England which decides the causes of
merchants by the general rules which obtain in all commercial matters relating to domestic trade, as for instance, in
the drawing, the acceptance, and the transfer of Bills of
Exchange.[41]

The *Lex Mercatoria* became part of national law, while maintaining its transnational character and authority, through the
patronage provided to it by emerging national political authorities. The *Magna Carta* of 1215 provided that 'All merchants
shall have safe conduct to go and come out of and into
England, and to stay in and travel through England by land
and water for purposes of buying and selling, free of legal
tolls, in accordance with ancient and just customs'. Such
ideas came to be reflected in reciprocal rights of individual
property holding and commerce provided for in treaties,
such as those which evolved among Italian cities from at
least the twelfth century on. So-called 'staple towns' in
fourteenth-century England, Wales, and Ireland—where
trade in wool, leather, lead, and other staple products was
conducted—were required to apply the *Lex Mercatoria* in all
matters relating to the staple, and they granted resident
foreign merchants political rights that today would be considered incredible. Such foreigners were legally entitled to
vote in elections for the local mayor, who was required to
have knowledge of the *Lex Mercatoria*, and composed half the
jury in all trials involving a merchant stranger and an
Englishman.[42]

The *Lex Mercatoria* was absorbed into English common
law in the seventeenth century, where judges, who were paid
out of litigation fees, initially treated it with some contempt.
Competition from Continental civil-law countries, however,
which frequently proved more accommodative to the *Lex
Mercatoria*, ultimately forced English judges to recognize
commercial custom in international trade in order to attract
cases.[43] In the United States, widespread early adoption of
the practice of commercial arbitration, as well as the history
of state jurisdictional competition, contributed to greater
acceptance of the *Lex Mercatoria* than in England. The US
Uniform Commercial Code thus reflects the fact that
business practice and custom are the primary source of
substantial law.[44] 'The positive law of the [American] realm',

Leon Trakman notes in his history of the *Lex Mercatoria*, 'was forced to conform to the mandate of the merchants, not vice-versa.'[45]

The Modern 'Lex Mercatoria'

The *Lex Mercatoria*, even in today's world of autonomous nation-states, still has vital importance as a form of commercial law. The *Lex Mercatoria* today is a combination of trade usages, model contracts, standard clauses, general legal principles, and international commercial arbitration, underpinned by a body of expert legal writing intended to facilitate its coherence and precision. It is arguably of considerably more consequence today than it was in medieval times, as non-simultaneous trade was much rarer then, owing to difficulties of enforcement where international merchants interacted only infrequently.

Of the modern *Lex Mercatoria*'s components, trade usage is the most important. Defined in the US Uniform Commercial Code as 'any practice or method of dealing having such regularity of observance in a place, vocation or trade as to justify an expectation that it will be observed with respect to the transaction in question',[46] its importance lies in the fact that commercial behaviour considered normal in a given industry will guide the application of both private arbitration and public common-law litigation. In other words, today, as throughout Western history, the way in which people freely choose to conduct commercial transactions with each other across borders is examined by both private and public tribunals in order to *discover* what the commercial law must be.

To what extent is the *Lex Mercatoria* truly 'law'? Legal scholars holding an 'autonomist' view of the governance of international commerce maintain that the fact that traders conduct cross-border business in a consistent manner and act as if bound by behavioural precedents is evidence of an autonomous legal order in operation[47] — a 'Grotian regime', in the vocabulary of international-relations scholarship. Those holding a 'positivist' view agree that the modern *Lex Mercatoria* is effectively law but insist that this is so *because* it has become codified in national laws.[48] They share with autonomists the conviction that international custom and standard forms of contract effectively create law unto themselves, and they note that private commercial parties routinely choose the law under which their relations will be governed and utilize international commercial arbitration— through bodies such as the London Court of Arbitration, the International Chamber of Commerce in Paris, and the World Bank's International Center for the Settlement of Investment Disputes—in lieu of state courts. Furthermore, commercial trade law has become substantially harmonized across nations through conventions on international commercial arbitration, institutional rules for arbitral tribunals, and legislation recognizing awards based on the *Lex Mercatoria*. The French Arbitration Decree of 1981, for example, forbids French courts reviewing arbitration awards from interfering with arbitrator decisions regarding applicable rules, provided that they are consistent with the choice of the parties. The decree reflects the fact that governments today compete to have both business and arbitration conducted within their jurisdictions—just as medieval lords did, generating revenues from sales levies and entry tolls associated with merchant fairs.[49] The force of the cosmopolitan principles of the *Lex Mercatoria* ultimately relies, however, according to the positivists, on the willingness of states to confront noncompliance with coercive sanction.[50] But this fact is entirely consistent with the centuries-old argument of natural law scholars, such as Grotius, that rulers traditionally obtained their legitimacy through their commitment to *enforcing* the law—law being coeval with society itself—and only undermined it through attempts to impose law which was not already recognized as such by the populace.

People around the globe today have been conditioned to see *governments* as the creators of cross-border commerce, in agreeing with other governments to remove trade barriers which their predecessors imposed to assert sovereignty. State prohibition of trade with foreigners is widely seen as the natural state of affairs, leading to the inference that globalization of business is being deliberately created by trade-liberalization policies rather than being ratified by them. But the development of the *Lex Mercatoria*, as with its conspicuous revival today, was driven from below by traders— stimulated, for example, by the rapid expansion of European agricultural productivity in the eleventh and twelfth centuries—rather than from above by rulers decreeing some hitherto unknown right to trade. And just as medieval trade could not have expanded and flourished without the foundation of a cosmopolitan private commercial law—standing in for conflicting and inappropriate local public laws—so globalization of trade today would never be possible on the basis of agreements among governments simply to allow private trade or to reduce taxes on it. A legal framework for the actual conduct of trade is necessary, and that framework is a spontaneous private creation.

Many anti-globalists see the deliberate creation of new law as necessary precisely to pre-empt the organic development of common international commercial practice and expectations and instead to dictate *ex nihilo* the form and scope of permissible facets of globalization. John Gray goes so far as to argue that the actual content of such law is less important than the fact that there be a regime capable of imposing it:

> A regime of global governance is needed in which world markets are managed so as to promote the cohesion of societies and the integrity of states. Only a framework of global regulation—of currencies, capital movements, trade and environmental conservation—can enable the creativity of the world economy to be harnessed in the service of human needs. The specific policies that should be implemented by such institutions are less important, for the purposes of the present inquiry, than the recognition of the need for a new global regime.[51]

If Gray were to be taken seriously, the coercive power that would have to be bestowed upon this new regime— regulating 'currencies, capital movements, trade and environmental conservation' with the express purpose of 'promot[ing] the cohesion of societies and the integrity of states'[52]—would be such that it is difficult to imagine what aspects of private interaction with foreigners could any longer be considered the prerogative of individuals themselves. Gray's thinking embodies the primal constructivist belief, which he fiercely derided two decades ago, that only actions that deliberately aim at purported common purposes can serve common needs. There is perhaps no other realm of global social interaction in which such thinking is so demon-

strably mistaken as in that of money. Historically, governments observing the political and economic importance of
money have chosen in consequence to monopolize it and in
the process have wreaked far more damage on people's
livelihoods than any private economic behaviour condemned
by Gray. As a matter of historical experience, it is also critical
to understand that Gray, and not the globalists, is the radical
in calling for the legal cart to be put in front of the commercial horse.

Global Private Law with Private Enforcement

In an article entitled 'Private Justice in a Global Economy:
From Litigation to Arbitration', Oxford political-economy
professor Walter Mattli traces the re-emergence of private,
nationless law, which is a striking and almost wholly neglected aspect of globalization. 'Today's scene', Mattli observes, 'calls to memory the flourishing era of arbitration
practices and institutions associated with the international
trade fairs of medieval Europe.' British Lord Justice Kerr in
1990 described the rise of international arbitration as 'something of a world movement'.[53] Roughly 90 percent of all
cross-border contracts now contain a private arbitration
clause.[54] Scholarly neglect of the phenomenon is largely a reflection of the myopic focus of international-relations writing
on what *governments* do, under the assumption that the way
in which private actors manage their commercial relations
cross-border must necessarily have been deliberately enabled
by governments.

The number of commercial arbitration forums has grown
about tenfold since the 1970s to over one hundred today.
One of the most popular of these, the International Court of
Arbitration (ICA), releases basic data, though infrequently,
on the volume of cases coming before it. ICA saw 580 filings
in 2003, up from 450 in 1997, 333 in 1991, an annual average
of 272 between 1977 and 1987, and an annual average of 55
between 1923 and 1977. The 1,584 litigants in 2003 came from
123 different countries. The organization has over seven
thousand member enterprises across these countries.[55]

Just like the medieval merchant courts which sat in fairs,
markets, and seaport towns, today's private tribunals provide arbitrators with specialist industry knowledge to

resolve commercial disputes. In the absence of an agreement between the parties on the applicable rules of law, the arbitral tribunal determines them on the basis of the specific contract provisions and, importantly, general trade practice. In other words, the law *follows* accepted behaviour in the industry, rather than *dictating* it. Tribunals often deal with highly technical matters, such as intellectual property in software, where applicable public law can be very limited, as illustrated in a seminal 1983 case involving IBM and Fujitsu. The privacy, speed, and flexibility of arbitration, relative to public courts, are major attractions for commercial enterprises, just as they were in medieval private courts: medieval sea merchants, for example, typically demanded that cases be settled 'from tide to tide according to the ancient law marine and ancient customs of the sea... without mixing the law civil with the law marine'.[56] And just like the medieval merchant courts, arbitration forums like ICA rely on reputation and commercial ostracism as enforcement tools. ICA decisions have a strong record for implementation, with only about 6 percent of awards being challenged by the losing party in a national court and 0.5 percent ultimately being set aside by such a court.[57]

As successful as arbitration has been in the private sphere, states have proven exceptionally reluctant to use it; or where they have used it, they have typically asserted absolute immunity when it comes to enforcement. Hostility to arbitration is sustained by the doctrine of inviolable state sovereignty.

Global Private Law with Public Enforcement

Public common-law courts are also used to adjudicate and enforce private law, particularly where the question is well defined, the law is clear, and the benefits of clarity outweigh those of flexibility. This is typically the case in the international financial markets, where the subject of dispute is typically whether one party has defaulted on an obligation.

There is no better example of James Bennett's international common law in operation than the global market in financial instruments. As far back as 1842, US Supreme Court Associate Justice Joseph Story wrote that 'The law respecting negotiable instruments may be truly declared in the language of Cicero, adopted by Lord Mansfield... to be in great measure, not the law of a single country only, but of the commercial world'.[58] Today, it is the over-the-counter (OTC) derivatives market that is the embodiment of global private law.

The OTC derivatives market is an interbank market for two types of financial contract in particular, known as swaps and options — promises to trade one set of future financial flows for another, in a given currency or across currencies. At the end of 2007, the notional value of interest-rate swaps, cross-currency swaps, interest-rate options, credit-default swaps, and equity derivatives outstanding was $454 trillion, or twenty-six times what it was in 1995 and 525 times what it was in 1987. OTC derivatives account for 83 percent of aggregate-derivatives trading, the remainder being traded on organized exchanges.

Whereas $454 trillion is a staggeringly large number, it is important not to overstate its economic significance. Notional values vastly exceed the actual risk exposure that market participants take. For example, a swap of a variable interest rate for a 5-percent fixed rate on a $10 million notional amount commits the parties to annual payments to each other of about $500,000, with differences in future payments depending on how interest rates move in the future. Consequently, the typical derivative involves a credit exposure equal to only a small fraction of its notional value.[59] Nonetheless, booming portions of this market, in particular credit-default swaps, have seen a dramatic increase in counterparty risk, which has thereby compelled major participants to collaborate in the establishment of centralized trade netting and clearing facilities of the type found on organized exchanges.

What is truly remarkable about the size of this market and its growth is the fact that it has no territory. It is not a US market or a UK market or even an 'offshore' market. Its legal foundation is a privately produced document of about thirty-two pages — unimaginably brief by the standards of US statutory regulation — laying out the common rules for each derivatives transaction and specifying that any dispute resulting from the transaction will be adjudicated by a common-law English or New York State court, as per the specified preference of the parties. This 'ISDA Master Agreement' can be downloaded for free from the website of the International Swaps and Derivatives Association,[60] a global industry body, founded in 1985, with about 670 member institutions located in 50 countries.

The fact that people from around the globe, the vast majority of whom have never met, would agree routinely to exchange millions of dollars in financial assets based on thirty-two downloadable pages of Anglo-American market and legal jargon, unauthorized by any sovereign body, and to subject any subsequent disputes to a UK or New York court is nothing short of an astounding sociological phenomenon. Just how astounding was brought to life in the mid-1990s, after passage of the French language law colloquially called '*la loi Toubon*', after the name of the French culture minister. The law (subsequently partially struck down by the French constitutional court) caused a brief panic in the French financial markets in appearing to undermine the legal validity of English-language contracts such as the ISDA Master Agreement. Whereas one might suppose that French bankers would prefer French-language contracts, at least among themselves, this is not the case where a common understanding of the legal meaning of French contract provisions is absent. An ISDA contract is understood, in the deepest sense, by virtue of a global pattern of behaviour having established itself around the contract's repeated bilateral exchange—such behaviour having been reinforced by decisions of common-law UK and New York courts.[61]

This phenomenon of global private law developing around financial contracts has been virtually ignored by legal scholars,[62] which is testimony to the degree to which the profession has been trained to think of law as being the exclusive handiwork of governments. The effect of this mindset is that there is little general knowledge of the degree to which growing international exchange is producing enduring patterns of common behaviour and expectation, which are in turn forming the basis for new law.

What is striking about the financial markets in an age of instant global communication is that they could only have been created and sustained internationally on such a scale to the degree that all the primary elements of Grotius's natural law among peoples had come to be widely accepted among the myriad dispersed participants, irrespective of their cultural upbringings: the sanctity of private property, contracting in good faith, accepting responsibility for harm to another, and sanction in accordance with harm done. The banker in London and Dubai may have vastly different understandings of the good life and the origins and purpose of existence, but they must nonetheless adopt a common commitment to fair dealing in order to participate in the same global commercial network. Those who do not are invariably obliged to depart, as no one will deal with them.

Past and Future Linked

> The view that law transcends politics — the view that at any given moment, or at least in its historical development, law is distinct from the state — seems to have yielded increasingly to the view that law is at all times basically an instrument of the state, that is, a means of effectuating the will of those who exercise political authority. (Harold Berman[63])

The technology of modern globalization is clearly new and consequential, socially as well as economically. Computerization and the internet in particular have vastly lowered communications and production costs, enabling the creation of new global markets and supply chains and changing the way each of us lives his or her life in consequence. Innovations in telegraph and shipping technology in the late nineteenth century were comparably important in expanding global commerce and changing lifestyles.

Dubious, however, is the popular notion that modern globalization is new in its challenging of timeless tenets of state sovereignty and authority. The constructivist mythology which emerged in the seventeenth and eighteenth centuries, that law worthy of the name must be, and must have been, consciously *designed* to achieve specific ends has in our time come to dominate popular thinking and has been bluntly confronted by the spontaneous, 'unauthorized' emergence of economic and social orders across national legal jurisdictions. Scholars and the public intelligentsia who reflect on the palpable manifestations of globalization are typically struck by its emergence in an institutional vacuum — national law appears impotent, and supranational law is yet to emerge. The implication frequently drawn is that there is therefore something fundamentally illegitimate about globalization.

Yet the history of law in the Western world, going back to ancient Greece, shows clearly that it is not possible to separate the activity of private exchange from the evolution of law and the evolution of thought about law. It is property that first gives rise to established notions of justice among people. Trade is much older than states; indeed it is older than agriculture itself.[64] Principles of just interaction emerge only after sentiments of mutual commercial interest take hold. And it is specifically in dealings with foreigners that it was necessary for law to develop that was independent of any ruler's will. Good law was always old law, and old law is what emerged by dint of its consistency with what people came to expect as just behaviour from others. Legitimacy is the cornerstone of stable government, and rulers established legitimacy by demonstrating appropriate reverence for the law and the ability to enforce it.

The glue that melded the Greek and barbarian peoples under the Macedonians and Romans was commerce. The creation of the Hellenistic world, the earliest 'globalization', was founded on a historically remarkable degree of economic freedom underpinned by the development of a Roman civil law, which was almost entirely the product of law-finding by jurists, rather than legislation.

The fact that belief in a 'natural law' rooted in the intrinsic social nature of human existence, true irrespective of even the wishes of God or gods, persisted from Chrysippus to Grotius with few credible intellectual challenges is testimony to a powerfully enduring conviction that a healthy society cannot be governed by the unfettered will of legislators. But what relevance can that have to our day and age, when practical people know full well that legislators can and will use their powers to control international commerce as they wish? The answer lies in Hume's observation that it is *commerce itself* that gives rise to symmetrical sentiments among people of different nations that there are identifiable principles of just conduct between them. Legislation does not give rise to such sentiments. New rules may or may not be enforceable, but they do not change what people view as being just or unjust behaviour between them.

Sovereign legislatures are, of course, generally empowered to ban virtually any and all forms of exchange with foreigners. Irrespective of current passions against 'outsourcing' to foreigners or receiving capital flows from them, however, an art director in New York will never see it as just for her government to stop her contracting a website designer in Buenos Aires, nor will the designer see it as just for his government to restrict his access to foreign money. As Hume believed of all international law, any sustainable bonds of cooperative human behaviour will ultimately be fashioned on shared feelings of economic interest. Globalization is simply what we choose to call the ongoing spontaneous creation of such bonds of shared interest across borders.

---

1   This paper is based on chapter 2 of a book by the author: Benn Steil and Manuel Hinds, *Money, Markets, and Sovereignty* (New Haven, CT: Yale University Press, 2009).

2   John Micklethwait and Adrian Wooldridge, *A Future Perfect: The Challenge and Hidden Promise of Globalization* (New York: Random House, 2000): 336.

3   See Martin Wolf, *Why Globalization Works* (New Haven, CT: Yale University Press, 2004).

4   See Deepak Lal, *Reviving the Invisible Hand: The Case for Classical Liberalism in the Twenty-First Century* (Princeton, NJ: Princeton University Press, 2006).

5   Thomas L. Friedman, *The World is Flat: A Brief History of the Twenty-First Century* (New York: Farrar, Straus and Giroux, 2005): 8.

6   Thomas L. Friedman, *The Lexus and the Olive Tree* (New York: Anchor, 1999): 469–70.

7   Regarding Mill, this would be the Mill represented by 'On Liberty', rather than the Mill reflected in the more statist 'Principles of Political Economy'.

8   Sophocles, *Antigone* (ca. 442 BC). Translated by R.C. Jebb at http://classics.mit.edu/Sophocles/antigone.html.

9   See Phillip Cary, 'Lecture 13', in *Great Minds of the Western Intellectual Tradition*, part 2 (video production) (The Teaching Company, 2000).

10   The period beginning in 312 AD with Constantine's conversion to Christianity may be likened to the torso, or the conjunction of the traditions of Jerusalem and Athens. Medieval scholastic thought may be said broadly to represent the intellectual merging of theology and philosophy. It is commonly dated to begin in the early sixth century – with the ascendance of the scholar Boethius and his

injunction 'as far as you are able, [to] fuse faith with reason' — and to end in the fourteenth century with the thinking of William of Ockham, who rejected this conflation and insisted on a radical separation between matters of fact and faith. The Renaissance, reclaiming and renovating the classical tradition, may then be likened to the left arm, and the Reformation, reclaiming and renovating the biblical tradition, to the right arm. Finally, modernity, the head, positions reason and faith as antagonists: with the Enlightenment, reason comes to despise faith, while in the Romantic epoch, faith re-emerges as an elemental, pre-rational, human-centred truth, beyond and prior to reason.

11 See George H. Sabine, *A History of Political Theory* (New York: Holt, 1937).
12 As quoted in Sabine, *History of Political Theory*: 150.
13 See Walter Mattli, 'Private Justice in a Global Economy: From Litigation to Arbitration', *International Organization*, 55 (Autumn 2001): 919–47.
14 'Survey on the Legal Profession', *The Economist* (18–24 July 1992): 17.
15 As quoted in Douglas A. Irwin, *Against the Tide: An Intellectual History of Free Trade* (Princeton, NJ: Princeton University Press, 1996): 21.
16 Francisco Suárez, 'De Ligibus, Ac Deo Legislature, 1612', in *Selections from Three Works of Francisco Suárez*, S.J. 2 (Oxford: Clarendon Press, 1934): 347.
17 As quoted in Irwin, *Against the Tide*: 22–3.
18 See, for example, Peter Stein, *Roman Law in European History* (New York: Cambridge University Press, 1999).
19 See Sabine, *History of Political Theory*.
20 *Laws*: III, 1, 2. As quoted in Sabine, *History of Political Theory*: 166.
21 Thomas Aquinas, *Summa Theologiae: A Concise Translation*, ed. Timothy McDermott (Westminster, MD: Christian Classics, 1989): 90.1.
22 Friedrich Hayek, *Law, Legislation and Liberty: A New Statement of the Liberal Principles of Justice and Political Economy*, 1 (Chicago, IL: University of Chicago Press, 1973): 82.
23 Sabine, *History of Political Theory*: 433.
24 In spite of Gray, in his recent anti-globalist incarnation, expressing profound contempt for Enlightenment thinkers such as Thomas Jefferson, it is notable that he shares with Jefferson a respect only for law determined and imposed from above, by an empowered legislature with a precise social end in mind. Jefferson loathed common law. See, for example, Jefferson's letter to Edmund Randolph (18 August 1799), http://odur.let.rug.nl/~usa/P/tj3/writings/brf/jefl128.htm
25 See Ian Hunter and David Saunders, 'Introduction', in *Natural Law and Civil Sovereignty: Moral Right and State Authority in Early Modern*

Political Thought, ed. Ian Hunter and David Saunders (New York: Palgrave Macmillan, 2002).

26 Hugo Grotius, as quoted in Sabine, *History of Political Theory*: 423.

27 *Ibid.*: 424.

28 See Hunter and Saunders, 'Introduction'.

29 As quoted in Martin Wight, *Systems of States* (Leicester: Leicester University Press, 1977): 127.

30 J.B. Condliffe, *The Commerce of Nations* (New York: Allen & Unwin, 1951): 832.

31 Sabine, *History of Political Theory*: 158.

32 James C. Bennett, *The Anglosphere Challenge: Why the English-Speaking Nations Will Lead the Way in the Twenty-First Century* (Lanham, MD: Rowman & Littlefield, 2004): 250.

33 *Dr. Bonham's Case* (1610) 8 Co. Rep. 107a, 118a. As quoted in Ian Williams, 'Dr. Bonham's Case and "Void" Statutes', *Journal of Legal History*, 27 (August 2006): 111–28, 111.

34 Hubert Védrine, *France in an Age of Globalization*, trans. Philip H. Gordon (Washington, DC: Brookings Institution Press, 2001): 17.

35 Condliffe, *The Commerce of Nations*: 23.

36 See, for example, Harold J. Berman and Colin Kaufman, 'The Law of International Commercial Transactions (Lex Mercatoria)', *Harvard International Law Journal*, 19 (Winter 1978): 221–77.

37 Clive M. Schmitthoff, 'International Business Law: A New Law Merchant', *Current Law and Social Problems*, 129 (1961).

38 See Jarrod Wiener, *Globalization and the Harmonization of Law* (London: Pinter, 1999).

39 See Harold J. Berman, *Law and Revolution: The Formation of the Western Legal Tradition* (Cambridge, MA: Harvard University Press, 1983).

40 See, for example, Berman, *Law and Revolution*; and Henry Mather, 'Choice of Law for International Sales Issues Not Resolved by the CISG', *Journal of Law and Commerce*, 20 (Spring 2001): 155–208. Available online at http://www.cisg.law.pace.edu/cisg/biblio/mather1.html.

41 As quoted in Berman, *Law and Revolution*: 342.

42 See Berman, *Law and Revolution*.

43 See, for example, Bruce L. Benson, 'The Spontaneous Evolution of Commercial Law', *Southern Economic Journal*, 55 (January 1989): 644–61.

44 See Benson, 'Spontaneous Evolution'.

45 Leon E. Trakman, *The Law Merchant: The Evolution of Commercial Law* (Littleton, CO: Rothman, 1983).

46 See, for example, Oliver Volckart and Antje Mangels, 'Are the Roots of the Modern Lex Mercatoria Really Medieval?', *Southern Economic Journal*, 65 (January 1999): 427–50.

[47] See, for example, Thomas E. Carbonneau, ed., *Lex Mercatoria and Arbitration: A Discussion of the New Law Merchant* (Dobbs Ferry, NY: Transnational Juris, 1990).

[48] See Wiener, *Globalization and Harmonization*.

[49] See, for example, John Gerard Ruggie, 'Territoriality and Beyond: Problematizing Modernity in International Relations', *International Organization*, 47 (December 1993): 139–74, 154–5.

[50] Clive Schmitthoff is the primary advocate for this positivist view of the *Lex Mercatoria*. For a literature review, see Wiener, *Globalization and Harmonization*.

[51] John Gray, *False Dawn: The Delusions of Global Capitalism* (New York: New Press, 1998): 199–200.

[52] *Ibid.*: 199.

[53] Mattli, 'Private Justice': 920.

[54] See, for example, Volckart and Mangels, 'Roots of the Modern *Lex Mercatoria*'.

[55] Data from International Court of Arbitration; Mattli, 'Private Justice'.

[56] W. Mitchell, *An Essay on the Early History of the Law Merchant: Being the Yorke Prize Essay for the Year 1903* (Cambridge: Cambridge University Press, 1904).

[57] See W. Laurence Craig, William W. Park and Jan Paulsson, *International Chamber of Commerce Arbitration*, 2nd ed. (New York: Oceana, 1990); René David, *Arbitration in International Trade* (Boston, MA: Kluwer Law and Taxation, 1985).

[58] *Swift v. Tyson*, 16 Peters (41 U.S.) 1, 19 (1842).

[59] See, for example, Financial Economists Roundtable, 'Statement on Derivative Markets and Financial Risk' (26 September 1994) for an overly sanguine perspective: http://www.stanford.edu/~wfsharpe/art/fer/fer94.htm

[60] Available from http://www.isda.org/

[61] To be sure, the utility of the ISDA Master Agreement could be diminished in jurisdictions that refused to confirm the enforceability of certain of its provisions. Dozens of countries, however, have given assurances that its provisions would, if challenged, be enforced as law, with some countries, such as France and Mexico, passing legislation drafted by ISDA itself. See Frank Partnoy, 'ISDA, NASD, CFMA, and SDNY: The Four Horsemen of Derivatives Regulation?', *Brookings-Wharton Papers on Financial Services* (2002): 213–52.

[62] Frank Partnoy is perhaps alone in calling attention to its importance. See Partnoy, 'ISDA, NASD, CFMA, and SDNY'.

[63] Berman, *Law and Revolution*: 38.

[64] See, for example, Friedrich Hayek, *The Fatal Conceit: The Errors of Socialism* (London: Routledge, 1988): 38–47; Richard E. Leakey, *The Making of Mankind* (New York: Dutton, 1981): 212.

Louis W. Pauly

Supraterritorial Obligations, the Global Economy, and the Changing Politics of Responsibility

Pressures to create new instruments to govern global risks are coming at policymakers from all sides. Financial shocks, footloose weapons of terror, fast-spreading pathogens—all suggest the need for innovation in risk mitigation, burden sharing, and crisis management. Functionalists foresee the inevitable migration of requisite authority to govern such risks to regional and systemic levels. Sceptics argue for the reassertion of government at the more feasible level of the nation-state and for voluntary cooperation with other governments to the extent necessary. Pessimists don't see any prospect for effective control at any level.

All three positions lead us nowhere. Choices are required. Many of the challenges facing us involve global risks that cannot decisively be addressed at levels below the system as a whole, and there aren't any solid historical precedents or otherwise plausible reasons for expecting a kind of non-political mechanism to deliver results. A more hopeful and more realistic argument is proposed here, one using the natural-law tradition of moral theorizing and the disciplined use of reason to understand the current and likely continuing transformation of political authority in a dynamic, reflexive, and increasingly global context.

This paper begins in a manner akin to a weekend spent with former president George W. Bush at his ranch in Crawford, Texas. It starts with a brush-clearing exercise, focused on the concept of political responsibility. After tying that concept to the rightly valued principles of individual and collective autonomy, it moves on to terrain any libertarian might comfortably occupy, contrasting responsibility with the idea of accountability actually practised at the international level in the regulation of the market economy and the management of associated crises. Here the argument leaves the ranch and parts company with the most fervent promoters of spontaneous market solutions to global problems. It acknowledges that the organization of world politics remains decisively influenced by the human will to power and an associated proclivity to violence. It contends that real-world polities are unable to liberate themselves entirely from territorial imperatives but are still quite able to conceive and to implement responsible policies to govern global risks.

Such policies are today designed through collaborative mechanisms across conventional political boundaries and are led by one or more key states. Both leaders and followers are becoming habituated to working together, however reluctantly. They do so mainly through domestic decision-making structures that are ever more open to external considerations. Tomorrow, deeper and more complex collaboration will be required, and it likely will reflect a distinct variability and diversity in systemic requirements across issue-areas.

Autonomy and Responsibility

Debates about the meaning and the implications of globalization prompt deeper reflection on the responsibility of individuals and groups of individuals for the impact of their choices on other individuals and other groups. Here we find ourselves on the ancient terrain of natural law. Little wonder, then, that this well-developed tradition of thought is today piquing fresh interest.

Responsibility is meaningless in the absence of the concept of autonomy.[1] Only individuals and groups possessing some requisite degree of autonomy can make decisions for which they may be held responsible. Decisions aimed at governing risks, global in nature or not, therefore must be understood against the necessary prior condition of freedom. 'Man is made in the image of God', states St. Thomas Aquinas in the *Summa Theologiae,* and therefore he 'is intelligent and free in judgment and master of himself'. John Finnis persuasively asserts that even an atheist convinced that all things are permitted must nonetheless 'appreciate that he is "responsible" — obliged to act with freedom and authenticity, and to will the liberty of other persons equally with his own — in choosing what he is to be; and all this, because, prior to any choice of his, man is and is-to-be free'.[2]

Most human beings in most human societies most of the time place a high value on their personal autonomy and on the autonomy of the social group closest to them; justifying that collective autonomy is their shared sense of the common good. In short, free persons embedded in communities organized around the common good are in a position to shape the conditions of their existence to the fullest extent possible and without external interference.

Personal and collective autonomy as put into practical effect in our time to harness, direct, and contain power arose out of the idea of individualism. As Charles Taylor puts it, 'The picture of society is that of individuals who come together to form a political entity against a certain pre-existing moral background and with certain ends in view'.[3] Actual societies, of course, are not all constructed the same way or with the same results, and they hold very different understandings of individualism and of how individuals come together around the common good, not just the dominant Eurocentric one familiar to Aquinas. In any case, the autonomous individual wherever he lives must in some basic way be capable of self-government, or literally 'giving himself laws'. And something similar must apply to collectivities of individuals if they are to be considered meaningfully autonomous. This sense of autonomy has developed into the modern notion of the sovereignty of the people and related ideas of self-government and self-determination.

Political institutions codify and make routine the expression of autonomy and sovereignty through the creation of a 'society', of a public sphere, and arrangements for governing activities within it. For the most part, however, when people today refer to 'society', they are thinking of nation-states that exercise collective autonomy and have institutionalized individual autonomy within themselves through practices such as citizenship. The ideological foundation of these societies is nationalism, whether manifested in civic or ethnic forms. There isn't any reason, however, to think that nation-states are the only human social and political formations capable of promoting autonomy, or that nationalism provides the only solid ground for self-government (certainly, ethnic nationalism suggests its limits).

Systemic change places significant pressures on actual political institutions; it creates demands for new ways of ordering the world, perhaps across societies that rest on different understandings of individual and collective autonomy. Sometimes it gives rise to straightforward and even anticipated challenges that societies acting alone cannot address well and that encourage states to act in cooperation with one another. This is commonly known as internationalization. In this light, human beings still separated by boundaries and barriers of various kinds are adapting existing institutions and creating new ones as they seek to bring order to their increasingly complex and increasingly shared lives.

Globalization, as distinguished from internationalization, may be defined as the transformative growth of many, and potentially crosscutting, connections among people living anywhere and everywhere on the planet. Although historical antecedents are easy to identify, globalization is today quite reasonably associated with various and coincident innovations that have taken place in critical technologies, in communication and transportation systems, and in the artistic and literary realms of social reimagining. Many of these connections take a supraterritorial form. In ever more profound ways, globalization ties together across national boundaries what people do, what they experience, how they perceive that experience, how they imagine their lives and future prospects, and how they discern and manage risks. To use the language of natural law, globalization can in principle change quite profoundly both the reality and the perceptions of the common good. Since human beings exist as individuals-in-community, globalization can force basic transformations in identity.

Supraterritoriality is, in fact, a distinguishing characteristic of many of the connections being formed across the world today. Sometimes through spontaneous action not hindered by states, but other times in consequence of intentional state policies pursued after the man-made catastrophes of the era from 1914 to 1945, a growing minority of individuals, disproportionately but not exclusively based in advanced industrial countries, now live and work in a political space decisively shaped by global flows of reward and risk. In contrast, the vast majority of the world's population continues to live and work in the political space of defined places, even as certain now-global flows, from pathogens to volatile capital, affect them profoundly.[4] (The current situation is not unique, but it is more complicated and dynamic than that of the past. Consider, for example, the flow of pathogens in the first era of global exploration and its impact on indigenous societies.) The space of defined places remains decisively but not entirely shaped by the territorial imperatives of states.

The denser the space of flows becomes, and the greater the challenge of holding the allegiance of empowered and mobile elites, the more difficult it becomes for existing international institutions to address problems of global order. At the same time, the space of defined places becomes more difficult to isolate. The image as well as the reality of supraterritoriality in the very processes that sustain — or endanger — life itself cannot help but force a reimagining of global risks and their effective management, and of the institutions or of new institutions that address them.[5] History, ideology, habit, and vested interest all stand in the way of this reimagining.[6]

The very ideas of human autonomy and the common good, however, clarify the stakes involved. Autonomy is the principle that confers legitimacy on collective decision making. The extent to which specific manifestations of the principle are universally applicable is contentious. Nonetheless, it is difficult to discern an alternative principle upon which to base respect for the decisions of others.

Many would associate political autonomy in this sense with the onset of modernity in Europe. Over a century ago, Georg Simmel argued that the oppressiveness of medieval institutions gave rise to the idea of the pure freedom of the individual based on their 'natural' equality.[7] This eighteenth-century idea of individualism, he added, came to be complemented by another version of individuality in the nineteenth century, that of the particular and irreplaceable person. Such an idea, rearticulated and developed by philosophers since Simmel, has become incorporated into what Taylor calls the 'social imaginary': 'the ways people imagine their social existence, how they fit together with others, how things go on between them and their fellows, the expectations that are normally met, and the deeper normative notions and images that underlie these expectations.'[8] In the West, such an imaginary is translated into a specific notion of autonomy: people have 'a right to choose for themselves their own pattern of life, to decide in conscience what convictions to espouse, to determine the shape of their lives in a whole host of ways that their ancestors could not control'.[9] Again, such a conception readily can be translated into the older language of natural law. Behind shifting forms of shared civic life lie changing perceptions of the common good.

This view of individual autonomy is complementary to collective autonomy in the sense that in modern societies, free individuals decide together upon the rules and the forms through which they will be governed. The idea of collective autonomy is therefore anchored in individual autonomy, though more of one does not imply less of the other. As Simmel noted, the larger the collectivity involved, the more individual autonomy is available, at least in theory: 'Individuality in being and action generally increases to the degree that the social circle encompassing the individual expands.'[10] For larger collectivities, individuals create ever more complex governing institutions, which, in principle, can even expand the freedom of the individual to choose a particular pattern or way of living. In principle, Adam Smith would not have disagreed.

By the early twentieth century, however, when Simmel was still writing, this fortunate complementarity of individual and collective autonomy seemed increasingly belied by practice. The very institutions that were supposed to free the individual operated on the basis of a technical rationality that frequently left the individual in what Max Weber called an 'iron cage'. The technologies required for these institutions to function could narrow and flatten human lives. As Pope Leo XIII diagnosed in his famous 1891 encyclical, *Rerum Novarum*, the advent of narcissistic individualism in an excessively materialist culture was anti-thetical to true freedom. This centring on the self could give rise to an indifference to participation in self-government, the realization of collective autonomy, thus opening the way to a modern form of despotism.[11] Drawing on Alexis de Tocqueville, Taylor comes to the same conclusion: collective autonomy could come to be placed in the hands of paternalistic governments, where everything is run by an 'immense tutelary power'.[12] Ironically and perversely, individual autonomy could be fundamentally compromised. On this point, I think, neither Friedrich von Hayek nor Aquinas would have disagreed.[13]

Sovereignty and Authority in Practice

Again, the tradition of moral reasoning associated with natural law asserts that human beings are by nature free social animals inclined toward the common good, which is what ultimately justifies collective autonomy. Rightly conceived, the defence of collective autonomy depends upon the defence of individual autonomy. The reverse also applies. Sustaining individual autonomy requires appropriately calibrated collective autonomy over the longer term. This means that there must be a realm for politics and, in principle, that politics can vary depending upon the nature of the common good required in order for autonomy to be achieved and sustained. In short, the boundaries around collective autonomy are not fixed. This fact requires distinguishing collective autonomy conceptually from the modern legal understanding of state sovereignty.

If, as commonly believed, sovereignty consists of 'being constitutionally apart, of not being contained, however loosely, within a wider constitutional scheme', then it becomes an absolute condition, and it is either present or absent.[14] It also becomes a unitary condition. Within a defined territory, only one authority, the state, is in the position to make final, binding decisions. The degree to which states actually can in practice advance collective autonomy depends upon certain preceding conditions. First, within a given territory, there must be a polity, an imagined community in which sovereignty is vested through constitutive arrangements of some sort. Second, there also must be a functioning state capable of establishing authority in the territory, backed by a monopoly on the legitimate use of coercive violence. Third, that state must have a bureaucracy sufficiently able to implement laws and policies and to gather necessary fiscal and material resources. Fourth, the territory in which the polity exists must have an adequate supply of such resources to enable it to defend and maintain the society it claims the right to govern. And fifth, this notion of sovereignty also implies that no external authority claims a competing right within the defined territory.

As Stephen Krasner and many others have pointed out, such a situation rarely describes the real world, and when the real world is like this, the cause of autonomy, individual or collective, has never been served.[15] The fact is that states always have found it difficult to control or regulate the movements of goods, capital, people, and ideas across their frontiers. In such circumstances, they may use their legal prerogatives to enter into explicit or implicit contracts with other states to establish interstate authority structures to try and control such flows. This, again, is the world of internationalization, of interdependence, where societies voluntarily cooperate in the belief that they will actually thereby be in a position to give themselves effective laws.

Globalization and Political Legitimacy

Internationalization generally refers to the expansion of transactions of various kinds across borders and the resulting political reactions. It depends upon and even reaffirms nation-states as the basic actors in the system.[16] Globalization, in turn, entails a basic transformation in social and political perceptions, a transformation with wide-ranging impact that accompanies a profound deepening of individual and collective connections. Making those connections becomes virtually irresistible because of profound, often discontinuous, changes in the ways in which information, technologies, ideas, disease, environmental conditions, and destructive weapons spread out from their points of origin, and in the speed with which they spread. If the planet were a human brain, internationalization would signify an increase in normal functioning through established neural networks, while globalization would suggest the construction of new networks, innovative ways of thinking, and the reconstruction of personal and social identities.

Of course, the processes of internationalization and globalization have coexisted for several centuries, although their relationship to one another continually has changed. They are not mutually exclusive nor zero-sum processes in the sense that as globalization increases, internationalization decreases, and vice versa. They may complement one another, they may occur simultaneously without necessarily influencing one another, or they may contradict one another.

Historians of globalization argue that in the seventeenth and eighteenth centuries, globalization and internationalization tended to coexist. Non-national identities and loyalties were seen to complement a sense of nationality; state borders were porous; the transnational corporations of the day, such as the British East India Company, linked consumers and producers across continents; cosmopolitan thinking flourished among intellectuals.[17] Whereas in this period most territories were subject to multiple systems of rule, the situation changed as national sovereign states began to gain 'exclusive authority over a given territory and at the same time this territory was constructed as coterminous with that authority, in principle ensuring a similar dynamic in other nation-states'.[18] Significantly driving this development were power-seeking and war, or as political realists since Thomas Hobbes have surmised, the security dilemma: the drive to make one polity secure within a given territory necessarily induces insecurity outside of it. More evocatively, Charles Tilly captured the irreducible core of the process in the title of his brilliant essay, 'War Making and State Making as Organized Crime'.[19] State claims to overarching authority, in short, bumped into one another. That no spontaneously generated countervailing force could be counted upon to contradict such claims and ameliorate their destructive effects was proven in modern times during the month of August 1914, and we still live in the shadow then cast.

As Benn Steil and Manuel Hinds note, states eventually asserted their authority over markets and market economies that had arguably established themselves long before.[20] This changed the common understanding of market behaviour as spontaneously derived from human nature to that of a politically constructed activity. Welding political control to an assertion of legitimacy by right of the inherent autonomy of a particular form of collectivity we now call the nation, the nation-state 'imposed its system of more rigidly bound territories, languages, and religious conventions on all international networks'.[21] A.G. Hopkins adds that the cosmopolitanism that was a marked feature of the preceding two centuries was 'corralled, harnessed and domesticated to new national interests'.[22] Where property rights earlier had been grounded in nature, now even land 'was converted to property, property became the foundation of sovereignty; sovereignty, in turn, defined the basis of security'.[23]

In the economic realm, older and looser economic linkages gave way to more formal agreements between states, or they were simply redefined through coercion. Compliance, nevertheless, was something else. The full range of rights that eventually came to be associated with citizenship, Charles Tilley argues,

> came into being because relatively organized members of the general population bargained with state authorities for several centuries, bargained first over the means of war, then over enforceable claims that would serve their interests outside of the area of war, and thereby helped to enlarge the obligations of states to their citizens. The leverage broadened the range of enforceable claims citizens could make on states even more than it expanded the population who held rights of citizenship… White-hot bargaining forged rights and obligations of citizenship.[24]

Scholars do not agree on when the tipping point occurred. But sometime after 1945, supraterritorial pressures clearly began asserting or reasserting themselves upon the intellectual foundations of these rights and obligations of citizenship. Nor do scholars agree on whether or when such pressures became sufficiently important that the historic grip of nationality and internationality began to weaken. Indeed, some argue that just such a grip is actually tightening right now. Eventually, however, and notwithstanding self-defeating efforts to turn back the clock, many close observers see the development in recent times of a companion system of rule developing alongside the rule of nation-states. Marx's analysis of the inexorability of capitalist growth certainly opened one prominent way to think about such a development, but today other traditions of thought lead to the conceptual linkage of scientific and technological innovations with positive as well as political consequences.

Few scholars doubt, however, that today's very highly developed corporate globalization would have been possible without the use of the sophisticated economic and technological capabilities nurtured over the past century by certain key states and then promoted inside other states. Sometimes by accident and sometimes by design, leading states—the United States in particular—supported the creation of the nodes and the material infrastructure for supraterritorial connectivity.[25] And whether irony is justified or not, that infrastructure, now embedded within interacting states, in turn begins to challenge the way that state institutions themselves mediate demands for individual and collective autonomy.

With internationalization, the realization and securing of collective autonomy became primarily the responsibility of nation-states, a few of which shaped informal empires. Their expansion in the nineteenth and the twentieth centuries meant that imperial states significantly influenced the degree to which peoples in many other territories could exercise their collective autonomy. American power in the contemporary era tends to be indirect and informal. Peter Katzenstein offers the term *imperium* to characterize this type of rule: the conjoining of power that has territorial and non-territorial dimensions, with the territorial dimension relating to internationalization and the non-territorial to globalization.[26] Whatever term we use, as globalization-influenced forms of rule conflict with traditional patterns of territorially based nation-states, the degree to which collective autonomy is present or absent becomes more difficult to assess.

The intensification of internationalization in the nine-teenth century meant that the degree to which people actually possessed individual autonomy came to depend heavily upon the nature of rule in the state within which they were citizens or subjects. Other factors were obviously important — relative wealth, gender, access to food, and physical well-being, to name but a few — but they were variously available depending upon the state. Associated processes of individualization — the spread of state-enforced private-property rights, the expansion of the electoral franchise, and the growth of material consumption — all contributed to the transformation of the values of autonomy in a direction of self-fulfilment, especially the fulfilment of appetites. Globalization, in turn, encourages the questioning, and ultimately the broadening, of claims to collective autonomy, and it thereby challenges the state's monopoly even within a given territory. It also impinges upon considerations of individual autonomy. I may be free to move, but that does not mean I escape heightened global risks.

Lines of responsibility begin to break down under conditions of globalization. Where it once made sense to speak of autonomous individuals exercising their personal responsibility to govern themselves through collective political instruments resting on self-evident sources of legitimacy, it now makes less sense when a blurring of responsibility now occurs all around us. This blurring long has been anticipated within certain polyglot and otherwise complicated societies where collective bonds were already attenuated. In hierarchical and unitary societies such as that of Great Britain, the idea of responsible government and its full meaning was easy to see in practice. In the more diverse and pluralist United States, meanwhile, intentionally divided sovereignty, checked-and-balanced power centres, and the deliberate opacity of the dividing line between society and the state always has rendered direct political responsibility ambiguous. (Perhaps this ambiguity explains the exceptional reliance of the United States on religion to remind Americans of a traditional obligation of stewardship, which must ultimately rest on a sense of personal responsibility for all members of the social collectivity to which one belongs.)

Beyond Limits to Solidarity?

To the extent that the expansion of global opportunities and risks erodes social and political boundaries without providing new sources of collective identity, it blocks the reconstitution of political and social responsibility. That I am my brother's keeper becomes a mere sentiment, even for those who believe it. It begins to seem a worthy aspiration routinely realized only by saints, of whom I personally know but a few. If the term 'international community' has become a nearly meaningless figure of journalistic speech, then what hope is there that the term 'global community' could become meaningful?

Since we actually live in St. Augustine's City of Man, there doesn't seem to be any way of avoiding the necessity of bringing just such a principle face-to-face with the truly pressing and now truly global risks, threats, challenges, and opportunities. As difficult as it seems, this means reconceiving actual modes of government. Not governance — that way of putting it, perhaps intentionally, obfuscates the issue. I mean government. Globalization forces a move out of analytical comfort zones. Effective problem solving, risk mitigation, and the search for maximum, feasible degrees of autonomy must now take us to many places, some below, some alongside, and some above the analytical level of the nation-state. But we must get there from the existing practice of cooperative decision making within and across the nation-state itself.

The key feature of institutional adaptation and innovation in the search for solutions to problems of collective action is *increasing complexity*. The building up and the breaking down of institutions for coordinating the actions of discrete governments is certainly part of the long story of internationalization. The League of Nations, commercial unions, monetary standards, and federations have come and gone. Even where reform actually has been achieved, erosion and constant adaptation seem more common than stability. The trend is clearly evident in the international institutions established by the victorious allies after World War II. Globalization, however, suggests deeper and more profound changes in the relationships constitutive of institutions aspiring to authoritative social ordering—relationships between individuals and among large groups of individuals.

There is nothing inevitable about those relationships creating governing structures that sustain what is best. Reshaping old institutions and fostering new ones require basic agreement on principles and the willingness of leaders and followers to make trade-offs between principles that are competing or contradictory. The transformative processes of globalization do not necessarily make it any easier to achieve such agreements or engineer such trade-offs. In fact, by making the multi-polarity of the world increasingly visible, whether in terms of economic power, cultural systems, or social practices, they render more and more inconceivable a world where institutions are simply designed, adapted, and directed by the states that have led the world since 1945. In such a context, the multifaceted concept of autonomy and the question of precisely who is responsible to whom in our new circumstances provide important metrics for setting achievable goals and defining realistic limits.

Edgar Grande and I contend that what we are witnessing and participating in is a *complex and partly contradictory transformation* of authority that remains up to this point centred on the state. This transformation 'affects all aspects of public authority, in particular the distribution of political decision-making power across territorial levels; the relation between public and private actors; and the definition of public functions'.[27] The new complexity is most evident today in the case of the European Union, where the sharing of sovereign prerogatives in a rapidly evolving system of decision making is subtle, impossible to dismiss, full of dissonance, and constantly challenged by events. The disintegration of that system is not inconceivable; it is just ever more unlikely.

Along this line, even if we accept a protean conception of sovereignty-in-practice, it seems reasonable to assert that access to the structures of the state today still creates the surest possibility for any specific community to make a claim to collective autonomy across a full range of areas of life. But globalization multiplies the situations in which states find themselves pushed to delegate their authority, to share it, and increasingly, to accept a reduction in their scope for unimpeded action. Plausible claims of responsibility encompassing but necessarily now exceeding claims bounded by state frontiers can only rest on new, or rediscovered, foundations of autonomy. But if those foundations are to be as stable as earlier ones, the citizens of still-discrete states must come to see them as just and right.

Nearly a century after Simmel wrote about it, economic sociologists would note without controversy that modern market society, organized as it has been around relatively autonomous nation-states, has produced more prosperity for more people than any other social and political formation in history. As Neil Fligstein observes, for example, 'It has done so by creating the conditions for social exchange between large groups of human beings, often separated across large geographic spaces'.[28] Those conditions for social exchange include shared understandings that are stable, efficient, and perceptibly just enough to be repeated. Since the dawn of modernity, human beings separated from one another by space and time, as well as by more artificial boundaries, have repeatedly reconstituted such understandings.

To combine the language of economics and the language of politics, the world's most prosperous societies have managed to combine economies of scale and scope with the defence of autonomy, defined in both collective and individual terms. Although there isn't any single model of a perfectly balanced society, the various societies constituting the advanced industrial world, along with growing parts of the emerging industrial world, are exemplary of the constant struggles necessary to attain and maintain that delicate balance. They seek, first, stable points of equilibrium among the prosperity produced by an integrated market; second, the stable social ordering created by a sense of collective belonging; and third, the fulfilment associated with the freedom both to escape wants and to make personal choices. Quite apparently, not all of their citizens have enjoyed all three outcomes equally. Even for those coming close, however, globalization now shakes the ground under their feet. We have only to recall the tragic history of the twentieth century and reflect on the various global risks humanity is now obviously facing to realize that things could get very much worse for all of us.

If, as noted above, the denser the space of flows becomes, and the greater becomes the challenge of holding the allegiance of elites within territorially bounded societies, then the more difficult it is for existing states and the international institutions they created to address problems of global order. At a certain point, institutional adaptation seems likely to be superseded by the necessity to create new kinds of institutions, albeit based on recent experience and on the habits of collaboration nurtured within heretofore successful states. On this point, it is worth clarifying and then extending a distinction already implied.

Accountability, Responsibility, and a Global Order

At the level of the system, accountability is not always entirely synonymous with responsibility. As Robert Keohane explains, accountability in its fullest sense entails both the sharing of information concerning actions, decisions, or behaviour of some sort *and* the exercise of sanctions.[29] In politics, the relationship is quite clear inside functioning democracies, where governments may be said to be accountable if citizens are entitled to information upon which to base their judgments and are empowered to punish those they have authorized to decide. Democratic governments thereby have been constrained by acceptance of the idea that citizens are ultimately responsible for their own decisions. The accountability of their government to them makes exercising that responsibility feasible for the autonomous collectivity, which is defined by citizenship. At the level of the global system as a whole, however, not only is full information likely to be unavailable, but the ability to seek redress of grievances or to sanction leaders is weak or non-existent. The idea of accountability, however, is not completely irrelevant.

In the post-1945 period, the deepening of economic interdependence among legally separate nation-states occurred in consequence of both policy design and the reassertion of cross-border markets (in truth, as Steil suggests, such markets were never actually extinguished in World War II). A set of collaborative political institutions and habits of interstate collaboration developed in tandem, their principal objective being to hold the separate nation-states accountable to one another.

Even as the practices of those institutions evolved, however, the weakness of any sanctioning mechanisms defined the compromised nature of systemic accountability. Enshrined, for example, in the early informal consultations process and later treaty-based surveillance procedures of the International Monetary Fund, accountability for the international impact of macroeconomic policy choices was only as robust as the willing deference of member-states to the rather weak practice of peer review.[30] Especially when no borrowing from the Fund occurred, members were legally bound to subject themselves to surveillance, but they also retained their capacity to ignore external criticism. Accountability in this sense did represent something new under the sun, but it did nothing to obviate the clear lines of legal *responsibility* of the officials to their respective nation-states. In other words, they remained accountable to one another but *responsible* only to the citizenry they formally represented. To be called to account internationally was one thing. To be held responsible domestically was quite another.

Internationalization did not erode norms of responsibility; indeed, it preserved and arguably even strengthened certain autonomous collectivities endowed with resources of power. But again, globalization suggests something else. By redefining the social group, shifting identities, spreading novel risks, opening new possibilities for movement and imagination, reinforcing habits of collaboration, and effectively transcending territorial divides, globalization extends outward nascent bonds of transnational responsibility.

An expansive form of accountability is to interdependent governments what a fully realized form of responsibility is to global government. With this analogy in mind, a global civil society and a global polity would be implied if human beings began acting as if they were responsible to and for one another, without restriction. If they acted this way, their actions would suggest that they were beginning to see themselves as stewards of a common legacy facing shared risks. They could, however, only take requisite policy actions capable of enduring enforcement if they retained a degree of autonomy.

Long before the term *globalization* was invented, Jacques Maritain anticipated this central truth. 'If world political society is someday founded,' he wrote, 'it will be by means of freedom. It is by means of freedom that people will have been brought to the common will to live together.'[31] That such a society would call forth its own 'supra-national' state, or body politic, seemed in principle obvious and unproblematic to Maritain. He did not see such a development as inconsistent with a continuing 'multiplicity of nations'. He could not imagine that new polity structured like a tight federation, and he lived long enough to be disappointed with experiments such as the United Nations. Still, he envisaged the gradual emergence of a transnational body politic and apparatus for self-government grounded in a sense of the common good of one people, which would supersede the sense of the common good characteristic of today's distinctive polities. To be sure, Maritain was tapping here into a distinguished vein of political thought, one that long preceded the rise of the modern state itself. But the modern state was for him the necessary starting point. Following this line of thought, if we seek a solid grounding for a greater sense of responsibility in an era of global risks, of a sense of stewardship for the shrinking planet human beings inhabit together, and for a reasonable basis for collaborative action, then we need not start from scratch.

As a first step in seeking this solid grounding for a greater sense of responsibility, we might envisage nations loosening their grip on certain practical rights and obligations, at least with regard to certain necessarily transnational policy spaces. Think climate change, inexpensive and easily transportable biological and chemical weapons, or cascading financial instability resulting from inadequately coordinated macroeconomic policies. By the very fact of having to live together, human beings haven't had any reason to confront the practical problems of globalization and thus haven't had any reason for reimagining (self-) government. As the level of common risks and challenges begins migrating from one level of our shared human experience to another, authoritative solutions will migrate too. There isn't any basis in political history, however, for imagining that this migration must occur through functional necessity. Uncertainty, mistakes, ignorance, irrationality, venality, and even malice—all undercut the logic of functionalism.

There was, after all, nothing inevitable about the rise of the nation-state itself. It emerged as an unintended consequence of policy decisions taken in Europe during the fourteenth and fifteenth centuries. As Hendrik Spruyt emphasizes, it solved certain problems in collective action at definite historical moments, problems mainly fiscal and military in nature, and it did so more effectively than its main competitors, city-leagues and city-states. Moreover, it inherited mainly by accident certain functions that were once managed by empires.[32] The nation-state was hardly perfect. Nevertheless, once leading nation-states began joining together in concert to address whatever problems happened to confront them, they began to construct an international system. Eventually, the success of this system drove out of existence alternative surviving forms of polity. Just as its predecessors and competitors finally faded into distant memory, however, there is no good reason to view this particular form of polity as immutable.

Indeed, we seem now to be living through a period of complex political reconstitution. The best evidence is provided by the reactions to it, which are mostly negative. Many, on the political 'right' as well as the 'left', desperately seek an escape back to the comfortable past, the world of known boundaries. Resisting such flights of fancy, some see disorder and a regrettable coming apart as perhaps a necessary step toward the reformation of political authority. Certainly the reactions of leading states to the prospect of a systemic financial meltdown in 2007 and 2008 suggested that they all believed outcomes such as depression, global war, terror-induced closure, and environmental catastrophe were entirely conceivable. After all, this is human history we are discussing, not some kind of mechanical machinery or biological organism.

The sounds of underlying political reorganization may be faint and dissonant, but they are becoming audible. In the search for practicable measures to deal with problems of collective action and especially to govern global risks, the nation-state seems caught up in a new political architecture. Institutionally differentiated but also structurally integrated, the state remains essential, but it is not sovereign in any sense other than a conventionally legal one. The state, whether alone or in simple concert with other states, increasingly is no longer the entity making effective decisions. The growing involvement of various types of organizations and non-state actors cannot be ignored. This can threaten constitutional democracy, but this is an empirical matter subject to question. There is certainly evidence that even existing multilateral organizations can actually empower diffuse minorities against vested interests, protect vulnerable populations, and enhance democratic decision making in leading states.[33]

It long has been quite clear that the member states of the European Union were embarked on an historic venture to create a novel and workable regional system of authority. The temptation for scholars interested in the international implications of this development long has been simply to place this case in an analytical box labelled 'federalism'. This labelling has the advantage of protecting inherited intellectual categories and economizing on intellectual energy. It has the distinct disadvantage, however, of missing the actual complexity of our current situation and foreclosing on the possibility of meaningful analogies.

Think more generally about the scale and complexity of the economic resources required to address fundamental security challenges now emanating from central Asia. If Americans can seriously tackle those challenges on their own, no one has explained that clearly to the taxpayer. In truth, the generation and coordination of effective responses appear to require a remarkable degree of economic, intelligence, policy, and military coordination across several continents. The need for much more intensive transnational cooperation has become much more obvious, not less, and authoritative structures for effective decision-making continue to evolve in response to this reality. In this and in other readily identifiable policy arenas, the process of reconstituting political authority has not come to a halt. Just as we should expect, however, it is clarifying points of convergence and conflict among interests, ideas, and values.

Recent events provide a glimpse of something more than deeper cooperation among existing polities. In the financial realm, in the absence of clear arrangements for systemic burden sharing, at the moment of crisis in 2007 and 2008, we witnessed leading states arguably 'exceeding their authorities' on an ad hoc basis to halt both national collapse and systemic contagion. In the United States, this translated into using taxpayer funds awkwardly and indirectly to bail out foreign banks. In the European Union, certain outrageous breaches of implicit and explicit obligations — for example, by Ireland — and coercive policy reactions — for example, by Great Britain — all forced the idea of negotiating new *ex ante* burden-sharing agreements back onto the regional agenda.[34] Although it is possible to force analysis of such incidents back into conventional statist categories, the tensions so vividly witnessed in financial markets in 2007 and 2008 again more plausibly suggest a harking back to an older tradition. As Terry Nardin puts it, sovereignty conceived simply as the power to decide — so apparently clear in emergencies —

> misunderstands law, which is not simply coercion by another name but a distinct kind of association, association in terms of non-instrumental rules, in which coercion is justified only to secure observance of the rules that are the basis of association, and whose ultimate ground is that they prevent one person from interfering arbitrarily with the choices of another.[35]

In this regard, perhaps an even clearer glimpse of the future came in 2003, when in response to the rapid spread of SARS, the World Health Organization (WHO) made decisions it had failed to make in earlier incidents that raised the possibility of a global pandemic. Although the authors of a recent study of transnational threats couch their overall analysis in what I have called here the camp of internationalization, which entails the straightforward need for more intense cooperation among established state authorities, they use a jarringly dissonant language when they describe this particular incident:

> A key part of the story was that Director General Brundtland pushed for WHO to exert autonomy and influence beyond its authority and mandate. SARS was not covered under existing International Health Regulations, but WHO demanded cooperation and openness nonetheless. Brundtland issued travel warnings and advisories without the legal

authorization to do so and amidst some criticism from member states.[36]

The fact that the member states of WHO retrospectively conferred legitimacy on their acquiescence to such creative policymaking does not diminish the basic point. At least in this particular, and particularly important, policy arena, human beings across diverse communities using available instruments redefined and rationalized their sense of the common good and of the authority necessary to defend it.

Reason, Responsibility, and Self-Government

Surely the Americans who ratified the Articles of Confederation in 1781 to govern thirteen former colonies on the Atlantic coast, as well as Upper and Lower Canada if they had agreed to join in, would have been surprised if they had come back one hundred years later to find their confederal system replaced by a complex new system combining unitary and federal principles in the government of a now continental society. The drafters of the new Constitution that replaced the Articles also likely would be surprised if they came back today to see their document interrelated significantly to adapt it to changing circumstances, geographical expansion, and systemic demands. In many other places in the world today, sovereignty remains an important legal principle, but its actual application is now enmeshed in increasingly complex domestic and international networks of expectations, claims, and obligations.[37] Contemporary scholars perhaps therefore will be forgiven if they are not surprised by the idea that political authority in our world can be and is being reconstituted by human beings struggling to cope with challenges and certain clear and evermore-present dangers confronting them.

It would be hard to argue with President George W. Bush on this point:

> The events of September 11, 2001, fundamentally changed the context for relations between the United States and other main centers of global power, and opened vast, new opportunities. With our long-standing allies in Europe and Asia, and with leaders in Russia, India, and China, we must develop active agendas of cooperation lest these relationships become routine and unproductive... We can build

> fruitful habits of consultation, quiet argument, sober
> analysis, and common action. In the long-term, these are the
> practices that will sustain the supremacy of our common
> principles and keep open the path of progress.[38]

It would be even harder not to follow his successor toward the following reasonable conclusion:

> We are a nation of Christians and Muslims, Jews and
> Hindus — and non-believers. We are shaped by every
> language and culture, drawn from every end of this Earth...
> [and] we cannot help but believe that the old hatreds shall
> someday pass; that the lines of tribe shall soon dissolve; that
> as the world grows smaller, our common humanity shall
> reveal itself; and that America must play its role in ushering
> in a new era of peace.[39]

We cannot reliably move to common action based on our common humanity, however, unless we combine practical reason with a deeper insight that some thinkers trace to the tradition of natural law. A belief in impermeable boundaries around human solidarity cannot survive scrutiny, certainly not under conditions of globalization. At the same time, it would seem unreasonable to oppose the practical imperative of political decentralization, or subsidiarity, whenever feasible and constructive. Also unreasonable would be to disconnect responsibility and autonomy as we consider practical implications. We must freely assume responsibility for reimagining and then actually building a *political* society that is both integrated and stable on the largest geographic scale necessary to achieve the common good. It cannot be induced. But consider the options of either doing nothing or of trying to turn the clock back.

In the face of global risks, the urge to seek avenues of retreat is understandable. Even as sage a guide as Robert Skidelsky recently opined:

> In this new climate, national politicians are likely to reach for
> ideas and influences that until recently would have seemed
> exotic. The idea, for example, that economic growth does
> not, beyond a certain point, make people happier... Rich
> countries could probably abandon the globalist project with-
> out much damage to their material standards and with
> possible gain to their quality of life. Rejecting the inevit-
> ability of market-based globalisation would not necessarily

be harmful — especially if it were accompanied by a reassertion of democracy at a national level.[40]

The thought is sincere, but the immediate consequences of
implementation are all too easy to imagine counterfactually.
Would Germany and Japan have been reconciled to world
order after 1945 in the absence of rapid economic growth on
a cross-continental scale? Would the Soviet tyranny have
collapsed and the Chinese system begun a difficult process of
reform in a less-interdependent world focused on raising
measurable living standards? Would the less-than-adequate
level of financing flowing from industrial to developing
countries really be increased in a low-growth environment?
To be sure, 'our' environmental challenges might be less
ominous in the immediate term, but would 'their' environmental situations be more tolerable or 'ours' less threatening
in the long run?

The Realistic Alternative

Aspiring to the restoration of a moral balance is quite
admirable. But unless we can imagine a realistic alternative,
a reversal of supraterritorial economic, social, and political
ambitions is not easily defensible. Modern markets can only
be self-regulating in the abstract. As underlined above, actual
markets coexist with the struggle for power, for the raw
capacity to coerce others and to defend oneself against being
coerced by others, and that unfortunate coincidence seems to
define the practical limits of the idea of spontaneous and
peaceful social ordering. It does so just as global risks and
changing perceptions of the common good demand a reimagining of workable forms of authority to govern dynamic
and reasonably free societies. This reimagining does not
imply the rapid obsolescence of currently existing forms of
authority, but it does suggest at the global level what Europeans in their own region call a new and necessarily variable
geometry of political responsibility and social obligation.

Economic growth and the wealth it generates have
proven empirically to be necessary conditions for the sustainability of individual and collective autonomy. Responsible government now rests on the foundation they provide.
Sustainable growth, moreover, now seems conditioned on
transformative technological innovation, the fruits of which

rapidly must be shared across the system. The truly sufficient condition for both individual and collective autonomy, however, must be the wisdom to exercise political responsibility and extend outward the boundaries around real political lives—to provide a secure foundation of legitimacy for deep transnational collaboration in those policy arenas where it is required to reduce and manage evermore-obvious global risks. In this stark new context, whether one calls such authoritative collaboration government or not, it is more than reasonable to continue believing that humanity can give itself laws.

---

1   Parts of this essay draw on and develop sections of a chapter written with my friends and colleagues William Coleman and Diana Brydon. See William D. Coleman, Louis W. Pauly and Diana Brydon, 'Globalization, Autonomy, and Institutional Change', in *Global Ordering: Institutions and Autonomy in a Changing World*, ed. Louis W. Pauly and William D. Coleman (Vancouver: University of British Columbia Press, 2009): 1–20. Coleman crafted key distinctions concerning the nature of globalization, and he continues to influence my thinking on the modalities of practical decision making in this context. Brydon decisively shaped our thinking on autonomy and its manifestations. Although we never discussed the tradition of natural law as we developed the larger project of which our book was a part, it is now clear to me that we should have done so. For constructive comments on that theme as developed in this essay, I am grateful to Joseph Boyle. Edgar Grande and I are engaged in a related new project on the governance of global risks and, as usual, I have learned much from his insights.

2   John Finnis, *Natural Law and Natural Rights* (Oxford: Clarendon Press, 1980): 127, 90.

3   Charles Taylor, *Modern Social Imaginaries* (Durham, NC: Duke University Press, 2004): 3.

4   See Manuel Castells, *The Rise of the Network Society*, 1 (Oxford: Blackwell, 1996).

5   See Amartya Sen, *Development as Freedom* (New York: Anchor, 1999).

6   See Ulrich Beck, *World Risk Society* (Cambridge: Polity, 1999).

7   See Georg Simmel, *On Individuality and Social Forms*, ed. Donald N. Levine (Chicago, IL: University of Chicago Press, 1971): 219.

8   Taylor, *Modern Social Imaginaries*: 23.

9   Charles Taylor, *The Malaise of Modernity* (Toronto: Anansi, 1991): 2.

10   Simmel, *On Individuality and Social Forms*: 252.

11   For an accessible overview and analysis of 'Rerum Novarum', see Pope John Paul II, 'Centesimus Annus' (1 May 1991).

12   Taylor, *Malaise of Modernity*: 9.

13   See Bruce Caldwell, *Hayek's Challenge: An Intellectual Biography of F.A. Hayek* (Chicago, IL: University of Chicago Press, 2004); Erik Angner, *Hayek and Natural Law* (London: Routledge, 2007).

14   Alan James, 'The Practice of Sovereign Statehood in Contemporary International Society', in *Sovereignty at the Millennium*, ed. Robert Jackson (Oxford: Blackwell, 1999): 35–51, 39.

15   See Stephen D. Krasner, *Sovereignty: Organized Hypocrisy* (Princeton, NJ: Princeton University Press, 1999).

16   See Peter J. Katzenstein, *A World of Regions: Asia and Europe in the American Imperium* (Ithaca, NY: Cornell University Press, 2005): 17.

17   See A.G. Hopkins, ed., *Globalization in World History* (London: Pimlico, 2002): 24–6.

18   Saskia Sassen, *Territory, Authority, Rights* (Princeton, NJ: Princeton University Press, 2006): 6.

19   See Charles Tilly, 'War Making and State Making as Organized Crime', in *Bringing the State Back In*, eds. Peter B. Evans, Dietrich Rueschemeyer and Theda Skocpol (Cambridge: Cambridge University Press, 1985): 169–91.

20   See Benn Steil and Manuel Hinds, *Money, Markets and Sovereignty* (New Haven, CT: Yale University Press, 2009).

21   C.A. Bayly, *The Birth of the Modern World, 1780–1914* (Oxford: Blackwell, 2004): 234.

22   Hopkins, *Globalization in World History*: 30.

23   *Ibid.*: 6.

24   Charles Tilly, 'Where do Rights Come From?', in *Contributions to the Comparative Study of Development*, ed. Lars Mjøset (Oslo: Institute for Social Research, 1992): 10. See Sidney Tarrow, 'Debating War, States, and Rights with Charles Tilly: A Contentious Conversation', *Contention, Change, and Explanation*, conference in honor of Charles Tilly, The Social Science Research Council, New York (3–5 October 2008).

25   See the work of Saskia Sassen, especially *Deciphering the Global: Its Scales, Spaces and Subjects* (London: Routledge, 2007).

26   See Peter Katzenstein, *World of Regions*: 2, 208. Also see Harold James, *The Roman Predicament: How the Rules of International Order Create the Politics of Empire* (Princeton, NJ: Princeton University Press, 2006).

27   Edgar Grande and Louis Pauly, eds., *Complex Sovereignty: Reconstituting Political Authority in the Twenty-first Century* (Toronto: University of Toronto Press, 2005): 5.

28   Neil Fligstein, *The Architecture of Markets: An Economic Sociology of Twenty-first-century Capitalist Societies* (Princeton, NJ: Princeton University Press, 2001): 3.

29   Robert O. Keohane, 'The Concept of Accountability in World Politics and the Use of Force', *Michigan Journal of International Law*, 24 (2003): 1121–41.

30   See Harold James, 'The Historical Development of the Principle of Surveillance', *International Monetary Fund Staff Papers*, 42 (December 1995): 762–91; Louis W. Pauly, *Who Elected the Bankers? Surveillance and Control in the World Economy* (Ithaca, NY: Cornell University Press, 1997).

31   Jacques Maritain, *Man and the State* (Chicago, IL: University of Chicago Press, 1951): 206.

32   See Hendrik Spruyt, *The Sovereign State and Its Competitors* (Princeton, NJ: Princeton University Press, 1994).

33   See Robert O. Keohane, Stephen Macedo and Andrew Moravcsik, 'Democracy-Enhancing Multilateralism', *International Organization*, 63 (Winter 2009): 1–31.

34   See Louis W. Pauly, 'Financial Crisis Management in Europe and Beyond', *Contributions to Political Economy*, 27 (2008): 73–89.

35   Terry Nardin, 'Theorising the International Rule of Law', *Review of International Studies*, 34 (1 July 2008): 385–40, 396.

36   Bruce Jones, Carlos Pascual and Stephen John Stedman, *Power and Responsibility: Building International Order in an Era of Transnational Threats* (Washington, DC: Brookings Institution Press, 2009): 156.

37   See Louis W. Pauly, 'Managing Financial Emergencies in an Integrating World', *Globalizations*, special issue edited by William Coleman, forthcoming.

38   The White House, 'The National Security Strategy of the United States of America' (September 2002): 28.

39   Barack Obama, *Inaugural Address* (20 January 2009).

40   Robert Skidelsky, 'Where Do We Go From Here?', *Prospect*, 154 (1 January 2009): 36–41, 39.

Samuel Gregg & James R. Stoner, Jr.

Natural Law and Property Rights[1]

The tradition of political philosophy does not begin aus-
piciously for advocates of property rights. Plato's *Republic*
famously forbids private property (and even private families) to members of the guardian and auxiliary classes —
those in the regime who are best by nature — and the dialogue is ambiguous over the status of property even among
the lower, 'money-making' classes. Property rights, Socrates
argues, interfere with the unity of the city, whose leading
members need to feel everything as one. And concern with
property seems to distract from the cultivation of virtue,
which is the best city's greatest end. When his interlocutors
complain that the ruling classes will be deprived of worldly
goods and thus of happiness, Socrates reminds them that the
happiness of the city as a whole is their object, not the
happiness of its parts. Besides, the account of the city and its
classes is drawn on analogy to an account of the soul and its
parts, so the denial of property to the ruling classes suggests
its irrelevance to the higher ends of the human being himself.

When Plato turns in the *Laws* to a more practicable city,
precisely what changes is the communism of the *Republic*. In
what is explicitly called the second-best city, there are to be
5,040 separate households, each with its own allotment of
land (slavery is now introduced). Still, estates cannot be

[1] Sections of this chapter are reprinted with permission from George-
town University Press. Copyright 1998 by Georgetown University
Press. James R. Stoner, Jr., 'Property, the Common Law, and John
Locke', in David F. Forte, ed., *Natural Law and Contemporary Public
Policy*, pp. 194–197; 201–207. www.press.georgetown.edu.

bought and sold, divided or combined, except under authority from the city, which aims to preserve the number of households and so the material basis of its citizenry. The common good, in other words, governs the allocation of property, and virtue, which is still the aim of the city, defines the common good.

This paper aims to provide an historical overview of the question of natural law in relation to property rights and to consider its implications for two important contemporary issues. In the first part, we identify two principal historical traditions of natural law—the classical and the modern—which are analytically distinct but can be profitably intermingled. Representatives of the classical tradition include Aristotle, the Roman jurists, Aquinas, later scholastics, and even Grotius and several authors in the Scottish Enlightenment. The modern tradition finds its origin in the writings of John Locke, though it soon drifts toward utilitarianism, the seeming opposite of natural law.

In the second part of the paper we look at the implications of natural-law thinking for two areas of law and policy that affect property rights: the nature and proper extent of government regulation of the free market, and intellectual property. These issues illustrate how natural law can supply a stable framework for thinking about property rights in the context of a global economy and of rapid technological change.

Property in Classic Natural Law

Let us begin with the classic account of natural law and property in the writings of Thomas Aquinas, looking back to his sources as need be. To say that property appears in his *Summa Theologica* only as an afterthought would be misleading, but in Aquinas's account of natural law, it does not exactly have pride of place. In the celebrated question 94, in the second article, where the basic precepts of natural law are sketched, property appears only by implication: '[W]hatever is a means of preserving human life and of warding off its obstacles belongs to the natural law.'[1] In the fourth article, theft is condemned as 'expressly contrary to the natural law', albeit in the context of explaining how, by the perversion of reason, some societies actually allowed it.

Finally, in the fifth article, on whether natural law can be changed, Aquinas directly raises the question of private possession. He answers an objection based on an authority who wrote that 'the possession of all things in common and universal freedom are matters of natural law'. Aquinas replies that these things are natural as nakedness is, and he is not making a case against clothes. He explains: '[T]he distinction of possessions and slavery were not brought in by nature but devised by human reason for the benefit of human life.' Property and slavery apparently belong not to natural law's 'most general precepts that are known to all' but to 'certain secondary and more detailed precepts which are, as it were, conclusions following closely from first principles'.[2] In this studied ambivalence or indirectness concerning property, one sees, perhaps, a reflection of Aristotle's complex account of money and money making, which he treats as at once necessary and yet in a sense unnatural. Aristotle is unambiguous in his support for private possession, however, most especially in his critique of the Platonic scheme, and of course he taught that some men are by nature slaves.[3]

Aquinas gives his more thematic account of property in his discussion of the virtue of justice, first in his discussion of right,[4] and then in his discussion of theft.[5] In the first passage, after establishing right as the object of justice, he distinguishes natural right from positive right and then natural right from the right of nations. Positive right depends upon agreement, either by the whole community or with the prince's decree. And while positive right cannot override natural right, it is often needed, apparently because of man's changeable—that is to say, imperfect, indeed corrupt—nature. The distinction between natural and positive right, of course, recalls the distinction between natural law and human law.

Aquinas's second distinction, between natural right and the right of nations, is more subtle; here natural right involves what is commensurate with another person. This commensurability takes two forms: an absolute form and a form 'according to something resultant from it'. His examples of the first form are the commensurability of male and female in procreation and of parent and child in the matter of

nourishment. His example of the second form is 'the possession of property':

> For if a particular piece of land be considered absolutely, it
> contains no reason why it should belong to one man more
> than to another, but if it be considered in respect of its adapt-
> ability to cultivation, and the unmolested use of the land, it
> has a certain commensuration to be the property of one and
> not of another man, as the Philosopher shows (*Polit*. ii. 2)...
> [T]o consider a thing by comparing it with what results from
> it, is proper to reason, wherefore the same is natural to man
> in respect of natural reason which dictates it. Hence the jurist
> Gaius says (*Digest* 9): *Whatever natural reason decrees among all
> men, is observed by all equally, and is called the right of nations.*[6]

The right of nations (*ius gentium*) thus appears not as the
opposite of natural right but as one of its forms, and property
seems rather to belong to it than to natural right, strictly
speaking. Whether the right of nations corresponds perfectly
to the 'secondary and more detailed precepts' derived from
natural law — or whether it attaches to only one form of
these — is not immediately clear.

Curiously, it is in the discussion of theft that Aquinas
finally raises the important questions, 'Whether it is natural
for man to possess external things?' and 'Whether it is lawful
for a man to possess a thing as his own?' He answers the first
of these queries with a distinction: only God can possess the
nature of things, as they obey His will, but 'as regards their
use... man has a natural dominion over external things,
because, by his reason and will, he is able to use them for his
profit, as they were made on his account'. He cites for this
last point both Aristotle's *Politics* and Genesis 1.

The second question is also answered in the affirmative,
and again with a distinction between power and use, but
now to different effect. Man's power 'to procure and dispense [exterior things]... [means] it is lawful for man to
possess property'. There are three reasons this is so, all
silently drawn from Aristotle's critique of the *Republic*: man
is more careful to procure what is for himself alone, human
affairs are conducted in more orderly fashion if each man is
charged with taking care of some particular thing himself,
and a more peaceful state is ensured to man if each one is
contented with his own. But if ownership here means that

the power to procure and dispense is to be private, use is still to remain common, at least so far as an owner's readiness to share with those in need—primarily himself and those in his care. The distinction between possession and use can be found as well in the *Politics,* but Aquinas again makes no reference, and for good reason. Aristotle's chief example is common use among friends, under the guidance of the virtue of liberality; for Aquinas, all in need apparently have a claim to use, under the aspect of justice.

In short, Aquinas endorses the right of private property as an element of natural law only in a qualified way. It belongs to the secondary precepts of natural law, the *ius gentium,* which are based not immediately upon man's natural inclinations but upon reflection on human experience, and which are devised for human benefit. Property is a right, in the language of one modern commentator, only to the private 'administration' of things, not necessarily to their private 'enjoyment', since private ownership is limited by the duty of sharing with the needy.[7] Moreover, in his brief consideration of commerce—in the questions under the general heading of justice concerned with cheating and usury[8]—Aquinas makes clear his adherence to the doctrine of the just price and his loyalty to the classical condemnation of usury. He cites in a critical passage both the *Politics* and the *Ethics* for the proposition that money was invented for the sake of exchange and so was meant for 'consumption or alienation', not for 'use' or hire, leaving usury 'by its very nature unlawful'.

This last passage makes clear some distinctions between Aquinas's way of thinking and views of money in modern market economies. Its distance from modern socialism—which insists on public administration even as it indulges private enjoyment—is also apparent, however. At least this is the case with such versions of socialism influenced by Marx, which have little use for considerations of nature, without which Aquinas's account of natural law makes no sense. If money remains in a sense unnatural for Aquinas (as it was for Aristotle), the conclusions of human experience—from which the rights of property derive—are not, to his mind, like the findings of modern-day social science, subject to continuous amendment and likely to be reversed with each passing generation. Human laws can indeed be changed as human reason discovers more about the truth, but he does not say the same even for the secondary precepts of the natural law, however easily the latter 'can be blotted out from the human heart either by evil persuasions... or by vicious customs and corrupt habits'.[9] Above all, for Aquinas, as in a way even for Aristotle, the first source of all good things is nature or providence, even though man's own contribution is acknowledged; the question of property is thus in the first place a question of the distribution or the exchange of goods that man finds ready to hand.

Natural Law and Property in the Late-Scholastic, Early-Modern Period

The natural-law treatment of private property in the early-modern period represents a broad continuation of the treatment found in Aquinas's works on the subject. Particular emphases, however, did begin to develop. One sees, for example, in the late-scholastic writings not only an affirmation of common use and private ownership but also a pronounced critique of common ownership.

Domingo de Soto (1494–1560), for example, underlines Aquinas's point about the tendency of common owners of a piece of property to shirk their responsibilities, but he also stresses other particular negative moral effects. Common ownership, he maintains, tends to corrode the virtue of liberality, not least because 'those who own nothing cannot be liberal'.[10] Tomas de Mercado (1530–1576) stresses that people tend to be more naturally inclined than the state to care for their home. 'If universal love', he writes, 'will not induce people to take care of their things, then private interest will. Hence private goods will multiply. If they remain in common possession, the opposite will be true.'[11] Other late scholastics, such as Juan de Mariana, underline the abuses that occur when things are owned in common. Speaking of his own religious order (the Jesuits), he exclaims, 'Certainly it is natural for people to spend much more when they are supplied in common than when they have to obtain things on their own. The extent of our common expenses is unbelievable'.[12]

None of these observations undermine Aristotle's or Aquinas's position on common use and private ownership. Indeed, they elaborate their points. Nor, it should be observed, did any late-scholastic writer believe that private property was absolute. Without exception, they endorse Aquinas's strictures on private property becoming 'common' in situations of extreme need.[13] Some late scholastics such as Martín de Azpilcueta (1491–1586) do, however, argue that even in cases of extreme need, it is not proven 'that extreme need makes the needy the absolute owner of the neighbor's good. It only gives them a right to use them if it is necessary to escape the need'.[14]

Some of these late-scholastic emphases, we may speculate, owe something to external factors. One was the emergence of the modern state, which, especially after the sixteenth-century religious schisms, had become increasingly powerful. The state was now more inclined to impose heavier taxation or to debase the currency to reduce government debts, many of which came from the costs of waging war. In their powerful criticisms of the negative economic and moral effects of such policies, Mercado and Mariana explicitly link their arguments to considerations about unjust infringements of private ownership of property, with Mariana going so far as to describe currency debasement as a form of theft.[15]

This question of the state's power vis-à-vis private ownership may also help explain some seventeenth- and eighteenth-century northern European natural-law treatments of private property. Here we find more divergence of opinion compared to the late-scholastic writers, although writers such as Hugo Grotius (1583–1645), Samuel von Pufendorf (1632–1694), Gershom Carmichael (1672–1729), and Francis Hutcheson (1694–1746) are far closer to the scholastic approach than otherwise suspected. In *De Iure Praedae*, for example, Grotius thinks that it is 'permissible to acquire to oneself, and to retain, those things which are useful for life'.[16] But because all things have been given by God to 'the human race, not upon individual men, and since such gifts could not be turned to use except by private occupation, it necessarily followed that what had been seized on should become his to each'.[17] From this understanding is derived the right to property: 'Let no one occupy what has been occupied by another.'[18] Pufendorf takes a similar line, arguing that while things are given to humanity in common, God allows people to use their reason to work out the best way of realizing common use, and generally, people had resolved that private property was the best way to do so. He does, however, add that expressions of property rights would become more diverse as the concept was applied over time to more and new things, commerce expanded, and social and economic life became more sophisticated.[19]

This maturation of natural-law reasoning about property *rights*—especially in terms of protections from undue interventions from the state—is especially evident in the writings of Carmichael and Hutcheson, often described as forefathers of the Scottish Enlightenment. While, as will be illustrated, both were influenced by Locke, they also clearly saw themselves as working in the natural-law tradition. Carmichael even acknowledges in his *Synopsis Theologiae Naturalis* (1729) that he found 'the doctrines of the Scholastics, or rather of the more ancient among them... much more correct and more consonant with sound reason, as well as with sacred scripture, than the doctrines that are opposed to them today'.[20]

Carmichael held that God does not appear to have assigned any one particular external non-human thing to any one particular human being. Property needs therefore to be secured by some type of human action—specifically 'by human labor'—and 'more closely adapted for human purposes'.[21] On this basis, he proceeds to identify different categories of property rights, most notably *'real* or *personal'* rights.[22] Real rights involve possession and use of things (that is, property), to which corresponds the obligation of others not to disturb them in their use of things. Personal rights are about those things and services conditionally owed to us[23] through mediums such as contracts. Neither real nor personal rights in Carmichael's schema are 'absolute'. They may be created, exchanged, transferred, or abolished, but he stresses that this should normally occur through voluntary consent.

Hutcheson's line of reasoning about property is similar. Human reason contains clear evidence of what God desires of human beings.[24] The first precept is to worship and obey God. The second is that 'we ought to promote the common good of all, and that of particular persons, while it in no way obstructs the common good'.[25] In his view, it is through people pursuing their advantages without harming others or violating the natural law that the common good is advanced: 'He who profits one part without hurting another plainly profits the whole.'[26] Hutcheson then argues that there are so many 'enjoyments and advantages' that all people desire and can procure for themselves 'without hurting others, and which 'tis plainly the interest of society that each one should be allowed to procure, without obstruction from others'. It follows that 'each man has a *right* to procure and obtain such advantages and enjoyments'.[27]

In delineating different property rights, Hutcheson replicates Carmichael's real and personal rights.[28] Initially he is somewhat dismissive of Lockean theories of property,[29] arguing that we should focus upon what are the human and just conditions that allow us to say that one person owns certain goods to the exclusion of others. Nonetheless, he does argue that the natural fruits of a person's labour are the foundation of merit that provides one person with a basic title to particular property.[30] In part, he may be forging an argument against David Hume's position that property emerges as a result of the usefulness of a convention that eventually receives endorsement and codification in law. While not dismissive of these factors, Hutcheson clearly believes that the causes of property can be identified beyond the realm of conventions and the useful. It involves consideration of what principles and causes demonstrate that it is human, just, and 'requisite also to the maintenance of amicable society' (that is, the common good) for people to own things and to use them to the exclusion of others.[31]

Locke's New Account of Property

It was the genius of John Locke to introduce a new understanding of property and a new account of natural law in a way that seemed only slightly to shift emphasis in the traditional understanding. Or at least they seemed to resemble it sufficiently to assuage those who wanted to believe in its continuity — which is why it makes sense to speak of some of his chronological successors as closer to his predecessors. Locke's art is subtle enough to confuse contemporary commentators who, acquainted with the less-abashed modernity descended from him and unfamiliar with the forebears he quietly abandoned, think his doctrine of property essentially the same as Aquinas's.[32] This view has the advantage of focusing attention on what Locke says about the public good, indeed on all those elements of his language that he derives from the natural-law tradition, but it is important to concentrate as well on the differences, lest erudition blind common sense. First, in contrast to Aquinas and the Aristotelian tradition, Locke distinguishes the grounds of slavery and property, treating slavery as against nature, except in punishment, and property as unmistakably natural; his redefinition of the end of government follows from this change. Second, Locke understands property to consist less in the distribution of what man is given than in the creation of his labour and ingenuity; what for Aristotle and Aquinas was a concession to man's intractable preference for himself is to Locke the key to unlocking human potential.

Locke's tactic of making concessions to tradition even while developing a novel idea is exemplified by a passage in his *First Treatise* often cited to establish the traditional character of his ideas on property. Locke admits that God has given a man's 'needy Brother a Right to the surplusage of his Goods; so that it cannot justly be denied him, when his pressing Wants call for it', referring to this claim as a title given by charity. This seems a reiteration of Aquinas's requirement that goods be reserved for common use, even if assigned to private administrators.

What is important to recall, however, is the context of the passage, which is not to limit the right of property *per se* but to insist on the strict separation of the claim to own and the claim to rule—a separation Locke intends more to limit government than to disenfranchise property. Indeed, in the next paragraph, he allows the 'rich proprietor' to extract a contract of obedience from the needy in exchange for food, insisting only that the relationship results from consent and not be seized as a matter of right, making clear that the title to charity might be pleaded but might not be enforced.[33] Moreover, as has been recently argued, the claim to charity can be raised only by those without capacity to labour[34] — but to see this we must proceed to the *Second Treatise*, where Locke develops his theory of property and government in a positive rather than a critical frame.

Locke begins his *Second Treatise* with a definition of political power, which he develops by elaborating what he calls, like Thomas Hobbes, the state of nature. This 'state of perfect freedom' and 'also of equality' is a condition of men living together without government — that is, without a common judge. But it is not a state of licence, Locke insists, because men are under the law of nature: 'And Reason, which is that Law, teaches all Mankind, who will but consult it, that being all equal and independent, no one ought to harm another in his Life, Health, Liberty, or Possessions.' Reason arrives at this conclusion by reflecting that men are 'his Property, whose Workmanship they are', namely, that of 'one Omnipotent, and infinitely wise Maker'. And this yields to each of them the duty '*to preserve himself*' and 'as much as he can, *to preserve the rest of Mankind*', at least so far as 'his own Preservation comes not in competition'.[35] Except perhaps by the doubts that might be raised at the prospect of competition for survival, this beginning seems traditional enough; Aquinas, after all, had followed the classical tradition in listing self-preservation as the first precept of natural law.

Locke, however, does not proceed to the other precepts, and only occasionally does another ever appear in the *Second Treatise*.[36] Instead, he introduces what he calls his 'very strange Doctrine' that every man in the state of nature has the executive power of the law of nature. Although this makes each the judge of his own cause, where he is apt to prefer himself, Lockean reason does not conclude that nature appoints men to live under a common judge or government. He quotes Richard Hooker, the Anglican Aquinas, for the traditional view that 'to supply those Defects and Imperfections which are in us, as living singly and solely by our selves, we are naturally induced to seek Communion and Fellowship with others, this was the Cause of Men's uniting themselves, at first in Politick Societies'. As if to highlight his departure, he adds, 'But I moreover affirm, that all Men are naturally in that State [of nature], and remain so, till by their own Consents they make themselves Members of some Politick Society'.[37]

Six chapters and 108 sections ensue before Locke's men are ready to consent to 'Politick Society'. And although much of the intervening text has to do with the historical origins of government and with the family, before Locke goes even so far, he considers—following Aristotle's order if not his theory—slavery and property. Aristotle distinguished the mastery of slaves from political rule, but the union of the naturally ruling and naturally ruled was indicative of the natural character of the household and so of the city. For Locke, as there is nothing natural about government, so slavery in the state of nature is narrowly confined: captives in a just war may be enslaved by a victor who forebears killing them, but no man has a right to sell himself into slavery. He repeats, now with some indirection and without mention of the Deity, that a man 'cannot take away his own Life'. And then, further undermining slavery and seeming to contradict the reason he just relied upon, he explains without condemnation that whenever the slave 'finds the hardship of his Slavery out-weigh the value of his Life, 'tis in his Power, by resisting the Will of his Master, to draw on himself the Death he desires'.[38]

Locke's account of property and its acquisition likewise departs from Aristotle's discussion of household management and acquisition as an ancillary art limited by need and use. Indeed, chapter five of the *Second Treatise*, 'Of Property', is one of the most celebrated passages in the history of political theory. The first thing to notice is that Locke treats property strictly in the context of the state of nature, that quasi-historical, quasi-theoretical condition in which human beings are considered as free and equal individuals, subject only to natural law, living and judging for themselves alone. Now and again he 'slips' and speaks as though property belongs to a family, but strictly speaking the family is not introduced until later; here Nature is 'Mother', and what she offers belongs 'equally to all her Children'. Actually, Locke begins with a couple of sections that acknowledge that 'God... hath given the World to Men in common', but He is quietly retired, for reasons we will soon see, and the 'spontaneous hand of Nature' takes His place.

The question with which Locke begins is how, out of this common, 'Men might come to have a *property* in several parts of that which God gave to mankind in common, and that without any express Compact of the Commoners'. His answer is, by his labour, which he wholly owns, since 'every Man has a *Property* in his own *Person*'. The first indication that Locke has left God out of the argument is his silence on the question of how man can have property in something said a few chapters before to be God's property, namely, himself. James Tully's suggestion that this is unproblematic, since man's property in himself means only to exclude other men and so can coincide with divine proprietorship, is unsatisfactory, not only because Locke makes no such assertion, but also because it avoids the question of whether God, who gave men the world in common, gave each sole ownership of himself, rather than, say, giving men to one another's care.[39]

In any event, Locke believes that 'the first gathering' is enough by way of labour to give man property in what he takes from the common, for it is enough to 'exclude the common right of other Men'. The only qualification is that this right to property in things taken from the common holds 'at least where there is enough, and as good left in common for others', and soon Locke finds a way to neutralize even that. Tully's assertion that 'the fundamental argument of the *Two treatises*' is 'that God gave the world to man as common property'[40] is true only in the sense that most buildings have their foundation in the ground: you need the ground to build, but the ground does not determine the kind of structure, at least if the architect is clever. The burden of Locke's theory of property is to show how the common is parcelled out, and its secret is that God in His wisdom did not give us very much.[41]

The key to Locke's argument is to understand why the requirement that 'enough and as good' remains is no serious obstacle to privatization. That the argument holds with air and water is self-evident and unproblematic; there is always (in normal circumstances) plenty more. But land and its fruits seem otherwise and often scarce enough to make Locke's case far less than universal in its application. Moreover, he adds that 'Nothing was made by God for Man to spoil or destroy', suggesting a traditional limit on just acquisition, if also suggesting natural scarcity, against the presumption of 'enough and as good'. Then, with characteristic indirection, he writes, as if digressing: 'To which let me add, that he who appropriates land to himself by his labour, does not lessen but increase the common stock of mankind.' It is an elegant argument he makes: if cultivated land is ten times more productive than prairie, heath, or forest, to cultivate ten acres is to produce the *natural* yield of one hundred, so one 'may truly be said, to give ninety acres to Mankind'.

Within the paragraph, the ratio of productivity has grown to one against one hundred, and within a few pages, it is one against one thousand. In the early days of economic development, as we would say, there was thus always 'enough and as good', since enclosure was the seed of plenty. In more crowded modern times, land may not be so plentiful in the settled areas, but America is wide open, and Locke has even heard of land for the taking in Spain. Besides, he suggests, in a developed — or rather, continually developing — economy, there are numerous profitable uses for human labour, even if land grows scarce. As he writes in one of his most celebrated sentences, contrasting the relative achievements of nature and human industry in providing human needs and wants, 'a King of a large and fruitful Territory [in America] feeds, lodges, and is clad worse than a day Labourer in *England*'.[42]

What makes possible such development, of course, is the invention of money, that is, of a durable good that has its value from 'the tacit Agreement of Men'. Here, rather than in appropriation from the common, is the locus of consent in economic matters for Locke, and it has the happy consequence not only of facilitating the complex exchanges upon which an industrious society depends, but also of solving the problem of spoilage, since durable money never rots. Introduced by consent, itself the product of labour, money can be amassed without prejudice to any man, according to Locke — '*the exceeding of the bounds of his* just *Property* not lying in the largeness of his Possession, but the perishing of any thing uselessly in it' — although perhaps to the annoyance of the 'Quarrelsome and Contentious'.[43] While for Aquinas, following Aristotle, the essence of money was its usefulness in exchange, for Locke it is its durability; Locke does not call this 'capital' yet, but he has clearly grasped the idea, and one is not surprised to learn that in his papers on interest, a sophisticated economics that anticipates the work of Adam Smith is in evidence.[44] Originating in tacit agreement, money, like real property, antedates government, even as it shares its basis in consent. Property, then, has a human origin, in labour or consent or some admixture of the two, but both issue naturally from the human personality for Locke, prior to any authoritative structure of command.

Locke makes clear that once governments are formed, property takes on a positive rather than a simply natural status; in his terms, men and nations 'have, by *positive agreement, settled a Property* among themselves, in distinct Parts and parcels of the Earth'. While the tacit agreement on valuing money ensures 'an inequality of private possessions' even without a fully formed civil society, 'in Government the Laws regulate the right of property, and the possession of land is by positive constitutions'. But Locke argues that natural law is not simply retired once government is formed. After all, it is the insecurity of property in the state of nature that helps give man the impetus to establish government in the first place. And the end of government, he repeats again and again, is the preservation of property, understood to encompass life, liberty, and estate. If property has its origin in man's natural labour, it gains security in society when defined by 'settled, standing rules' made by the legislature, rules that cannot be altered by absolute and arbitrary power.

That Locke is serious about the protection of property as the end of government becomes clear when he makes its violation a licence for revolt. From that standpoint, private property is the common good of the new republicanism, not just for the pleasures it offers but also for the protection of liberty it affords.[45] The paradox apparent in this standard reflects the great discovery, or great hope, upon which the modern science of political economy also was based, namely, that by pursuing his individual interest, a man might best contribute to the common wealth. In Locke this intimation does not take on the character of natural necessity, but it does reinforce natural law. Although the city does not exist by nature, a man's natural pursuit of his own preservation and development, when channelled in the matrix of industry and rationality that is civil society, tends to raise the lot of all.

Property and Utilitarianism

While the classical and early-modern natural-law tradition of reflection upon property demonstrates some concern for utility, it is as much concerned with reasoning about the substance of justice and the common good. A shift toward an almost exclusively utilitarian justification for property arises, however, with utilitarianism's emergence as a distinctive philosophical position. While utilitarian reasoning about property is usually associated with Jeremy Bentham, it initially acquired considerable momentum with David Hume. For Hume, the convention of property emerges because sufficient numbers of people desire to have stability of possession. Over time, these conventions facilitate more patterns of behaviour, many of which become recognized in law.[46] Thus, as Stephen Munzer observes, Hume believes that 'utility in the sense of common interest explains how private property arises'.[47]

There are certain parallels here between Hume's thought and that of Pufendorf, Carmichael, and Hutcheson, but there is at least one significant difference. The difference lies in their concepts of justice. Pufendorf, Carmichael, and Hutcheson argue to different degrees that private-property arrangements are generally just because they enable realization of the principle of common use that is self-evident to human reason. Hume, by contrast, argues for private property based on experience of its utility in regulating many people's relationship with those things that can be viewed as property. The two justifications are not necessarily in conflict, not least because the classical and early-modern natural-law traditions had a healthy regard for private property's efficacious character; reason and experience often confirm the wisdom revealed by the other. Nonetheless, the two do point to different ways of morally reasoning about the validity or otherwise of a social institution such as property.

With Bentham, however, a wider shift away from natural-law reasoning begins to open, and Hume's influence is significant. In his *Fragment on Government*,[48] Bentham specifically acknowledges how illuminating he found

Hume's claim that, in the final analysis, every virtue is derived from *utility*. In another place, Hume went so far as to state that 'public utility is the sole origin of justice'.[49] To Bentham's mind, 'Property is nothing but a basis of expectation; the expectation of deriving certain advantages from a thing which we are said to possess, in consequence of the relation in which we stand towards it'.[50] Human beings are able to anticipate the future, including the circumstances and conditions that minimize pain and maximize pleasure—that is, utility. Given that property creates stability and security that enhance people's ability to maximize their pleasure and minimize their pain, then it may be grounded in a concern for utility. With this theoretical explanation in place, Bentham proceeds to discuss the various ways in which different property arrangements and legal mechanisms (wills, contracts, title acquisition, etc.) best realize this function of property.

While there are certain similarities between the ways that Bentham and the classical and early-modern natural-law traditions considered the legal and economic implications of private property arrangements, their philosophical justifications for private property are profoundly different. This difference is exacerbated by Bentham's commitment to a rather 'hard' version of legal positivism, which essentially denies any necessary link between the demands of morality and the law. For the classical and early-modern natural-law schools, private property required legal recognition as a matter of justice and as part of the state's limited responsibility to uphold and promote the common good. This not only protected private property from encroachments from private actors, it also limited the state's ability to alter the rules and institutions of property in any given scenario.

The same, however, cannot be said of utilitarianism, especially when it is embedded in a framework of legal positivism. As John Finnis observes, legal positivism actually embodies a range of moral assumptions.[51] Even the twentieth century's most prominent positivist jurist, Hans Kelsen, conceded that 'by [legal] "norm" we mean something ought to be or ought to happen, especially that a human being ought to act in a specific way'.[52] That said, neither legal positivism nor utilitarianism has an *in-principle moral objection* to

substituting general common ownership for private property. If — as many socialists propose — collective property
arrangements minimize pain and maximize pleasure, and if
the state is entitled to revise property arrangements in the
interests of what it considers to constitute utility and
efficiency at a given moment, then the only obstacle left to
collectivized arrangements are arguments about efficiency.

Arguments about economic efficieny are important. The
track record of common ownership compared to private
property in facilitating long-term economic prosperity, for
example, is abysmal. Utilitarianism, however, cannot provide a basis for the interpersonal comparisons of utility that
are often important components of such arguments. Utilitarianism presumes that people can actually know all of the
possible effects of their actions and then decide — weighing
all the possible pleasures and pains proceeding from a
variety of possible actions — which act is likely to produce the
most pleasure. Such a calculation is simply impossible. If we
purport to *know* — not 'feel' — that one future embodies more
good (pleasure) than any of its alternatives, we are claiming
to understand the future in a manner beyond the cognitive
powers of human reason. Then there is the problem of
'incommensurability': the inability to reduce all experiences
and actions to one common measure in a way that meets the
demands of reason. We cannot, for example, weigh pleasures
and pains, because they have no common denominator. We
cannot reasonably claim to objectively measure the experience of unemployment against growth in wisdom, against
the death of a spouse, against a happy family.

As if aware of these objections, Bentham claims that
people could narrow the range of necessary calculations by
giving greater weight to that which brought them more
pleasure than to something that brought less. Here, however,
Benthamite utilitarianism encounters further problems. This
reduction of horizons, as Finnis explains, 'cannot be guided
by any *moral* principle of responsibility'. Put differently,
there are no morally objective criteria that can establish what
is greater pleasure or lesser pain. This means that in the process of narrowing, we will be guided primarily not by what
we reason but rather by what we happen to want.[53] In this
light, we should not be surprised that rule utilitarians such

as John Stuart Mill moved in later life toward strong limitations on private property—far stronger than those articulated by most classical and early-modern natural-law scholars—even favouring arrangements that might be considered 'socialist', with all of socialism's well-known negative effects upon human liberty and human dignity (not to mention economic prosperity). If it is judged that utility is better served by common ownership and/or heavy regulation, utility will be no barrier to diluting significantly private property rights in ways foreign to the classical and early-modern natural-law traditions.

Natural Law, Property, and Regulation

In light of this theoretical background, how might natural-law reasoning be applied to some modern property issues? Two questions likely to feature significantly in any discussion of property rights in the modern global economy are regulation and intellectual property.

Regulation is a perennially controversial subject. But apart from anarchists, relatively few disagree that the state has some role in organizing the rules that shape everyday economic life. Adam Smith certainly believed this to be the case. Contemporary arguments tend to be about the degree of regulation and its relative efficacy, and sometimes about the degree to which regulation should occur via government fiat versus through the various rights and responsibilities associated with private property and associated legal mechanisms, such as private contracts.

One issue rarely examined in these debates is the fact that utilitarianism does *not* provide a stable philosophical framework for thinking through the question of regulation in a coherent way. As an essentially incoherent philosophical position, utilitarianism—be it of the rule or act variety—will produce a generally arbitrary regulatory system in so far as it relies on governments making decisions based upon impossible calculations about the known and the unknown effects of certain regulatory acts. It might well be the case that adherence to, and reflection upon, natural-law principles of property provides a more stable foundation for thinking about the validity of different regulatory proposals, and perhaps even a simpler regulatory framework.

Contemporary examples of such natural-law thought being applied in a systematic manner to questions of economic regulation are difficult to identify. Perhaps the closest example may be found in the Freiburg School of Ordoliberalism, much identified with the economists Walter Eucken (1891–1950) and Franz Böhm (1895–1977). Eucken and Böhm were especially concerned with the issue of how to preserve freedom in complex social orders based primarily upon voluntary cooperation. Eucken was worried about the accumulation of power and was less convinced that the spontaneous interaction of people usually sufficed to produce a stable and flourishing social order. 'The experience of the last decades has shown', he contended, 'that business associations and interest groups have mastered the art of turning every politically influential ideology to their own purpose in a most effective manner.'[54] Cartels exemplified how private contracts, often with the support of the legal system and the government, were used to shelter sections of the economy from competition. This collusion of private and public power undermined essential market mechanisms such as free prices and paved the way for extensive economic intervention and, eventually, centrally planned economies.

Seeking to find ways to limit the ability of interest groups to capture state power, Eucken and Böhm drew upon both Scottish Enlightenment insights and natural-law reasoning to establish precise parameters that recognized the state's legitimate authority in questions of regulation while simultaneously limiting that authority to very specific tasks.

Undergirding Eucken's *ordo* framework—his *natürliche Ordnung* (natural order)—were eight 'constitutive' and four 'regulative' principles. The most essential constitutive principle required for free competition was an efficient and free price system. This ruled out policies such as exchange controls and monopolies. The other constitutive principles were a commitment to a stable anti-inflationary monetary system, open markets and free trade, protection of private property, freedom to contract (without allowing people to contract in ways that diminish others' freedom to contract), liabilities for people's formal commitments and choices (thereby tying risk to responsibility), constancy of economic policy (in the sense of avoiding decisions that create uncertainty), and acknowledging the interdependence of all of the constitutive principles.[55] Eucken sought to limit government interventions in the economy to what he called 'regulative principles' consistent with maintaining a free market, such as prohibiting the establishment of monopolies.[56] An economy controlled by monopolies and cartels effectively destroyed the liberty of other market participants, thus rendering meaningless the rule of law.[57]

Certainly these principles could be interpreted in purely positivist terms. There are different opinions as to whether this *natürliche Ordnung* reflects *Naturrechtsordnung*. Indeed, Eucken specified that his regulative principles were not derived from natural-law axioms. Yet at the same time, he defined his competitive order as a natural order that corresponds to the will of God.[58] At a minimum, one may say that none of the constitutive principles contradict any principles of natural law. In any event, they may well reflect a natural-law approach to regulation in significant contrast to more contemporary natural-law reflection upon regulation, which tends to focus on how regulation can contribute to the realization of distributive justice. It is, however, an open question as to whether this is an especially helpful focus.

As several natural-law scholars have observed in recent decades, distributive justice is not simply about need. It also concerns questions of merit, worth, desert, etc. This underlines a central problem with John Rawls' 'difference principle', that is, the claim that social and economic institutions—in particular, social and economic inequalities—always must be arranged to the advantage (in the sense of Rawls' 'primary goods') of the least-advantaged class (whomever they might be). Once considerations such as merit and desert are excluded, as Rawls insists they must be, then we cannot look backwards to judge who, for example, has worked harder or contributed more. The situation is further complicated by the fact that in an economic order in which literally millions of ongoing acts of exchange and entrepreneurship occur every day, it is impossible to identify (1) the sum total of wealth to be redistributed or (2) the point in time at which we can assess the validity of the precise distribution of goods. Either course of action necessarily involves making *arbitrary* judgments. Then there is the reality that the fact that someone owns more than another does not in itself mean that the principle of common use is somehow being violated. In sophisticated developed economies, the private wealth of those who have more is normally being used in myriad ways that enable others to make use of the same, still privately owned, wealth. This use may come in the form of investments that allow other businesses to grow, which in turn creates employment and allows people to develop the virtue of liberality, to give philanthropically, etc.

If these are legitimate concerns, then perhaps the more significant contribution that natural-law thought can make to issues of property regulation is twofold. One contribution, which would be consistent with both the classical and the early-modern natural-law traditions, might be to focus the distribution issue upon questions of extreme need. Debates about what constitutes real poverty and where precisely one draws the poverty line will continue, but the natural-law tradition offers firm guidance on what constitutes extreme need. If the state and the law are able to issue regulatory guidance on how to address this in a way that accords with the rather strict parameters outlined by figures such as Aquinas and Martín de Azpilcueta, this might address *part* of the distribution question without falling into the trap of arbitrariness. And it might leave it to private actors to actualize *their* responsibilities in distributive justice.

The second contribution may be to rethink the question of property and regulation from the standpoint of *natural law* and *natural rights,* as was especially evident in the late-scholastic and early-modern natural-law traditions. When it comes to the subject of rights, natural-law thinking is quite precise about the nature and the origins of rights in ways that are less evident in other intellectual traditions. A good example concerns the issue of free trade. The first to argue that liberty to trade privately owned goods and services — including capital — across national boundaries is not a privilege but rather a *right* was the sixteenth-century theologian and natural-law thinker Francisco de Vitoria in *De Indis et de Ivre Belli Relectiones* (1532). Here Vitoria states that the right to free trade is derived from the natural right of *free association* enjoyed by all people. Significantly, he made this argument in the context of insisting that the peoples of Latin

America should not be prevented from freely trading with European merchants by either the indigenous rulers or by the Spanish king. He even went so far as to describe laws inhibiting free trade between nations as 'iniquitous and against charity'.[59]

In one sense, this embodied the application of the Christian idea of universal brotherhood of all human beings to an economic issue. But it also reflected the natural-law insight that human flourishing cannot be realized without some association with others, be it the living or the long dead. This did not mean that there are no grounds for the state to regulate trade between countries. The state well might have prudential reasons to limit or even to forbid trade with particular regimes or countries. In the circumstances of a declared war, the government well may forbid trade with enemy countries. But the normative natural-law principle remains that as a form of legitimate, peaceful association that allows participation in a number of moral goods and involves no intention of harm to others, free trade is a natural right, with all the authority that natural law confers upon such a right.

Adherence to such a principle cannot but affect the regulation of property exchanges across and within natural boundaries. Moreover, it brings with it the added benefit of being an intellectually coherent position that is less easily swept aside or unduly limited by state fiat. A state bound by an adherence to natural-law principles is far less able to undermine free exchange, as opposed to a state that is only bound by considerations of convention and utility, both of which government officials can easily dismiss in the name of some dubious calculation of purported utility.

Intellectual Property and Natural Law

While the free exchange of material goods and services is a natural right, it is not immediately obvious that property rights in intellectual goods have natural-rights status. On the contrary, scholars of intellectual property commonly quote Thomas Jefferson's letter to Isaac McPherson, written in 1813 in response to an enquiry about the extension of a patent. He pronounces it 'a moot question whether the origin of any kind of property is derived from nature at all', noting that physical property begins with occupation, and concluding that 'stable ownership is a gift of social law, and is given late in the progress of society'. He then proceeds:

> It would be curious, then, if an idea, the fugitive ferment-ation of an individual brain, could, of natural right, be claimed in exclusive and stable property. If nature has made any one thing less susceptible than all others of exclusive property, it is the action of the thinking power called an idea, which an individual may exclusively possess as long as he keeps it to himself; but the moment it is divulged, it forces itself into the possession of everyone, and the receiver can-not dispossess himself of it. Its peculiar character, too, is that no one possesses the less, because every other possesses the whole of it. He who receives an idea from me, receives instruction himself, without lessening mine; as he who lights his taper at mine, receives light without darkening me. That ideas should freely spread from one to another over the globe, for the moral and mutual instruction of man, and improvement of his condition, seems to have been peculiarly and benevolently designed by nature... Inventions then cannot, in nature, be a subject of property. Society may give an exclusive right to the profits arising from them, as an encouragement to men to pursue ideas which may produce utility, but this may or may not be done, according to the will and convenience of the society, without claim or com-plaint from any body.[60]

Precisely as, in the formulation of thoughts, 'the opinions and beliefs of men depend not on their own will, but follow involuntarily the evidence proposed to their minds'—the opening words of Jefferson's draft statute on religious free-dom—so it is in the diffusion of thoughts; nature is not subject to human manipulation, at least not without distortion.[61]

This notion meshes perfectly with the constitutional treatment of the issue: 'The Congress shall have Power... To promote the Progress of Science and useful Arts, by securing for limited Times to Authors and Inventors the exclusive Right to their respective writings and Discoveries' (art. 1, sec. 8, clause 8). In this clause, what we call 'intellectual property' appears as a discretionary statutory right created for a util-itarian purpose; implicitly, copyrights and patent rights would be limited exceptions to the presumption against state-created monopolies. As it happened, the first Congress copied the British system from the 1710 Statute of Anne with regard to copyrights, allowing a fourteen-year copyright for published works and a fourteen-year renewal if the author was still alive at expiration, assigning all other published materials to the public domain. In 1831 Congress doubled the initial term and in 1909 doubled the renewal period. So at the beginning of the twentieth century, a work could be copyrighted for fifty-six years. The 1790 act had extended protection to works already in print as of the time of its passage, and subsequent extensions applied to works then under copyright.[62]

Patent law was separate. Also established in 1790, it originally allowed a single fourteen-year term. Its principles, though related to those of the copyright's, were considered distinct, since an inventor might choose to preserve his knowledge as a trade secret (as, for example, the formula for Coca-Cola remains today). A patent is a *quid pro quo,* it is generally said, whereby the inventor discloses to the public a full accounting of his invention and is thereby guaranteed a temporary exclusive right to its production or use. The disclosure in a patent allows others to build upon the knowledge of the first inventor; copyright, of course, involves disclosure in the act of publication itself.

But Jefferson's theory and early-American copyright and patent law is only half the story. If the origin of property is in labour and the origin of most value in human making, then the mind that initiates labour is the principal source of the natural right of ownership. For Locke, after all, although property originates in mixing labour with natural things, as his account progresses, the value of labour grows and that of nature diminishes. Although Jefferson, drawing his account of ideas from Locke, emphasizes the idea's independence from the mind that first discovers or develops it, it is easy to see how Locke's emphasis on the human origin of property could establish the opposite presumption: intellectual property might be considered property in its purest form and thus no less—maybe even more—deserving of protection than most other forms. Already at the time of the 1831 revision of copyright law in the United States, members of Congress were asserting that 'an author has an exclusive and perpetual right, in preference to any other, to the fruits of his labor' and that copyright is 'merely a legal provision for the protection of a natural right', a view repudiated by the Supreme Court a few years later but nevertheless obviously in circulation.[63]

French law had established a *droit d'auteur* even before the Revolution and reiterated it afterwards. And the French apparently took the lead in establishing the international Berne Convention for the Protection of Literary and Artistic Works in 1886, which in contrast to Anglo-American copyright law, established the right as soon as the work was finished, whether or not it was published or registered, and treated the right as a moral one. The US Constitution's reference to authors and inventors rather than to publishers and manufacturers might seem to draw upon the creative-property tradition, even as its reference to a 'limited time' might suggest a positive rather than a natural right. Only in 1976 did Congress align US copyright to the Berne Convention, dropping the requirement that copyright be registered and extending future protection until fifty years after the author's death. It meanwhile lengthened the term for works already protected from fifty-six to seventy-five years, a term extended for an additional twenty years in the 1998 Copyright Term Extension Act (CTEA).[64]

While patent law remained generally stable, copyright law was altered, not only to change the term of copyright and alter the moment (and maybe the theory) of its origin, but also to respond to technological developments. As Lawrence Lessig has pointed out, Congress's response to changing technology has been uneven, although not necessarily irrational.[65] Stage performances could not be copyrighted, only written scripts and scores, but audio and visual recording raised the question of whether a record or a film was like a performance or like a script or score. For musical recording, Congress established a licence fee: once a composer allowed a piece to be recorded, anyone else could record it, too, provided the owner of the copyright was paid a set fee. Radio can broadcast a performance upon paying a fee to the composer, although it need not pay the recording artist. Films can be copyrighted, but authors of books and scripts came to be accorded rights to control the making of films deriving from their written texts. Recordings can be copyrighted, too, restricting the rights of others to make copies for use or for sale.

Although all copyright law makes an exception for fair use, this has not been precisely delineated in law; video recording from broadcasts is permitted for temporary, private use, but sharing of copyrighted files over the internet has been a subject of extensive litigation and draconian punishment. Increasingly, encryption technology is being employed by the producers of cultural products to disable or to at least encumber the technical ability of others to copy, regardless of the question of legal right. And the global character of the internet has made all such questions matters of international concern, as the distribution of digital content is no longer bound by territorial space and its control; 'bootlegging' and 'piracy' are rampant, particularly outside the United States and Europe, despite international conventions and trade agreements.[66]

The United States Supreme Court issued a major opinion on copyright law in 2003 in the case of *Eldred v. Ashcroft*, notable more for the road not taken than for any substantive determination concerning the nature of copyright.[67] The case involved a challenge to the constitutionality of the 1998 CTEA, also known as the Sony Bono Act. The plaintiff, represented by a legal team headed by Lessig, argued that the extension of the term of copyright to ninety-five years meant that copyright protection was effectively perpetual, contradicting the Constitution's clear command that the right be established for only a 'limited time'. Moreover, since the matter at issue is expression, an underlying right protected by the First Amendment, the court ought to view the restrictions with 'heightened scrutiny', meaning that it should not presume constitutionality. Key to Lessig's argument was the purpose expressed in the copyright clause, 'to promote the progress of science and useful arts', which, he argued, cannot be achieved retroactively by rewarding authors beyond the incentives in place when their work was created. The court rejected the argument by a clear 7–2 margin. Applying the more lenient 'rational basis' test, they noted the history of congressional extension of existing copyrights and accorded Congress an ample presumption of legislative discretion, rejecting also the argument of the dissenters that the public was injured when it was deprived of the accretion of works in the public domain when copyright expired. That no work published since 1923 is now in the public domain or will become so without an explicit grant from its creator before 2018 seemed to the court to be a decision within Congress's authority.

Neither the court in *Eldred* nor its dissenters or critics made use of natural law or natural rights in relation to the issue, at least explicitly. Lessig makes a powerful argument in his book *Free Culture* that the current regime locks in place the dominant forces of contemporary popular culture and thus inhibits genuine cultural development, although his reasoning is largely utilitarian: most cultural creation throughout history has depended to a certain extent upon the borrowing and reworking of existing cultural artefacts. He nicely shows that even Walt Disney's iconic Mickey Mouse, who remains copyrighted with every extension, was introduced in the 1928 synchronized-sound cartoon film *Steamboat Willie,* which was a parody of a silent Buster Keaton film of the same year called *Steamboat Bill, Jr.* He argues that the increasingly intolerant law of copyright now punishes creative efforts that similarly employ emergent technologies to alter or transform cultural products, for instance by restricting the use of film clips even in documentaries and in work created from content available through the internet. Moreover, having discarded copyright registration and renewal while exposing artists to severe liability for copyright infringement, US law inhibits even efforts to copy and preserve decaying film and material from the era between 1923 and the invention of digital media, for it places the burden on would-be preservers to find the owners of old copyrights to material long since removed from public circulation and no longer available commercially—as is indeed the case with the vast majority of copyrighted material.

As for the digital age, if the problem of preservation is apparently solved, new problems of access are multiplying: a traditional book can remain on a library shelf for years and be read by multiple users without further fees to its author or its publisher—or it can be bought once and then resold without a further licence—but every use of an electronic database comes with the potential of a licence fee, and every access through the internet involves making some sort of electronic copy. Lessig argues for a limiting of copyright terms, a restoration of registration and renewal, a lessening of penalties for unauthorized use in areas where technology is emerging and the distinction between piracy and property is not yet settled, and the development of a 'Creative Commons' of freely licensed cultural products.[68] He recognizes, though, that there are powerful interests behind the current system and that the beneficiaries are not only the large corporations he condemns but successful artists, whose creative energies he does not want to deflate.

In light of this ongoing legal tussle, what can considerations of natural law bring to analysis of intellectual property rights? First, a sort of natural-right claim on the part of writers and artists seems to stand behind the intuition that supports copyright protection—and indeed supports its global claim, for true artistic achievement is universally recognized as a contribution to the heritage of humankind. This hardly makes the claim perpetual; it would seem odd to think that a natural right can outlast, at least by much, the natural life of the one who can assert it. Still, the modern culture of Enlightenment has flourished precisely in a context where individual initiative and creativity have been protected and rewarded, while efforts at state-dominated culture have typically been sterile or corrupt.

Second, natural law nevertheless suggests that cultural production has a social context that must itself be nourished and protected as a public good. Rare individual genius is not unheard of, but the greatest eras of science and culture in history—classical Athens, Renaissance Italy, Elizabethan England, late eighteenth- and early nineteenth-century Vienna, and the like—are moments of public patronage as well as private emulation. The concern for the common good of public culture that belongs to the older natural-law tradition thus seems needed to balance an acknowledged modern natural right to the rewards of creative endeavour. This is not the formula for a code but rather again an indication of the need for balance in the allocation of rights of property—and that the fulcrum is not some arbitrary index of utility but a complex understanding of the human good.

Conclusion

Critics of natural law often argue that, beyond articulating broad general principles, natural law struggles to offer more detailed direction when it comes to addressing complex policy issues, especially those with a substantial economic dimension. Our analysis of regulation and intellectual property, however, underscores the limits of such critiques. Although natural-law reasoning about property will not always provide a ready-made solution to any one regulatory issue or intellectual property claim, it does provide a *principled* way of thinking through these issues in ways that avoid the pitfalls of utilitarianism. And it simultaneously promotes the avoidance of decision making marked by profound arbitrariness. In this sense, it arguably incorporates a robust concern for justice into any issue in which property and property rights feature significantly. At the same time, it also grounds reflection on such issues upon an appreciation of human flourishing that goes beyond maximizing pleasure and minimizing pain. This assumes, of course, that there *is* such a thing as human flourishing grounded in moral goods that can be known to human reason and that people *can* freely choose various combinations of these goods in a non-arbitrary manner. Sceptics have always disputed both of these contentions. But that is to quarrel with the substance of natural law itself rather than its application. Should, however, the premises be accepted, then we see that denoting natural-law approaches to questions of property as impractical becomes a far more tenuous claim.

---

1   Thomas Aquinas, *The 'Summa Theologica' of St. Thomas Aquinas*, trans. Fathers of the English Dominican Province (London: Burns, Oates, and Washbourne, 1921): I–II, quest. 94, art. 3.

2   *Ibid.*: art. 5–6. That Aquinas consistently sees property and slavery as identical in status, citing Aristotle for both, appears in II–II, quest. 57, art. 3.

3   See Aristotle, *Politics*: I (1257a–1259a) and II (1260b–1266a); and on slavery: I (1256b26).

4   Aquinas, *Summa Theologica*, II–II, quest. 57.

5   *Ibid.*: quest. 66.

6   *Ibid.*: quest. 57, art. 2–3.

7   See Albert Broderick, OP, 'The Radical Middle: Natural Right of Property in Aquinas and the Popes', in *Natural Law*, I, ed. John

Finnis (New York: New York University Press, 1991): 155–87. First published 1964, *Solicitor Quarterly*, 3: 127–59.

8   Aquinas, *Summa Theologica*, II–II, quest. 77–8.

9   *Ibid.*: I–II, quest. 97, art. 1; quest. 94, art. 6.

10 Domingo de Soto, *De Iustitia et Iure* (Madrid: IEP, 1968): bk. 4, quest. 3, fol. 105–6.

11 Tomas de Mercado, *Summa de Tractos y Contractos* (Seville: 1571): bk. 2, ch. 2, fol. 19.

12 Juan de Mariana, 'Discurso de las Cosas de la Compañia', in *Biblioteca de Autores Españoles*, 31 (Madrid: Editions Atlas, 1950): 2–69, 64.

13 See Alejandro A. Chafuen, *Faith and Liberty: The Economic Thought of the Late Scholastics* (Lanham, MD: Lexington Books, 2003): 43.

14 Martín de Azpilcueta, *Manual de Confessoresy Penitentes* (Salamanca: 1556): 206.

15 See Juan de Mariana, 'Tratado Sobre la Moneda de Vellon', in *Biblioteca de Autores Espanoles*, 31 (Madrid: Editions Atlas, 1950): 560–601, esp. 586.

16 Hugo Grotius, *Commentary on the Law of Prize and Booty*, ed. Martine Julia van Ittersum (Indianapolis, IN: Liberty Fund, 2006): 10. First published 1603.

17 *Ibid.*: 11.

18 *Ibid.*: 13.

19 See Samuel von Pufendorf, *De Officio Hominis et Civis Juxta Legem Naturalem Libri Duo*, vol. 2, trans. Frank Gardner Moore (London: Wildy & Sons Ltd, 1964).

20 Gershom Carmichael, *Natural Rights on the Threshold of the Scottish Enlightenment: The Writings of Gershom Carmichael*, ed. James Moore and Michael Silverthorne (Indianapolis, IN: Liberty Fund, 2002): 229.

21 *Ibid.*: 94.

22 *Ibid.*: 78.

23 See *ibid.*

24 Francis Hutcheson, *A Short Introduction to Moral Philosophy*, ed. Luigi Turco (Indianapolis, IN: Liberty Fund, 2007): 104–5. First published 1747 by the University of Glasgow.

25 *Ibid.*: 109.

26 *Ibid.*: 110.

27 *Ibid.*

28 See *ibid.*: 145.

29 See *ibid.*: 137–8.

30 See *ibid.*: 139–40.

31 *Ibid.*: 137–8.

32 See James Tully, *A Discourse on Property: John Locke and His Adversaries* (Cambridge: Cambridge University Press, 1980); and his more recent *An Approach to Political Philosophy: Locke in Contexts* (Cambridge: Cambridge University Press, 1993): esp. ch. 3.

33   John Locke, *Two Treatises of Government*, ed. Peter Laslett (Cambridge: Cambridge University Press, 1988): treatise I, 42–3.

34   See Gopal Sreenivasan, *The Limits of Lockean Rights in Property* (New York: Oxford University Press, 1995): 102–5.

35   Locke, *Two Treatises*: tre. II, 6.

36   But see *ibid.*: tre. II, 56, where Locke says that parents are 'under an obligation to preserve, nourish, and educate the Children, they had begotten'. This is qualified in tre. I, 65, where paternal power 'so little belongs to the Father by any peculiar right of Nature, but only as he is Guardian of his Children, that when he quits his care of them, he loses his power over them'.

37   *Ibid.*: tre. II, 15.

38   *Ibid.*: tre. II, 23.

39   See Tully, *Discourse on Property*: 105–6.

40   *Ibid.*: 103.

41   The Locke quotations in this paragraph are from *Two Treatises*: tre. II, 25–8.

42   Locke, *Two Treatises*: tre. II, 31, 37, 43, 41.

43   *Ibid.*: tre. II, 36, 46, 34.

44   See Karen Iversen Vaughn, 'The Economic Background to Locke's Two Treatises of Government', in *John Locke's Two Treatises of Government: New Interpretations*, ed. Edward J. Harpham (Lawrence, KS: University Press of Kansas, 1992): 118–47.

45   Locke, *Two Treatises*: tre. II, 45–6. *Cf.* ch. 9 (esp. sec. 123), 11, 19. See also Harvey C. Mansfield, Jr., 'Responsibility Versus Self-Expression', in *Old Rights and New*, ed. Robert A. Licht (Washington, DC: AEI Press, 1993): 96–111; Thomas L. Pangle, *The Spirit of Modern Republicanism: The Moral Vision of the American Founders and the Philosophy of Locke* (Chicago, IL: University of Chicago Press, 1988).

46   See David Hume, *A Treatise of Human Nature*, ed. Lewis A. Selby-Bigge (Oxford: Clarendon Press, 1960): bk. III, pt. II, sec. II–IV, 484–516.

47   Stephen R. Munzer, *A Theory of Property* (Cambridge: Cambridge University Press, 1990): 194.

48   Jeremy Bentham, *A Fragment on Government: And an Introduction to the Principles of Morals and Legislation*, ed. Wilfrid Harrison (Oxford: Basil Blackwell, 1948).

49   David Hume, *An Enquiry Concerning the Principles of Morals*, ed. Tom L. Beauchamp (Oxford: Clarendon Press, 1998): 145.

50   Jeremy Bentham, *Theory of Legislation*, ed. Charles Kay Ogden (London: Routledge & Kegan, 1931): 111–12.

51   See John Finnis, 'The Truth in Legal Positivism', in *The Autonomy of Law: Essays on Legal Positivism*, ed. Robert P. George (Oxford: Oxford University Press, 1996): 195–214, esp. 204.

52   Hans Kelsen, *Pure Theory of Law*, trans. Max Knight (Berkeley, CA: University of California Press, 1970): 4.

53 John Finnis, *Moral Absolutes: Tradition, Revision, and Truth* (Washington, DC: Catholic University of America Press, 1991): 18.
54 Franz Böhm, *Wettbewerb und Monopolkampf* (Berlin: Carl Heymanns verlag, 1933): xi.
55 Walter Eucken, *Grundsätze der Wirtschaftspolitik* (Tübingen: JCB Mohr, 1952): 254.
56 *Ibid.*: 291–4.
57 See *ibid.*: 41–55.
58 See *ibid.*: 176.
59 Francisco de Vitoria, 'Relecciones Sobre los Indios', in *Restituto Sierra Bravo, El Pensamiento Social y Económico de la Escolástica* (Madrid: CSIC, 1975): vol. 2, 610–40, 622.
60 Thomas Jefferson, *Writings* (New York: Library of America, 1984): 1291–2.
61 *Ibid.*: 346.
62 See the review of copyright law in *Eldred v. Ashcroft*, 537 U.S. 186 (2003): 194–223; Lawrence Lessig, *Free Culture: How Big Media Uses Technology and the Law to Lock Down Culture and Control Creativity* (New York: Penguin Press, 2004): 133–6.
63 Quoted in *Eldred v. Ashcroft*, 537 U.S. at 236.
64 *Ibid.* at 195–6.
65 See Lessig, *Free Culture*, esp. ch. 4. The following account draws upon Lessig's discussion.
66 See, for example, the transcript of 'Panel #4: Intellectual Property and the Rule of Law', *Arizona Journal of International and Comparative Law*, 25 (2008): 357–78.
67 *Eldred v. Ashcroft*, 537 U.S. 186 (2003).
68 See Lessig, afterword to *Free Culture*: 275–306.

Edward Skidelsky

The Emancipation
of Avarice

Since 2008, we have seen a surprise revival of the term *greed*.
For many decades, the free-market right saw no harm in
making as much money as one could, while the left spoke
only of inequality and injustice: terms relating to distribution
rather than to motivation. Yet it was avarice, not inequality,
that was on display in the various oversights and abuses
leading to the financial meltdown. The vast bonuses, the
reckless risk-taking, the collusion of auditors and regulators—all fruits, it seemed, of that unlovely vice. Tabloid
journalists led the cry, followed shortly by clerics, happy at
last to be able to talk about something other than sex.

But although once again popular, the term *greed* is not yet
intellectually respectable. In the eyes of many economists,
greedy people are just agents with certain preferences acting
on certain incentives. Joseph Stiglitz, for example, has
insisted that 'those who misbehaved in the corporate and
financial world were not necessarily particularly venal, or
more venal than those who occupied their positions in an
earlier era; rather, their incentives were different, and their
behaviour responded to those incentives'.[1]

If anyone is to blame for the crisis, economists claim, it is
the politicians and the regulators who created those incentives, or even the economists whose false theories inspired
them. But this only pushes the problem back a step. Why did
so many politicians, regulators, and economists—some of
them very intelligent people— accept what in retrospect look
like manifestly bogus theories? Surely motives of ambition
and greed were at play here too, especially given the close

connection among intellectual, political, and financial elites in the developed world. And so the argument bounces back and forth. There seems to be no easy reconciliation between the popular view of the crisis, in which motives such as greed occupy centre stage, and more 'serious' discussion, which focuses exclusively on institutional design.

This incoherence in our response to the financial crisis is not an accident. We are inheritors of two traditions of thinking about wealth, which lie side by side in our minds without mingling. On the one hand, we have it on ancient and venerable authority that the love of money is the root of evil and a sure path to corruption and servitude. Western travellers to China, where cash is given in pretty red envelopes to children and burnt in effigy before graves, feel the residual force of the old Occidental distaste for the 'filthy lucre'. Yet these ancient classical and Christian traditions have been overlaid by another, dating back to the Enlightenment, for which wealth creation is a perfectly innocuous or even benign activity — provided, of course, it is confined within legal limits. This latter attitude is ensconced in centres of political power and mainstream economics. It rules our thinking heads, if not our feeling hearts.

Hence we find the odd inconsistency in our response to the financial crisis. While cries of 'greed' dominate the popular media, serious thinkers are occupied with working out how we can go back to amassing wealth as quickly as possible.

The following essay explores the origins of this inconsistency. It shows how the concept of avarice, having dominated moral discourse about wealth for millennia, was sidelined over the course of the eighteenth century, clearing the ground for the emergence of modern economics. And this revolution was accompanied by another, even deeper revolution of ethical thought, which eventually was to become known as utilitarianism. So comprehensive has been the triumph of this twin revolution that sophisticated minds today find it hard not only to see the love of money as a vice, but to see how anything *like* the love of money ever could have been regarded as a vice. 'Greed' has been relegated along with 'lust' and 'perversion' to the lumber-room of moral language, where only priests and rabble-rousers seek to rummage.

And this of course is a great comfort to those who *are* greedy. Here as elsewhere, economic theory serves, as Percy Bysshe Shelley put it, to 'lull the oppressors of mankind into a security of everlasting triumph'.[2]

Avarice Before the Enlightenment

The philosophers of the eighteenth century confronted a formidable legacy of thinking on the subject of accumulation, almost all of it hostile. This hostility was based not merely on aristocratic or monkish prejudice, as is often alleged, but on the reasonable supposition that the only intrinsically valuable thing in the world is a good human life. Money, and the goods purchasable with money, have value only in so far as they are conducive to such a life. To pursue them beyond this point is irrational. Thomas Aquinas puts it with his usual dry clarity: 'The desire for material things as they are conducive to an end is natural to man. Therefore it is without fault to the extent that it is confined within the norms set by the nature of that end. Avarice exceeds these limits and is thereby sinful.' Aquinas adds that avarice 'darkens the soul' by 'putting love for money above love for God' and compares it to idolatry.[3] However, these theological embellishments are not essential to his argument, which can be stated in purely secular terms.

Aquinas's remarks on avarice summarize a long tradition of thinking on the subject, stretching back to ancient Greece. The legends of Midas, Croesus, and Erysichthon taught Greeks to see the pecuniary passion as sterile and violent. Philosophers such as Aristotle contrasted *pleonexia,* the restless desire for more, with *autarkia,* the tranquil self-sufficiency of the sage.[4] Roman moralists swelled the theme. 'Neither burning heat, nor winter, fire, sea, sword, can turn you aside from gain', declaimed Horace to the miser. 'Nothing stops you, until no second man be richer than yourself.'[5]

Christian authors drew freely from this classical tradition, particularly Aristotle's image of compound interest as a kind of monstrous birth. 'Repeatedly, by the most vile cunning of usury, gold is born from gold itself', runs Gratian's *Decretum,* the foundation of Western canon law. 'Never is there satis-faction; never will there be an end in sight for the greedy.'[6] Examples might be multiplied. For pagans and Christians alike, the miser's sin lay primarily in his insatiability, his incapacity for rest. In a society that took its measure from the eternal identity of God or the circling stars, this ceaseless striving after more seemed tantamount to a breach in the cosmic order.

Nowhere does Aquinas (or any of the authors he draws on) suggest that avarice might be redeemed by its beneficial social effects. Not only did he not perceive any such effects, but even if he had, he could not have accorded them any moral significance. Explanation of this point requires a brief excursus into Aquinas's theory of acts and ends. An act, for Aquinas, has two ends: one 'proximate', which is what makes it the kind of act it is, the other 'ultimate', which is what the agent aims at in acting. If either end is bad, the act as a whole is bad. A good ultimate end cannot redeem a bad proximate end; thieving to help the poor is still thieving. Acts furthermore have consequences that, though foreseen, are not ends of either kind but mere 'double' or side effects. These can sometimes render a good act bad but never a bad act good (praising a little girl is kind, but less so if done in earshot of her jealous sister. Taunting a little girl is never kind, even if it warms her sister's heart). Finally, acts have consequences that are neither intended nor foreseen. These come under the heading of accidents, and they are morally indifferent.

It should now be clear why Aquinas was uninterested in the possible benefits of avarice. If an act is of an intrinsically bad sort, then any good consequences flowing from it, whe-ther intended, unintended but foreseen, or unintended *and* unforeseen, are morally irrelevant. The act is vitiated from the start; nothing can redeem it. Aquinas knew from Scrip-ture that bad acts sometimes have good effects. If Adam had not sinned, Christ would not have come into the world. But to permit evil for the sake of future good belongs exclusively to divine providence. We humans must take our bearing not from God's providence but from His law, which forbids evil absolutely.

If some pre-Enlightenment thinkers damned avarice as harmful to individual happiness or salvation, others condemned it as politically divisive. Crucial here was the ancient vision of the polity as a teleologically ordered whole, in which the public good is not just the product but the ultimate *end* of private actions, the 'toward-which' they are directed. A bridle maker, to use Aristotle's example, aims at ease and agility in the cavalryman, the cavalryman at victory in war, and victory in war at the freedom and glory of the *polis*.[7] Each small action is connected through a long chain of final causality to the greater good. In a society so conceived, the avaricious man is an outsider, because his actions, even if they happen to further the common good, do not in any sense *aim* at that good but only at his own enrichment. He is a permanent potential subversive, if not an actual criminal. To the extent that the spirit of avarice and luxury prevails in a nation, patriotism and virtue will wither away.[8] (Classical republican rhetoric tended to focus on 'luxury' rather than 'avarice', but the distinction between the two was not clear-cut.)

This 'classical republican' critique of avarice could (and often did) conflict with the ethical-theological critique outlined above. From the standpoint of the *res publica*, personal happiness or salvation might seem just as selfish a goal as monetary gain, while from the standpoint of salvation, devotion to the *res publica* might seem sheer tribalism. But there was no necessary opposition between the two viewpoints. Mainstream Christian thinkers recognized the health of the political community as a genuine if subordinate good (the political common good) and so could embrace a modified version of the classical republican critique. 'No vice is worse [than avarice],' wrote John of Salisbury, 'especially in those who are at the head of states or hold any public office.'[9] And all pre-Enlightenment thinkers agreed that avarice, whether primarily a spiritual or a political evil, is at any rate an *intrinsic* evil. Even if it has habitually bad effects, it is not bad because of these effects but because of what it essentially is: a deflection of the will from its proper end—be that God, the public good, or some combination of the two.

None of this is to say that pre-Enlightenment attitudes to commerce were uniformly hostile. From the late twelfth century onward, schoolmen and friars strove to develop ethical principles appropriate to the emerging commercial society. Textbooks such as Johannes Nider's fifteenth-century *De Contractibus Mercatorum* advised merchants on how to make a living without endangering their souls. Still, the general attitude of this literature to commerce was one of accommodation to a distasteful worldly reality.[10] Trade, like sex, was viewed as an inherently perilous activity, with its own distinctive temptations and vices. Its practitioners needed to be constantly on guard if they were not to fall victim to these things. Nothing could be further from the outlook of many modern economists, for whom all commercial activity, provided it remains on the right side of the law, is morally unimpeachable. An intellectual revolution lay between these two attitudes. It is to this revolution I now turn.

Avarice in the Enlightenment

The intellectual revolution that interests me here is not that famously described by Max Weber. For whatever the unique features of the Protestant work ethic, it was undeniably still an *ethic*—that is, a valuation of economic acts, like human acts in general, as intrinsically good or bad. The Puritan divines refer freely to avarice, sloth, luxury, and so forth, even if they use these terms somewhat differently than did their medieval predecessors. The thinkers of the Enlightenment, by contrast, assess economic acts in a radically new way, as good or bad in virtue of their *consequences*. A long and tortuous path connects the Reformation to its Enlightenment successor.[11] Nonetheless, since my interest is in the terminus of this path—the advent of modern economics—I shall confine myself to the secular Enlightenment, leaving to one side its religious hinterland.

In his *Fable of the Bees* of 1714, the Anglo-Dutch essayist Bernard Mandeville put forward an outrageous suggestion. What if the 'private vices' of avarice and luxury are transformable, through skilled political management, into the 'publick benefits' of wealth and industry? With a satiric eye on contemporary England, Mandeville pictures a hive of vicious but prosperous bees:

> The Root of Evil, Avarice,
> That damn'd ill-natur'd baneful Vice,
> Was Slave to Prodigality,
> That Noble Sin; whilst Luxury
> Employ'd a Million of the Poor,
> And odious Pride a Million more:
> Envy it self, and Vanity,
> Were Ministers of Industry.[12]

Mandeville's paradoxes were widely denounced as immoral. But he was not a solitary eccentric. In Naples, a few years later, the philosopher Giambattista Vico put forward an almost identical thought in his *New Science*:

> Out of ferocity, avarice, and ambition, the three vices which lead all mankind astray, [society] makes national defence, commerce, and politics, and thereby causes the strength, the wealth, and the wisdom of the republics; out of these three great vices which would certainly destroy man on earth, society thus causes the civil happiness to emerge. This principle proves the existence of divine providence: through its intelligent laws the passions of men who are entirely occupied by the pursuit of their private utility are transformed into a civil order which permits men to live in human society.[13]

Here was a radical break with the ancient social vision. The public good was no longer an end but an *effect*, no longer something to be aimed at but merely engineered. Patriotism was superfluous. Institutional machinery would do the job instead. Neither Mandeville nor Vico had any clear idea how this machinery might work in practice—the one speaks vaguely of 'the State's Craft' while the other appeals to providence—but they were both convinced that some such machinery must exist. Their faith in social causality was as little empirical as Galileo's faith in physical causality.

Why were Mandeville's and Vico's paradoxes only proposed in the early eighteenth century? Two reasons spring to mind. First, the rise of commercial Holland and England had impressed upon thinkers the increasingly close relationship between economic and political power. Henceforth, it seemed that avarice and luxury might have to be tolerated, encouraged even, for the sake of the public revenues. Second, Newton's recent explanation of planetary movement as the accidental offspring of gravity and inertia, as opposed to a manifestation of cosmic reason, encouraged philosophers to treat civic order in like fashion, as an unintended by-product of private actions.

Nonetheless, both Mandeville and Vico remained conventional in so far as they continued to talk about avarice and its companions as 'vices'. It was this that gave their thesis its air of paradox: they seemed to be suggesting that evil should be encouraged for the sake of the public good. Few in the eighteenth century could swallow such a suggestion. 'It seems upon any system of morality', wrote David Hume in 1752, 'little less than a contradiction in terms, to talk of a vice, which is in general beneficial to society.'[14] Two courses were open. Either the benefits of avarice could be denied and the derogatory epithet retained, or else, more radically, the benefits could be admitted and the activity redescribed so as to remove any taint of vice.

Tory Aristotelians such as Lord Bolingbroke excepted, the most seminal writers of the era opted for this latter, revisionary course. Increasingly, the acquisition of wealth was described in language suggestive of a benign if unheroic pastime. 'There are few ways in which a man can be more innocently employed than in getting money', was how Dr. Samuel Johnson famously put it. *Le doux commerce*, a late seventeenth-century French epithet popularized by Montesquieu, was echoed in English and Scottish descriptions of commerce as 'polishing' or 'softening'. The term 'avarice' was sidelined in favour of the more neutral 'interest' or 'self-love'.[15] It was retained, if at all, only for pathological or criminal forms of acquisition such as hoarding or swindling. Hume's essay 'Of Avarice' equates avarice with miserliness — traditionally only one of many species of avarice — and depicts it as a marginal, somewhat ludicrous vice, fit more for 'wit and humor' than serious reproach.[16] Adam Smith uses the word only six times in the whole of *The Wealth of Nations* and then only in connection with specific misdeeds, such as theft or debasing coinage, or with foolish, self-defeating conduct.[17] When referring to the motive underlying ordinary economic activity, he uses the colourless term 'interest'.

The phasing out of 'avarice' and related terms — a process substantially completed by the time *The Wealth of Nations* appeared in 1776 — had the effect of stripping economic activity of its ethical character, of rendering it morally indifferent. Legal infractions such as theft and fraud were still censored, of course, but not as expressions of the acquisitive drive so much as breaches of general principles of justice. This was a radical shift of perspective. For Aristotle and Aquinas, acts of avarice form a natural continuum ranging from the trivial to the viciously criminal. Aristotle's list of the avaricious includes pimps, usurers, profiteers, dicers, petty thieves, and brigands; Aquinas numbers restlessness, fraud, perjury, and violence among the 'daughters' or effects of avarice.[18] For the thinkers of the Enlightenment, by contrast, there is a clear-cut binary division between lawful and unlawful economic acts, and everything lawful is innocuous. Morality no longer pervades economic life from within but constrains it from without.

This transformation of attitudes to wealth creation cleared the ground for the new science of political economy. Having been de-moralized, so to speak, economic acts became open to analysis and assessment in terms of their effects, intended or otherwise. They could enter into a calculus. It now made sense to ask, for instance, whether it might not be more beneficial in the long run to let corn prices fluctuate freely, even in a famine, than to regulate them — a question that could not have been decently posed when the duty to feed the poor was regarded as absolute.[19] Without this prior de-moralization of economic activity, Smith's enterprise would have been unthinkable. Aquinas, for instance, would have regarded it as akin to an earnest discussion of the benefits of cutting up a hospital patient and distributing his organs among others.

The Deeper Ethical Implications

What were the deeper ethical implications of this revolution in economic attitudes? Aquinas, as you may recall, had condemned acts of avarice as bad in and of themselves, regardless of their 'ultimate intention' or their expected but unintended consequences. Sacking a loyal worker to increase profits is wrong, even if done with the aim of amassing funds for charity and in expectation of future benefits to society. From the new perspective, however, *all* expected

consequences of the sacking—whether intended proxim-
ately, ultimately, or not at all—contribute equally to its
ethical value. What matters is the aggregate. So long as our
employer can expect any suffering caused by his action to be
outweighed by its indirect social benefits, he has nothing to
reproach himself with. Responsibility for promoting the
good has been shifted onto an impersonal causal mechanism.
He is free to pursue his own interest—legally, of course, and
within the framework of a properly functioning market
economy.

This new method of moral reckoning was to become
famous as *utilitarianism*, but it is more aptly called *consequentialism*.[20] For what is crucial is not the stress on utility or
happiness—that, after all, had been central to many ancient
ethical theories—but the insistence on pooling or aggregating
all the expected consequences of an action. Utilitarianism is
just one of many species of consequentialism, although it has
always been the dominant one, no doubt because its chief
good, happiness, has the double advantage of appearing
both self-evidently desirable and uniquely quantifiable, in
principle if not in fact. If consequentialism holds that the
moral value of an act is determined by the sum of its expected consequences, utilitarianism adds that the only relevant consequences are pleasures and pains. This limitation is
not inherent in consequentialism. The Russian nihilist Sergey
Nechayev commended as moral everything favourable to the
revolution. G.E. Moore defined as 'right' all actions tending
to bring about good states of mind. Both were consequen-
tialists but not utilitarians.

Utilitarian reasoning was at first confined to its native
sphere of trade and industry. Adam Smith had a distinctly
non-utilitarian appreciation of goods such as national
defence and personal wholeness; his friend Hume continued
to ascribe intrinsic as well as instrumental value to benevolence. Both men, moreover, were more concerned with
explaining moral sentiments than with reforming them.
Nonetheless, the seed was sown. In suggesting that consequences might in some cases be aggregated, Smith and
Hume had hit upon a principle of universal application that
was ready to burst the bounds within which their own good
sense had confined it. Utilitarianism swiftly evolved into a

comprehensive system of normative ethics, applicable not just to economic but to all human acts.

Meanwhile, economics itself moved in an increasingly formalistic direction, eclipsing Smith's own ethical and socio-logical concerns. There was nothing accidental about this development. The colourful panorama of Smith's economics concealed a hard calculus of consequences; once this essence was grasped, the rest fell away as superfluous. Those who invoke Smith against the formalism of contemporary econ-omics do well to bear this in mind.

The discipline of economics has long since severed ties with utilitarianism in its classical, Benthamite form. The maximand is no longer conceived as a distinct mental state but as the satisfaction of preferences or the realization of certain 'capacities'. Nonetheless, the consequentialism in util-itarianism — the insistence on pooling the various conse-quences of an act, regardless of their intentional status — remains integral to any form of economic analysis. This is why economics has no use for 'avarice' or other terms designating acts and motives as intrinsically good or bad. From the economic point of view, the value of an act or a motive depends upon the particular chain of effects to which it gives rise, which varies from situation to situation. The same drive that leads to mass starvation under conditions of monopoly leads to general affluence under conditions of competition. Everything depends upon the institutional context.

A Humanly Supportable Ethics

But although enshrined in economics and cognate fields, consequentialist thinking has never captured the popular imagination, and it is fiercely resisted by the churches. Here is the explanation — to return to where I started — for the con-flict between popular and academic accounts of the financial crash. While one side calls in strident tones for justice, the other scrutinizes causes and consequences. A parallel conflict can be seen in the sphere of sex, where popular thinking con-tinues to regard certain acts and desires as perverse, while much educated opinion tends to the view that if no one is harmed, then nothing is wrong.[21]

According to a familiar progressivist narrative, non-consequentialist intuitions are a theological relic, destined to give way in time to a more enlightened standpoint. I believe, conversely, that they are the natural and indispensable basis of any humanly supportable ethics. They can be suppressed only fitfully and with considerable intellectual effort. An economic training is very serviceable to this end. It takes, for instance, a thorough drilling in the law of comparative advantage to be able to regard with complaisance the spectacle of a company 'off-shoring' hundreds of jobs from Sheffield to Mumbai. 'The invisible hand theory was a great relief to CEOs', writes Joseph Stiglitz, 'for it told them that by doing well (for themselves) they were doing good (for society). Not only should they feel no guilt in greed; they should feel pride.'[22] What the rich and powerful once sought in divine providence, they now find the market mechanism—assurance that their good is the public good, and that all is for the best in this best of all possible worlds.

Does the traditional ethical view of economic life have any future? The prospect, it must be admitted, looks bleak. Modern economics has built up a formidable body of theory from which thick evaluative terms are in principle excluded. 'Avarice' and 'usury' last made a serious appearance in the work of John Maynard Keynes, but they were swiftly disowned by his disciples, who viewed them like medieval gargoyles on an otherwise splendid hydraulic machine. Today, ethics impinges on economics only exogenously, in the formulation of policy goals and side constraints. The question of how to fulfil these goals, within these constraints, is a purely technical one. There is no space for an ethics of specifically *economic* acts and motives.

From a modern point of view, the most distasteful feature of traditional economic thought is its *pedagogic* ambition. The writings of Aristotle and Aquinas express an aspiration to mould people's characters, to make them less greedy, more generous, and so forth. Modern economists, by contrast, take people as they are, not as they ought to be. Their ambition is limited to changing outward conduct; they have no desire to transform the soul. Contrary to popular myth, economists do not treat all people as self-interested. They assume only that (1) most people are not indifferent to material incentives and that (2) this gives us some leverage over their behaviour. They pride themselves on the minimalism of this approach. The old aspiration to forge character strikes them as both utopian and despotic.

There is hard-won wisdom in this outlook. In complex, fractured societies, the attempt to rule through direct, moral exhortation can easily lead to tyranny. Material incentives have become an indispensable tool of government; even the Stakhanovites required extra pay. Nonetheless — and here the traditional outlook remains valid — reliance on incentives need not imply indifference to questions of character and motivation. Incentives can be understood not just techno-cratically, as tools for channelling self-interest this way or that, but pedagogically, as instruments for fostering virtue. A favourable incentive structure makes it easier to do good, or at any rate, harder to do evil. It minimizes temptation. T.S. Eliot put it well when he defined a Christian society as one so structured that, for ordinary believers, 'the difficulty of behaving as Christians should not impose an intolerable strain'.[23]

A further example may help illustrate the point. It is generally acknowledged that raising judges' salaries makes them less vulnerable to corruption. But why? An economist would say that it reduces their incentive to take bribes. I would say that it reduces the strain upon their virtue. These terminological differences matter. The economist's formul-ation implies that judges merely weigh up costs and benefits (some of them 'psychic', a rational-choice theorist might helpfully add). Yet in fact we expect judges to do the right thing for its own sake, without second thought. Although we know that their integrity may be subverted if they are under-paid, we do not deem it any less genuine on that account. Virtue does not have to be infinitely robust to count as virtue.

This compromise allows us to embrace an orthodox economic analysis of the financial crisis while avoiding the reductionism about motives that normally accompanies it. We can condemn deregulation, easy money, bonuses — what-ever our favourite culprit is — without thereby suggesting that the City is free of vice. We can acknowledge distortions in the incentive structure without insinuating a view of bankers as helpless laboratory rats. 'A financial system cannot be built around the assumption that participants in it are saints', writes Philip Booth in this volume.[24] That is true, and it is why incentives matter. But it does not follow that a financial system can be *indifferent* to the moral character of its participants. Systems are only as good as the individuals who compose them. Even if we cannot ask bankers to be saints, we can ask them, as we once did, to be gentlemen.

1   Joseph Stiglitz, *The Roaring Nineties* (London: Allen Lane, 2003): xviii.

2   Percy Bysshe Shelley, preface to 'The Revolt of Islam: A Poem in Twelve Cantos', in *The Poetical Works of Percy Bysshe Shelley*, 1 (Boston, MA: Houghton, Mifflin, and Co., 1883): 189–99, 194.

3   Thomas Aquinas, *Summa Theologiae*, 41, trans. T.C. O'Brien (London: Blackfriars, 1972): 243.

4   For ancient Greek attitudes toward money, see Richard Seaford, *Money and the Early Greek Mind: Homer, Philosophy, Tragedy* (Cambridge: Cambridge University Press, 2004).

5   Horace, Satire I, 39–40. In Horace, *Satires, Epistles and Ars Poetica*, trans. H. Rushton Fairclough (London: Heinemann, 1961): 7. I am grateful to Steven Kennedy for this reference.

6   Gratian, *Corpus iuriscanonici*. As quoted in Anne Derbes and Mark Sandona, 'Barren Metal and the Fruitful Womb: The Program of Giotto's Arena Chapel in Padua', *Art Bulletin*, 80 (June 1998): 274–91, 277.

7   Aristotle, *Nicomachean Ethics*, trans. Christopher Rowe (Oxford: Oxford University Press, 2002): 95. The same teleological structure is set forth in Gracie Fields' well-known Second World War song: 'But it's the girl that makes the thing that drills the hole that holds the ring that makes the thing-ummy-bob that makes the engines roar. And it's the girl that makes the thing that holds the oil that oils the ring that makes the thing-ummy-bob that's going to win the war.'

8   See Christopher J. Berry, *The Idea of Luxury: A Conceptual and Historical Investigation* (Cambridge: Cambridge University Press, 1994).

9   John of Salisbury, *Politcraticus*. As quoted in Lester K. Little, 'Pride Goes Before Avarice: Social Change and the Vices in Latin Christendom', *American Historical Review*, 76 (February 1971): 16–49, 20–1.

10 See Max Weber, *The Protestant Ethic and the Spirit of Capitalism*, trans. Talcott Parsons (London: Routledge, 1992): 73: 'But even when the doctrine was still better accommodated to the facts, as for instance with Anthony of Florence, the feeling was never quite overcome, that activity directed to acquisition for its own sake was at bottom a *pudendum* which was to be tolerated only because of the unalterable necessities of life in this world.'

[11]   For a penetrating analysis of these connections, see Charles Taylor, *A Secular Age* (Cambridge, MA: Belknap of Harvard University Press, 2007).

[12]   Bernard Mandeville, *The Fable of the Bees: Or Private Vices, Publick Benefits*, 1 (Oxford: Clarendon Press, 1924): 25.

[13]   Giambattista Vico, *Scienzanuova*. As quoted in Albert O. Hirschman, *The Passions and the Interests: Political Arguments for Capitalism Before its Triumph* (Princeton, NJ: Princeton University Press, 1977): 17.

[14]   David Hume, 'Of Refinement in the Arts', in *Essays Moral, Political and Literary* (London: Grant Richards, 1903): 287.

[15]   The genealogy of 'interest' and 'le doux commerce' is traced by Hirschman, *Passions and Interests*: 31–66. 'Self-love', originally an Augustinian term of opprobrium, was transformed by Jean-Jacques Rousseau, and Adam Smith following him, into a neutral term designating a natural regard for one's own welfare. For details, see Pierre Force, *Self-Interest Before Adam Smith: A Genealogy of Economic Science* (Cambridge: Cambridge University Press, 2003): 57–67.

[16]   See Hume, 'Of Avarice', in *Essays Moral, Political and Literary*: 563–7.

[17]   See Adam Smith, *The Wealth of Nations*, 1 (Oxford: Oxford University Press, 1904): 30, 437; Smith, *Wealth of Nations*, 2: 114, 117, 335.

[18]   See Aristotle, *Nicomachean Ethics*: 145; Aquinas, *Summa Theologiae*: 41, 261.

[19]   See E.P. Thompson, 'The Moral Economy of the English Crowd in the Eighteenth Century', *Past and Present*, 50 (February 1971): 76–136.

[20]   The term 'consequentialism' was coined by G.E.M. Anscombe in 'Modern Moral Philosophy', *Philosophy*, 33 (January 1958): 1–19. Anscombe for some reason names Sidgwick as the first consequentialist, but the doctrine is clearly present in Bentham and implicit in Hume.

[21]   See Jonathan Haidt, Silvia Helena Koller and Maria G. Dias, 'Affect, Culture, and Morality, or Is it Wrong to Eat Your Dog?', *Journal of Personality and Social Psychology*, 65 (October 1993): 613–28.

[22]   Stiglitz, *Roaring Nineties*: 14.

[23]   T.S. Eliot, *The Idea of a Christian Society* (London: Faber and Faber, 1939): 29.

[24]   See page 235.

Samuel Gregg

Money and Its Future
in the Global Economy

Money is coined liberty.
Fyodor Dostoevsky[1]

In the wake of the 2008 financial crisis, considerable
rethinking of the world's global financial architecture was
inevitable. Doubts were raised about the dollar's long-term
future as the world's reserve currency and proposals for a
global currency and a global reserve bank were floated.
There is nothing new about some of the proposals being
advanced. The world once possessed what was effectively a
global currency — the gold standard — during the first period
of economic globalization, which abruptly ended in August
1914. Long before a United Nations commission of experts
advocated a Global Reserve System in 2009,[2] John Maynard
Keynes argued for a world superbank in his 1933 pamphlet
The Means to Prosperity.[3]

Whatever measures are eventually implemented domestically and internationally, the risks should not be under-
estimated. Many reforms will understandably focus upon
preventing a recurrence of the 2008 financial crisis's precise
circumstances, even though our ability to predict the origin,
nature, and extent of the *next* major financial crisis is limited.
We need to be careful not to invest too much energy pre-
paring to fight the previous war. Moreover, if the law of
unintended consequences holds true, solutions designed to
address past problems will contribute to future difficulties.

Largely missing, however, from the present discussion about the global financial system's future is consideration of a crucial preliminary matter: what functions do we want money to perform in the global economy? Initially this seems a simple question with a relatively simple answer. Yet deeper reflection soon indicates that while money can serve several functions, not all are necessarily compatible with one another. This paper seeks to provide a framework for considering the different choices facing us concerning money's roles in economic life and the possible implications of these choices for the world's financial architecture.

Admittedly, developing such a framework involves abstraction, even simplification, and the choices faced by governments, central banks, and legislatures are rarely abstract or simple. The advantage of such frameworks is that they help to clarify the choices, issues, and trade-offs involved. They also remind us that the choices are not simply technical in nature. They have a normative dimension. This includes debates about the different weight accorded to liberty and equality, the issue of consumer sovereignty versus state sovereignty, questions about the proper functions of government, and the perennial dispute of how much significance we should ascribe to the economic 'short-term' and economic 'long-term' (not to mention what qualifies a perspective as short-term or long-term).

These are recurrent questions in political economy. They also are affected by debates about the nature of economic enquiry.[4] If, for example, economics develops a more sceptical view of the use of mathematics and econometrics as tools of predictive analysis, this will raise questions about the efficacy of governments and central banks trying to manage the quantity of money circulating in an economy. This will in turn affect those economic policies that treat money largely as one of several macroeconomic tools for managing entire economies.

In sketching a framework to explore these questions, I begin by demarcating a basic difference in emphasis about money's role: there are those who primarily see money as a tool of government policy designed to achieve certain results; others focus upon money's market functions and its unique capacity to reflect through prices the information that people need to make choices about what to buy and sell in light of scarcity. I then examine different ways in which the world's financial architecture variously reflects a *micro, market-centric* and/or a *macro, state-centric* conception of money.

Market-Oriented Money

The first lesson outlined in introductions to theories about money is that money's most basic function is as a medium of exchange. Money serves as a proxy for the value of real goods and services that are the objects of individual economic exchange. This forms the basis of money's three other functions: a store of value, a unit of account, and a standard of deferred payment. These functions allow money to serve as a conveyor of information through the price system. As prices increase and decline in response to consumer demand and the emergence of new and/or better products and services, the price information conveyed through the medium of money allows resources to be constantly reallocated to meet ever-changing needs. Money thus permits a coordination of millions of pieces of economic information dispersed among billions of individuals, allowing a type of order to be brought to the seemingly anarchic character of market economies.

If these are accepted as money's essential functions and roles, there are strong reasons to try to ensure that the value of money is maintained at a stable level over long periods of time. As Keynes noted, 'The importance of money essentially flows from its being a link between the present and the future'.[5] Considerable intellectual effort is thus devoted to ensuring that the supply of and demand for money does not operate separately from the actual supply of and demand for goods and services (i.e. the 'true' price relativities). This effort in turn translates into the type of monetary policy that seeks both to protect money's functions from disturbances emanating from the money supply and to prevent the supply of money itself from facilitating changes in the production and distribution of goods and services. The goal of monetary policy consequently becomes that of keeping the supply of money as 'neutral' as possible.

A number of normative concerns underlie this goal. One is facilitating liberty of exchange and economic security by reducing the uncertainty and risk that can flow from fluctuations in the value of money that have nothing to do with the relative valuation of different goods and services. Constant oscillations in the value of money undermine people's ability to discern what they find marginally preferable and marginally less preferable. Another normative conviction is that stable money means greater economic prosperity for more people, because many long-term contracts benefit from a confidence that the prices of goods and services will remain relatively constant over time. A third concern is for particular marginalized groups who may lack the financial sophistication and resources to navigate the waters of inflation or who are on fixed incomes (such as the elderly or the disabled). A fourth is an emphasis upon legal justice, inasmuch as a commitment to 'neutral' money reduces the opportunities for powerful interest groups to manipulate monetary policy to serve their own interests rather than the common good. Finally, an attachment to stable market-oriented money is often associated with scepticism about the utility of macroeconomics and a sense that money should be free to reflect microeconomic realities rather than macroaggregates based on broad statistical indices.

The concept of market-oriented 'neutral money' as a theoretical ideal was first articulated by the Swedish economist Knut Wicksell in 1898.⁶ It has been subject to a number of critiques; central is the claim that there is no truly *neutral* money. The concept of neutral money, it is argued, does not take into account factors such as time lags in the formation of prices. The same goods and services will not necessarily reflect the same prices at the same point in time. Money is a way of conveying value over time, but economic situations can change very quickly. Hence there will inevitably be some friction between the value of money and the supply of and demand for goods and services. The situation is complicated by the fact that there can be a disjunction between prices and the actual demand for goods and services, as in the case of the price rigidities that result from trade unions refusing to contemplate wage flexibility or businesses deciding to establish a cartel. Then there is the further difficulty that money itself assumes the quality of a commodity — and has therefore a commodity value different from that of the goods and services whose value it expresses. As the economist Friedrich von Hayek once observed, a perfect monetary stability could only be maintained if the flow of money remained constant, all prices were perfectly flexible, and the future movement of prices could be predicted in long-term contracts. The second and third of these conditions, he noted, are unlikely to be fulfilled.[7] From this standpoint, perhaps it is more reasonable to pursue 'stable money', minimizing friction and volatility in order to maintain some constancy in a given currency's *average* purchasing power.[8]

Another critique of market-oriented neutral money is that it diminishes the ability of governments or central banks to address economic downturns by loosening monetary policy or engaging in 'quantitative easing' (i.e. printing money), as well as from directly intervening to dampen an economic boom through raising interest rates. In short, market-orientated money establishes barriers to direct interventionist measures by the state. At this point a microeconomic view of money begins to conflict with a macroeconomic, state-oriented understanding of its functions.

State-Oriented Money

Until the 1920s, monetary policy was primarily concerned with securing a gold or a silver equivalent of the currency in circulation. It assumed a different complexion, however, once the argument began to gain traction that the state's control of the quantity of money could be used more directly to stabilize, increase, or deflate economic activity. After World War II, the cause of 'sound money' in Europe was at least temporarily displaced by a new political emphasis: ensuring full employment and an extensive welfare state. This strategy partly depends upon governments and central banks playing a central role in managing the money supply.

Today this line of thought is associated primarily with Keynes and the various schools of economics that bear his name. But other economists, such as the Stockholm School, were proposing Keynesian-like arguments about using the money supply to maintain effective demand as early as the 1920s.[9] Antecedents may even be found in the writings of the

Scottish-French economist and financier, John Law, who in the early eighteenth century argued for a type of state-driven monetary expansionism to provide prosperity. In Law's words, 'as this addition to the money will employ the people who are now idle, and those employed to more advantage, so the product will be increased, and manufacture advanced'.[10]

This view shifts from money as a medium of exchange and a means of coordination amidst a complex market, to money as one of several statistically traceable macroaggregates that the state can use to shape, even plan, economic life. Though money still serves the needs of individuals and companies, it becomes a means for state officials to pursue collective action—as found in expressions such as 'income multipliers', 'accelerator coefficients', and 'savings and spending ratios'.

Quite different moral imperatives are integral to this view of money. Perhaps the most prominent is the belief that the state should employ its control of the money supply in a more interventionist fashion to reduce wealth disparities, enhance equity in income distribution, prevent and ameliorate recessions, and even facilitate more-or-less lasting prosperity by decreasing or augmenting the aggregate of money expenditure—especially when economic catastrophe appears imminent (in such cases, even many sceptics of demand management are willing to contemplate monetary activism by the state). The intellectual architects of West Germany's economic liberalization in 1948, such as Wilhelm Röpke and Walter Eucken, were fierce anti-inflationists. In 1931, however, they had no hesitation in arguing for such action, while cautioning that it should be limited to answering the immediate crisis and not employed to the end of managing the economy over the long-term.[11]

The critiques of money as a tool of state economic policy are extensive. Perhaps the most prominent is that it facilitates the politicization of money. Once the state assumes direct responsibility for managing the money supply, it becomes difficult for governments and politicians to resist manipulating it for self-interested, short-term ends (such as re-election) or to benefit particular interest groups rather than the common good. State-managed money, it is held, gives governments the option of letting the inflation genie out of the bottle to boost short-to-medium-term employment at the expense of devaluing people's savings, shattering price stability, and undermining long-term employment growth.

This worry is not a post-Keynes phenomenon. Writing in the fourth century BC, the Greek philosopher Diogenes described money as the legislators' game of dice. Sixteen hundred years later, Bishop Nicole Oresme of Lisieux (1320–1382) assailed the widespread practice of currency debasement among European monarchs of the time. The king, he insisted in his *Tractatus de Origine, Natura, Jure et Mutationibus Monetarum*, did not own the polity's money. Instead he was its custodian, and his responsibility was to maintain the stability of its value.[12] In the early seventeenth century, the scholastic theologian Juan de Mariana wrote an entire treatise, *De Monetae Mutatione*, criticizing governments for depreciating currencies in pursuit of dubious ends.[13] For his pains, Mariana was charged with treason and sentenced to life imprisonment in a Franciscan monastery. Then, 152 years after Mariana's death, Adam Smith lamented in his *Wealth of Nations* that 'in every country in the world, I believe, the avarice and injustice of princes and sovereign states abusing the confidence of their subjects, have by degrees diminished the real quality of the metal, which had been originally contained in their coins'.[14]

A second set of critiques involves what has been called the knowledge problem. After World War II, aggregate income-expenditure models were increasingly used as the basis for macroeconomic forecasting. This practice was facilitated by the heightening sophistication of statistical analysis, which promised a more scientific management of fiscal and monetary policy.

Neoclassical formality can certainly clarify aspects of different economic problems, but the difficulty lies in how much we can realistically expect these aggregates, whose purpose is to eliminate or reduce complexity, to tell us about what is really happening in an economy. As Nobel Prize-winning economist Robert Solow once remarked, 'I could verify the existence of witches if you give me the chance every other year to tack on some variables in the regression'.[15] One former senior official of the Federal Reserve noted similar sentiments over fifty years ago:

> Statistics are necessarily expressed in totals and subtotals, while the course of human events is shaped by many millions of decisions which may not always fit into statistical categories. The broader the totals, the more violence they may do to reality... Conclusions based on impersonal aggregates may lead to policies that have disastrous personal consequences to many groups... Policy based on aggregates and aimed at shaping them tends towards an ever-increasing degree of centralized action.[16]

Economic activity and prosperity relies on knowledge of a range of factors, only some of which are quantifiable, and then only in limited ways. As Philip Booth writes, 'There is a tendency in modern economics to ignore variables that do not fit neatly into econometric models... [T]here may be many economic variables and processes that are not amenable to measurement or to modeling but that have important information content'.[17] This fact has immediate implications, Booth observes, for understanding something like the impact of money in creating inflation:

> It may be difficult for central banks (or financial market forecasters) to precisely model the impact of the money supply upon inflation, as relationships have become less predictable over time. This does not mean, however, that monetary aggregates are not a very important (indeed, possibly the most important) variable in determining inflation. It simply means that to understand the processes we have to interpret the data, and we may have to accept that any predictions we make are simply predictions of tendencies rather than of precise magnitudes.[18]

Governments or central bankers relying upon this type of information to make decisions about the money supply should concede that they are acting on limited knowledge. Even when econometrics establishes correlations between different sets of macroeconomic phenomena, there is always considerable—even heated—debate about the robustness of these correlations. Inevitably, central bankers start looking through all the information at their disposal for what they think will be the leading indicators of what is happening in the economy, and when it is time to raise or lower the discount rate. In 1997, for example, *Business Week* reported that the then-chairman of the Federal Reserve, Alan Greenspan, focused upon supplier delivery times, inventory levels, and measures that related wages and benefits to productivity.[19] If true, none of these indicators warned the Federal Reserve that it was keeping interest rates too low for too long during the 2000s.

There are, then, considerable differences between market-oriented and state-oriented views of money and its functions. It may seem that our choices are between an international central bank or a system where banks issue notes and operate without regard for national boundaries or fields of operation, relying on their own reserves. These, however, are not the only choices.

Internationalizing Money

With the re-emergence of a global economy following the accelerated economic and financial liberalization of the 1980s, discussion about establishing a truly global currency was bound to resurface. Since Bretton Woods, the US dollar has functioned as the world's reserve currency, even after the last tenuous link to a commodity ended when President Nixon effectively ended the gold standard on August 15, 1971. The dollar's ability to continue as the world's reserve currency since that time has rested upon confidence in the robustness of the American economy and the United States' continuing political and military strength. It follows that America's economic problems—such as its ballooning federal deficit under the G.W. Bush and Obama admin-istrations—have raised questions about how long the US dollar will function in this capacity.

The presumed great advantage of a single global currency would be the simplification of economic transactions between two or more nations. A single medium of exch-ange—that is, one money for one market— would thus be more efficient for a world economy understood as a global, integrated reality. A universal currency, it is argued, would mean that capital mobility would be directed more by pot-ential comparative risks associated with particular invest-ments, and less by concerns about the different value and stability of various currencies. To this extent, the efficacy of a global currency would rely upon and facilitate the free flow of capital, labour, and exchange across national boundaries. As one head of state wrote, 'One might ask whether in a globalized world economy a state has any real need for a national currency and a national bank'.[20]

One model for achieving an internationalization of money is what might be called *state internationalization*. Through the creation of a global reserve bank responsible for managing a global currency, all nation-states would ascribe to it some of their sovereignty — much as most European Union (EU) members have done with regard to the European Central Bank (ECB). This is more or less what the United Nations panel of experts recommended in its 2009 report. Here it should be recognized that economic and financial globalization has diluted national governments' ability to use their control of the money supply to manage domestic economies. Fluctuating exchange rates and traders' ability to transfer billions across national boundaries by pressing a key on a computer have, for example, reduced most governments' ability to control their national currencies.

The first difficulty for those advancing such proposals is that the objections to state institutions trying to control the money supply are even more applicable to a global reserve bank. When one reads the fine print of the United Nations 2009 report, one finds that its authors envisage such a bank using its influence over the money supply to engage in demand management for the world economy. But no matter how sophisticated the statistical information and mathematical resources at their disposal, no group of central bankers can know, for example, what is the optimal interest rate for the world in the present, let alone what it will be nine months in the future. Here one is reminded of Hayek's Nobel Prize speech, in which he noted that 'the Spanish schoolmen of the sixteenth century... emphasized that what they called the *pretium mathematicum*, the mathematical price, depended on so many circumstances that it could never be known to man but was known only to God'.[21]

Inevitably, a global bank would be reduced to making policy based on assumptions about aggregates even more detached from reality than the macroaggregates employed at the level of nations. Precisely because a global bank would have to think globally, it would rely on broad indices of global reserve ratios, global capital flows, global monetary aggregates, and global employment statistics that can only very roughly approximate economic reality. The bigger the aggregate, the more detached from reality become the numbers.

The second difficulty for an international central bank is that it could not be rendered even relatively independent from unwarranted political pressures. The United Nations report of 2009 did not even assume that such autonomy could or should be granted to a global reserve bank. Reflecting on proposals for a world central bank in the early 1960s, Röpke argued that such a bank's inevitable politicization would mean that it 'would have to serve the liquidity requirements of its more unsound clients'.[22]

The ECB is often cited as a prototype of a global central bank. It does, after all, conduct monetary policy for sixteen nations with often-different approaches to fiscal policy. The ECB, however, is somewhat unique, inasmuch as its formation was deeply influenced by the Deutsche Bundesbank, which from its very beginning stressed a strongly anti-inflationist approach to monetary policy. Thus according to EU law, the ECB's prime objective is 'to maintain price stability'. It also has the responsibility — crucially 'without prejudice to the objective of price stability' — to 'support the general economic policies' of the EU, specified by article 2 of the Treaty on European Union as 'a high level of employment and sustainable and non-inflationary growth'.[23] In technical terms, procedural monetary rules designed to serve the stability of money were given priority over the discretionary use of money as an instrument of state economic policy. This has not, however, stopped politicians such as French president Nicolas Sarkozy from repeatedly stating that the ECB's charter ought to be more aligned with France's *dirigiste* ways. Nor was this legislated independence apparently enough to prevent the ECB from succumbing to pressures from the governments of EU member-states in May 2010 to buy up the debt of European nations with intolerable debt burdens.[24]

A global central bank would more likely be given a charter somewhat akin to that of the Federal Reserve. The

Federal Reserve has the responsibility of 'conducting the nation's monetary policy by influencing the monetary and credit conditions in the economy in pursuit of maximum employment, stable prices, and moderate long-term interest rates'.[25] It is thus legislatively charged with realizing goals that are not only ascribed equal importance but which also may be incompatible in some circumstances. As the experience of the early 1980s illustrated, the Federal Reserve's pursuit of stable prices (i.e. fighting inflation) could only be achieved by accepting high unemployment for three years. In retrospect, this was surely the right decision. But whether it reflected the Federal Reserve adhering to all of its legislatively mandated responsibilities is another matter.

That is one model for achieving an internationalization of money. Is there any alternative to a global reserve bank and state internationalization when it comes to creating an international currency? It is easy to forget that such a situation was once more-or-less realized in the form of the gold standard. The gold standard might be called an instance of *market internationalization*, in so far as it avoided the state centralization of the money supply while simultaneously embodying the market-oriented priorities of stable money. The international gold standard was such that each unit of the currency circulating in a country could be equally used for payments in other countries. Its primary advantage was that its workings were driven by known rules, which meant that the decisions of governments and central banks about the money supply could be to a certain extent foreseen and thus predictable.

In its heyday between 1870 and 1914, the classic gold standard gradually linked the different currencies of major trading powers such as Germany, the United States, Britain, and France; all notes and coins of countries adhering to the gold standard were underwritten by and redeemable in specific weights of gold. The effects were twofold. First, the gold standard facilitated an unprecedented stabilization of prices. Thus as noted by Lewis E. Lehrman and John D. Mueller, from '1879 to 1914, [US] average annual CPI [consumer price index] inflation was 0.2 percent, with average annual volatility (up or down) of only 2.2 percent. No other standard comes close in combining low average inflation with low volatility'.[26] A second effect was that each unit of the currency circulating in a country could be equally used for payments in other countries. A common and stable universal currency was therefore created without any need for an international monetary authority.

Apart from generating monetary stability, the gold standard also automatically adjusted balance-of-payment deficits. If a country overextended itself by importing more than it exported, gold left the deficit country to cover the imbalance of payments against nations with surpluses. The money supply in the deficit country subsequently fell, thus reducing demand and providing a brake against inflation. The fall in demand also forced deficit countries to become more competitive. In surplus countries, the gold imports increased the money supply, augmented demand, reduced competitiveness, and thus gradually diminished the original causes of the gold inflows.

Central banks played a critical role in this process. Indeed the entire system relied on close cooperation among the world's central banks. In surplus countries, the gold standard required them to lower the discount interest rate charged to members of the domestic money system in order to reduce the gold inflow. This resulted in gold flowing back to deficit countries. Conversely, central banks in deficit countries would raise the discount interest rate, thereby reducing demand and averting potential inflation.

The gold standard emerged without conscious top-down planning and mirrored a period in which capital, labour, and trade moved relatively unhindered across national boundaries. For most of its history, it was a British-pound standard, upheld by confidence in the City of London's reputation and Britain's continued prosperity. Instead of being based on an international monetary authority, it was grounded, as Röpke writes, upon the unwritten agreements of nation-states 'to behave in matters of monetary and credit policy in such a way that this fixed and free coupling remained an undisputed permanent institution, irrespective of trade fluctuations'.[27]

The gold standard's origins lie partly in many societies' historical attachment to gold, especially in the Mediterranean and European worlds. Of course, there is no economic reason

why such a standard should be gold. As early as the late
1930s and early 1940s, economists such as Benjamin Graham
and Frank D. Graham were arguing for a new reserve
currency that could be embraced internationally and whose
basic unit would be redeemable against a fixed mixture of
warehouse warrants for a quantity of storable commodities.[28]
They envisaged a physical link being established between
real income and the money used to measure it. They did not,
however, resolve the issue of how we would determine
which commodities were put into the basket, at what ratio,
and at what price.

Moreover, there were disadvantages to the gold standard.
The most prominent was the slowness with which the gold
supply adjusted to real changes in demand. This impaired
gold's ability to function as a regulative mechanism. Sometimes the needed gold supply became available only some
time after it was actually needed. Hayek observed in the
1920s that 'self-regulating currencies secured by their con-
vertibility into a precious metal often bring their compen-
satory mechanism into play too slowly to prevent severe
economic fluctuations and create additional disturbances in
the economy because of frequent variations (due to extra-
monetary factors) in the value of their underlying metallic
standard'.[29]

Another disadvantage (at least from some governments'
standpoint) was that the international gold standard imposed a discipline upon governments that did not always suit
their short-term responsibilities – or in some cases, their self-
interests. In times of crisis, they might not only avoid the
painful effects of policies that would lower economic well-
being but adopt monetary policies to escape the gold standard's strictures that facilitated the same process of down-
ward adjustment. Governments were well aware that abandoning the gold standard would allow an expansion of credit
not possible under the pre-1914 automatic gold standard. In
this context, we should remember that gold is *not* money but
a store of value that needs to be exchanged for money, be it
paper or electronic. Governments can – and have – fixed the
ratio of gold to the currency. They have also abandoned gold
when it seemed necessary, or politically convenient, to do so.
To this extent, gold did not prove to be quite the long-term

brake on government influence on money and the money supply that many considered it to be.

Decentralizing Money

Market-oriented or state-oriented approaches to internationalizing money do not exhaust the options. Active decentralization of the money supply is another. One approach might be called *state-based decentralization* or more pejoratively, 'monetary nationalism'.

State-based decentralization involves governments abandoning any effort to harmonize different national monetary policies. In practice, it creates two sets of rules for the global monetary order: one allowing money to circulate freely within a country, the other forbidding or severely restricting the same free circulation of money across national boundaries. Governments would accept that the world's money supply will not be determined by the same means and according to the same principles that determine the amounts of money in circulation within a nation.

Governments typically embrace such nation-state-focused monetary policies to advance two priorities. One is insulating the nation from external financial shocks in the interest of maintaining social and political order. There is, however, little evidence that such policies, such as exchange and capital controls, are especially effective in realizing this end. A second priority is enabling the government to keep domestic interest rates as low as possible. This assumes that it has the will and the power to assert its claim to monetary sovereignty over and against globalizing trends. A government's capacity to do so lies in the link between money and the state's provision of an authoritative basis to its currency through its power of legal tender. The state could, for example, simply decree that all domestic or international transactions must be conducted in the currency it specifies.

Taken to its logical conclusion, the decentralization—or more accurately, disintegration—of the world monetary system along such lines would make the process of globalization very difficult to sustain. In a global economy, there are usually considerable dissymmetries between national-geographical regions and the market for a given good. Changes in the supply of and demand for goods and services in one area affect the supply-demand status of goods in others. If prices are to convey information quickly across the globe, money needs to be able to transmit this information in as frictionless a manner as possible. 'Monetary nationalism' impedes this transmission. Furthermore, it is possible that monetary nationalism would not reduce global volatility but increase it, as nations would encounter great difficulty accessing money and credit from abroad to meet urgent capital needs. In short, an approach that seeks to provide protection against external monetary shocks might actually undermine the prospects of long-term foreign investment, diminish the benefits that accrue from an international division of labour, and contribute to the international political instability typically associated with domestic economic volatility.

In its most overt forms, this mode of monetary decentralization manifests itself in war economies and the policies of economic autarky, such as those attempted by Communist and Fascist regimes in the inter-war and post-war years. A somewhat milder contemporary expression might be the monetary policies adopted by populist regimes such as Hugo Chávez's Venezuela. Even gentler forms might be seen in a government's efforts to regulate the flow of capital in the hope of reducing the effects of financial shocks emanating from other countries or limiting the risk of contagion.

Regardless of how state-oriented decentralization manifests itself, a critical political element is *sovereignty*. One reason traditionally given for the state's monopoly of the money supply is that it is an expression of national sovereignty. In the mid-fifth century BC, for example, Athens compelled her allies to adopt Athenian coinage — a move that signalled Athens' sense of the expanding territorial boundaries of its sovereignty. As the modern nation-state began emerging in the late thirteenth century and onwards, national sovereigns insisted on proclaiming their own distinctive units of account and then used them to proclaim an exchange value on any foreign monies that managed to circulate across their increasingly well-defined territorial borders.[30] The scholar who most developed the modern concept of sovereignty — Jean Bodin (1530–1596), also one of the leading theorists of royal absolutism — identified the right to issue coinage as a key element of sovereignty. This was not least because he thought the state should reserve to itself an authority to alter the value of money. In the early twenty-first century, some of the most contentious debates surrounding the euro have concerned its reduction of the national sovereignty of EU member-states adopting this transnational currency.

But is a state monopoly of the money supply truly essential to sovereignty? Historically speaking, a state's monetary sovereignty has rarely been total. Sociologist Geoffrey Ingham points out that 'coinages circulated promiscuously across ill-defined and insecure jurisdictions in later medieval Europe; local money was issued as late as the mid-nineteenth-century in Europe; and capitalist networks have always developed their own "private" media and means of payment—"near money" such as certificates of deposit'.[31] As late as the nineteenth century, a multiplicity of media of exchange, ranging from private bank money to corporate and government script, operated side-by-side in advanced market economies.[32] When Adam Smith listed what he regarded as the state's three primary economic responsibilities, he did not include the supply of money. In fact, the world has done without central banks and their monopoly of the money supply for most of history.

This history suggests that sovereignty does not require an irrevocable commitment to the state's monopoly of the money supply. This then opens the door, at least theoretically, to various forms of *market-oriented decentralization,* including free currency competition and/or the privatization of money.

There are historical precedents for more-or-less private money. Order was restored, for example, to the anarchy of circulating coinages in early medieval Europe by Italian exchange bankers using their own version of the Carolingian money of account as the basis for their bills of exchange. These bills were used in turn to finance the rapidly expanding trade of medieval Europe.[33]

In more modern times, 'private money' proposals have often been associated with Hayek, though other economists such as Gordon Tullock and Benjamin Klein began advocating such approaches several years before he did.[34] Even more recently, Benjamin J. Cohen and others have argued that new electronic and technological capacities are creating fresh possibilities for using money and securing its value through non-state means.[35] 'Virtual money', for example, has considerably diminished the nation-state's ability to exercise substantial control over the money it issues, despite the continued existence of legal tender.

In simplified terms, Hayek's schema for denationalizing money involves formally ending the state's money-supply monopoly and allowing banks to issue non-interest-bearing certificates and open check accounts based on their own trademark.[36] These certificates would function as currencies trading at variable exchange rates. To set a minimal legal requirement, banks initially would undertake to redeem their notes in deposits with a range of state currencies (e.g. one 'ducat' for two euros, one 'ducat' for three US dollars). In the long-term, however, they would focus on maintaining their currencies' purchasing power by linking it to a basket of commodities that they would change as the market's valuation of commodities changed to maintain the value of their currency. Banks would compete against each other as well as against state-issued currencies to maintain their currencies' value. As the governor of the Bank of England, Mervyn King, writes, the money of account would simply be 'a matter of public choice'.[37]

One initial step toward private money would be competition among state currencies in which the monetary authorities of different countries would be allowed to compete in domestic settings other than their own, and consumer sovereignty rather than state sovereignty would ultimately determine which moneys were used. This was once proposed by then-Prime Minister Margaret Thatcher as an alternative to the EU's single currency. Even today, more than one national currency functions as the generally acceptable medium of exchange in some border areas as well as in failed states, where most people prefer to use euros and US dollars rather than Congolese francs, Somali schillings, or Zimbabwean dollars.

The normative claims underlying the case for market-oriented decentralizations of the money supply mirror those of the market-oriented view of money: particularly that only markets can reveal how one secures the optimal quantity of money in the economy at any given time. They also reflect the conclusion that even the most benign and superbly staffed monetary authority will at some point make bad mistakes. The case for private money also assumes that going back to the gold standard as a way of restraining state irresponsibility in the area of money supply is no longer practical—not least because the gold standard's effectiveness relied heavily upon stigmatizing those governments who refused to obey its rules. In the end, the stigma proved insufficient to restrain governments from abandoning gold in times of crisis.

One unanswered question is whether private money would help address the problem of moral hazard that played such a significant role in the 2008 crisis, especially in the cases of government-sponsored enterprises such as Fannie Mae and Freddie Mac and of the 'too big to fail' financial institutions. Most of those proposing private money assume that its companies would be subject to the same laws of the marketplace as any other privately owned business—including being allowed to fail. It follows that private money would diminish the problem of moral hazard in so far as bankers would have more incentive to safeguard individual deposits and to assume prudent risk. Any organization issuing money could only remain viable by keeping the value of its money constant through regularly changing its assets to match the loans it has issued. This does not imply the complete absence of a legal framework. The distinguished nineteenth-century English jurist Lord Farrer argued that contract law, tort law, and criminal law were sufficient to adjudicate monetary crimes without invoking any special law of legal tender.[38]

There is no shortage of critiques of private money. Apart from opposition to diminishing the state's ability to use its money-supply monopoly to pursue macroeconomic objectives, there are a number of technical objections. One such objection that was made by Milton Friedman—interestingly, an early critic of private money—is 'that in the present circumstance of the world there are no assets which banks could acquire to match purchasing-power obligations'.[39] Another objection is that money's effectiveness as a unit of account and a coordination mechanism depends upon the unit meaning the same thing to different people at the same point in time. Private money, it is suggested, undermines money's function by creating so many 'numeraries' that financial communication would become harder.[40] One wonders, however, whether this apparent problem of financial asymmetry might not be overcome by technological developments that would allow such conversions to be calculated instantaneously.

It is also claimed that private-money scenarios would be plagued by Gresham's law that when 'good' and 'bad' money circulates in the economy, the bad money becomes the dominant money. Those expending money deal in the bad (artificially overvalued) money rather than the good (artificially demoted) money, because they generally keep any good money for themselves. Hayek's response is that Gresham's law only applies if the two kinds of money *have* to be accepted at the *state*-prescribed rate of exchange. When people are free to choose their currency in conditions of competition, the opposite will happen: good money will drive out bad money. Private issuers of currency would be under intense competitive pressure to maintain the value of their currency; moreover, any hint of dishonesty on an issuer's part would destroy their reputation.[41] Trust, competition, and reputation, it is assumed, would thus replace the legal-tender mechanism.

The two groups most likely to resist market-oriented decentralization in the global financial system would be governments and bankers. Governments would lose their ability to use their monopoly of the money supply to placate interest groups. Generally, state organizations tend to be reluctant to remove themselves from any arena they already control. In 1999, for example, the ECB specified that, with regard to private issuers of electronic money, all e-money had to be integrated into the existing system. It stated that,

> [I]ssuers of electronic money must be subject to prudential supervision; the issuance must be subject to sound and transparent legal arrangements, technical security, protection against criminal abuse and monetary statistics reporting; issuers of electronic money must be legally obliged, at the request of the holders, to redeem electronic money against central bank money at par; [and] the possibility must

exist for central banks to impose reserve requirements on all issuers of electronic money.[42]

Bankers also would resist any move toward market-oriented solutions, partly because they are familiar with the present system (though they forget that today's banking system has existed for only two hundred years) but more importantly because they would lose their present capacity to privatize their gains and socialize their losses. With no lender of last resort, bankers would become accountable for their actions in the same way that most other private business is held accountable — success or failure in the marketplace.

Conclusion

Despite the considerable opportunities for innovation created by the integration of the world economy, and the world financial system's startling growth over the past thirty years, there has been little significant alteration in money's global role. Almost all contemporary economies reflect often-uneasy compromises between market-oriented and state-oriented views of money. Whatever were the real causes of the 2008 financial crisis, the Great Recession has provided some short- and perhaps medium-term impetuses to a change in policy for those who primarily think of money as a tool of macroeconomic management. In the long-term, however, the practical feasibility of this conception of money is likely to be increasingly questioned in light of the decreasing significance of monetary sovereignty, the ongoing and presently unknown effects of the electronic/technological/internet age, and current concerns about mainstream economics' predictive powers, priorities, and tools of analysis. In short, those reflecting about money's future role should not let their imaginations be unduly bounded by circumstances and conditions ever-less relevant to an increasingly globalized economy. Despite the 2008 crisis, these longer-term questions will not disappear. Indeed they make it likely that, at some point, the monetary pendulum will swing back the other way. *Plus ça change, plus c'est la même chose.*

---

1   Fyodor Dostoevsky, *The House of the Dead*, trans. Constance Garnett (London: Heinemann, 1915): 16.

2   See United Nations, *Report of the Commission of Experts of the President of the United Nations General Assembly on Reforms of the International Monetary and Financial System* (New York: UN, 2009): 109–25; http://www.un.org/ga/econcrisissummit/docs/FinalReport_CoE. pdf

3   See John Maynard Keynes, *The Means to Prosperity* (London: Macmillan, 1933).

4   See Samuel Gregg, 'Smith Versus Keynes: Economics and Political Economy in the Post-Crisis Era', *Harvard Journal of Law and Public Policy,* 33 (Spring 2010): 443–64.

5   John Maynard Keynes, *The General Theory of Employment, Interest and Money* (London: Macmillan, 1936): 293.

6   See Joseph Schumpeter, *History of Economic Analysis* (New York: Oxford University Press, 1994): 1088. First published 1954 by Oxford University Press.

7   See Friedrich August Hayek, 'On "Neutral" Money', in *Good Money, Part 1: The New World,* vol. 5 of *The Collected Works of F.A. Hayek,* ed. Stephen Kresge (Chicago, IL: University of Chicago Press, 1999): 228–31, esp. 230.

8   Even efforts to stabilize the value of a currency through, for example, legislative fiat or a return of a country to the gold standard can produce significant injustices in so far as they may reward those who have been irresponsible and damage those who have been prudent.

9   See Gilles Dostaler, *Keynes and His Battles* (Cheltenham: Edward Elgar, 2007): 256.

10   John Law, *Money and Trade Considered: With a Proposal for Supplying the Nation with Money* (New York: Augustus M. Kelley, 1966): 36. First published 1705 by Heirs and Successors of Andrew Anderson.

11   See Samuel Gregg, *Wilhelm Röpke's Political Economy* (Cheltenham: Edward Elgar, 2010): 107–9.

12   See Nicolaum Oresme, *Tractatus de Origine, Natura, Jure et Mutationibus Monetarum* (1355), http://phare.univ-paris1.fr/textes/Oresme/Tractatus.html

13   See Juan de Mariana, SJ, *De monetae mutatione* (1609), in English at http://www.acton.org/publications/mandm/mandm_scholia_57.php#frm, under 'Scholia'.

14   Adam Smith, *An Inquiry into the Nature and Causes of the Wealth of Nations,* vol. 2 of *The Glasgow Edition of the Works and Correspondence of Adam Smith,* ed. R.H. Campbell and A.S. Skinner (Indianapolis, IN: Liberty, 1981): bk. 1, ch. 4, p. 10. First published 1776.

15   Arjo Klamer, *Conversations with Economists* (Totowa, NJ: Rowman & Allanheld, 1984): 136.

16   Emanuel Alexandrovich Goldenweiser, *American Monetary Policy* (New York: McGraw-Hill, 1951): 2–3.

17   Philip Booth, 'Learning from the Crash, and Teaching After It', in *Profit, Prudence and Virtue: Essays in Ethics, Business and Management,*

ed. Samuel Gregg and James Stoner (Exeter: Imprint Academic, 2009): 234.

18 *Ibid.*

19 See Dean Foust, 'Alan Greenspan's Brave New World', *Business Week* (14 July 1997): 44–50, esp. 48.

20 Hans-Adam II, *The State in the Third Millennium* (Liechtenstein: Van Eck, 2009): 136.

21 Friedrich von Hayek, 'The Pretence of Knowledge', lecture to the memory of Alfred Nobel (11 December 1974), http://nobelprize. org/nobel_prizes/economics/laureates/1974/hayeklecture.html

22 Wilhelm Röpke, *Against the Tide*, trans. Elizabeth Henderson (Chicago, IL: H. Regnery, 1969): 227. Chapter first published 1961.

23 European Central Bank, 'Objective of Monetary Policy', http:// www.ecb.europa.eu/mopo/intro/objective/html/index.en.html

24 See Samuel Gregg, 'Europe's Monetary Sins', *Public Discourse* (25 May 2010), http://www.thepublicdiscourse.com/2010/05/1332; John Taylor, 'Central Banks are Losing Credibility', *Financial Times* (11 May 2010).

25 Board of Governors of the Federal Reserve System, 'Mission' (6 November 2009), http://www.federalreserve.gov/aboutthefed/ mission.htm

26 Lewis E. Lehrman and John D. Mueller, 'Go Forward to Gold: How to Lift the Reserve-Currency Curse', *National Review Online* (15 December 2008), http://www2.nationalreview.com/monetary.html

27 Wilhelm Röpke, *International Order and Economic Integration*, trans. Gwen E. Trinks, Joyce Taylor and Cicely Käufer (Dordrecht: D. Reidel, 1959): 76.

28 See Benjamin Graham, *Storage and Stability* (New York: McGraw-Hill, 1937); Frank D. Graham, *Social Goods and Economic Institutions* (Princeton, NJ: Princeton University Press, 1942).

29 Friedrich August Hayek, 'Monetary Policy in the United States After the Recovery From the Crisis of 1920', in *Good Money, Part 1: The New World*, vol. 5 of *The Collected Works of F.A. Hayek*, ed. Stephen Kresge (Chicago, IL: University of Chicago Press, 1999): 71–151, 139.

30 See John Day, *Money and Finance in the Age of Merchant Capitalism* (Oxford: Blackwell, 1999): 59–109.

31 Geoffrey Ingham, *The Nature of Money* (Cambridge: Polity Press, 2004): 76.

32 See *ibid.*: 181.

33 See *ibid.*: 117.

34 See Gordon Tullock, 'Competing Monies', *Journal of Money, Credit and Banking*, 7 (November 1975): 491–7; Benjamin Klein, 'The Competitive Supply of Money', *Journal of Money, Credit and Banking*, 6 (November 1974): 423–53.

35 See Benjamin J. Cohen, *The Future of Money* (Princeton, NJ: Princeton University Press, 2004). Here we should note that an electronic, cashless economy is not the same as a moneyless economy.

36   See Friedrich August Hayek, 'The Denationalization of Money: An Analysis of the Theory and Practice of Concurrent Currencies', in *Good Money, Part 2: The Standard*, vol. 6 of *The Collected Works of F.A. Hayek*, ed. Stephen Kresge (Chicago, IL: University of Chicago Press, 1999): 128–229.

37   Mervyn King, 'Challenges for Monetary Policy: New and Old', *Bank of England Quarterly Bulletin*, 39 (November 1999): 397–415.

38   See Thomas Henry, Lord Farrer, *Studies in Currency, 1898: or, Inquiries Into Certain Modern Problems Connected with the Standard of Value and the Media of Exchange* (London: Macmillan, 1898): 43.

39   Milton Friedman, 'Currency Competition: A Sceptical View', in *Currency Competition and Monetary Union*, ed. Pascal Salin (The Hague: Martinus Nijhoff, 1984): 42–6, 43.

40   See Otmar Issing, 'Hayek—Currency Competition and European Monetary Union', *Institute of Economics Affairs, London* (27 May 1999), http://www.ecb.int/press/key/date/1999/html/sp990527.en.html

41   See Hayek, 'Denationalization of Money': 149–50.

42   European Central Bank, *Annual Report 1998* (Frankfurt am Main: European Central Bank, 1999): 105–6.

Gerald P. O'Driscoll, Jr.

Monetary Order for a Free Society

What role does money play in generating an overall order in society?[1] Is a monetary order necessary for a free society? Oxford economist Herbert Frankel argued that 'there is an intimate relationship between money and freedom; between the keeping of promises and the certainty of contracts; between social function and the rule of law'.[2] Many would agree with this, but modern monetary theory and practice are at odds with it.

In examining the question of whether a monetary order is necessary for a free society, I will draw upon a variety of sources. Not all fit neatly into the natural-law tradition, but almost all are consonant with it. I focus on two interrelated issues. First, are there laws of monetary development? Second, is there a morality of money?

Economic Law

In the history of economics, there have been contentious debates over whether there can be laws of economics. The mid-nineteenth century saw the emergence of the German Historical School. Its members rejected natural-law doctrines—in the sense of 'natural' referring to the nature of man and 'law' to the order that acting men evolve. Instead, they viewed each society as developing according to its own culture and historical situation. No general laws of economics were possible. Empirical-historical knowledge was the research programme.[3]

The rejection of the concept of economic laws brought a reaction from within the broad tradition of German economics. In 1871, the Austrian economist Carl Menger published the *Principles of Economics*.[4] As Bruce Caldwell put it in his biography of F.A. Hayek, 'what was most striking in Menger was how he put things together, how he gave a new and thoroughly systematic structure to various previously expressed notions concerning the effects of human action'.[5] Menger and those who followed in his footsteps consciously sought a sound philosophical basis for developing economic laws of human action. Moreover, from the beginning, the Austrian School (as it came to be called) was preoccupied with the laws by which money operated.

In the twentieth century, Ludwig von Mises (1966) was most identified with pursuing Menger's programme of developing the laws governing human action or purposeful behaviour. Yet in his major work, *Human Action,* he at one point dismisses natural law out of hand, saying the idea 'is quite arbitrary [and] such discussions are not open to settlement'. A few pages later, he equates economic law with the 'laws of nature' (for example, those of physics and biology) and argues that man must recognize these regularities 'if he wants to succeed'. He then articulates 'the reality of natural law, namely, the fact that [man's] power to attain chosen ends is restricted and conditioned'.[6]

Mises is thoroughly modern in his ambivalence toward natural law. I would maintain he was correct when he implicitly equated natural law with the 'laws of nature'. He accepted what Joseph Schumpeter characterizes as 'explanatory natural law'[7] and Alejandro A. Chafuen as 'the laws of nature'.[8] We would now say that Mises accepted the positive analysis of natural law. He rejected 'normative natural law' in the sense of morality, as it was understood by figures ranging from Aristotle to Aquinas. For now, let us return to Menger and his analysis of the origin of money.

The Evolution of Money

Menger analysed the development of money in the larger context of the evolution of institutions. In *Problems of Economics and Sociology*, he raises what he describes as 'the most noteworthy' problem of the social sciences: 'How can it be that institutions which serve the common welfare and are extremely significant for its development come into being without a common will directed toward establishing them?'[9] He employs invisible-hand reasoning not just to endogenous variables, such as prices, wages, and interest rates, but also to institutions.

Institutions develop not as the result of human design ('not the result of socially teleological factors'), he argues, but as the outcomes of individual human actions ('the unintended result of innumerable efforts of economic subjects pursuing *individual* interests').[10] Among modern Austrian school economists, Hayek most consistently followed Menger in explaining undesigned social institutions.[11]

Menger fit his theory of money as the product of evolution into this framework:

> As *each* economizing individual becomes increasingly more aware of his economic interest, he is led by this *interest, without any agreement, without legislative compulsion, and even without regard to the public interest,* to give his commodities in exchange for other, more saleable, commodities, even if he does not need them for any immediate consumption purpose. With economic progress, therefore, we can everywhere observe the phenomenon of a certain number of goods, especially those that are most easily saleable at a given time and place, becoming, under the powerful influence of *custom,* acceptable to everyone in trade, and thus capable of being given in exchange for any other commodity. These goods were called *Geld* by our ancestors, a term derived from *gelten* which means to compensate or pay. Hence the term *Geld* in our language designates the means of payment as such.[12]

This single paragraph is packed with theoretical issues. 'More saleable' commodities are those with smaller bid-asked spreads, which are, hence, more liquid. Before taking up the 'Theory of Money' Menger had developed 'The Theory of the Commodity', an analysis of the holding of stocks of goods for sale. The willingness to do so depended on the progress from economic self-sufficiency to production for the market on order, to production for the market on speculation.[13]

Menger outlined an historical process by reasoning through the consequence of the pursuit of individual interests. Historically, silver and gold have generally been the goods that became the 'means of payment' (with many variations along the way). Gold and silver are valuable and highly marketable. He solved a theoretical problem that has eluded even modern theorists, the simultaneous deter- mination of the money good and its market value. In Menger's analysis, what became money was always a good with prior market value. Its use as money enhanced the demand for it and increased its value in a gradual process over time.[14]

German philosopher Georg Simmel, influenced by Menger's analysis, also analysed money as the outcome of voluntary exchange. In *Two Philosophies of Money: The Conflict Between Trust and Authority*, S. Herbert Frankel analysed and elaborated upon Simmel's contributions. In Frankel's words, 'Money is not a consciously created artifact, but grows out of, reflects, and in turn affects the ever-changing relationships between individuals and the society which they compose'.[15]

That view, which also captures the essence of Menger, contrasts with the State Theory of Money, first articulated by Georg Friedrich Knapp in the late nineteenth century and endorsed by John Maynard Keynes. In its simplest form, it rejects any market (or 'catallactic') analysis of money in favour of a command or 'chartalist' theory. In this under- standing, money doesn't have any intrinsic value, and the state determines what will serve as money — hence the term 'fiat money' — and its power is often ascribed to its ability to determine what is legal tender for obligations owed it.[16] As Keynes wrote in his *Treatise on Money*, 'the Age of Chartalist or State Money was reached when the State claimed the right to declare what thing should answer as money to the current money-of-account — *when it claimed the right not only to enforce the dictionary but also to write the dictionary*. Today, all civil- ized money is, beyond the possibility of dispute, "chartalist"' (the italics were added by Frankel).[17]

Frankel has sport with Keynes over the idea of the state's being able to write a dictionary and enforce its usage on the public: 'Nobody has ever been able to force a single word on to society which the individuals composing did not wish to use.' Money and language each evolve spontaneously. The state has most influenced money when it approves a commodity or money already chosen by economic transactors. Silver coinage is an ancient example, and dollarization is a modern one.[18]

There isn't any question, of course, that modern states now exercise a degree of control over money exceeding that in almost any other area of developed economies. The 'Chartalist Theory of Money' now undergirds most modern monetary theory. The question for the remainder of this paper is whether the modern theory and practice of money produces a monetary order that is consistent with a free society.

A Free Monetary Order

The monetary system is an undesigned social order. That order has been described by Hayek in the first volume of his *Law, Legislation and Liberty* as 'a state of affairs in which a multiplicity of elements of various kinds are so related to each other that we may learn from our acquaintance with some spatial or temporal part of the whole to form correct expectations concerning the rest, or at least expectations which have a good chance of proving correct'.[19]

In *The Economics of Time and Ignorance,* M.J. Rizzo and I present the idea of 'pattern coordination', in which 'there is coordination of plans but not actual activities'. Two co-authors who agree to meet each week to discuss a book project are coordinated, for example, but there is an inherent unpredictability of what exactly they will say and do. The meeting is predictable but not its content. There is coordination and order but not equilibrium.[20]

This is a good way of understanding Menger's idea of a free monetary order: it is the product of money freely chosen. Such an order, writes Frankel in his *Two Philosophies of Money,* 'implies the possibility for individuals of choosing between a multiplicity of conflicting goals or ends'.[21] It is an abstract order in that it is not oriented to the achievement of specific goals but the maximal possibility of achieving individual goals. Michael Polanyi in *The Logic of Liberty*[22] and Hayek in *The Constitution of Liberty*[23] have referred to it as a 'spontaneous order'. Hayek quotes Polanyi: 'The actions of such individuals are said to be free, for they are not determined by any *specific* command, whether of superior or public authority; the compulsion to which they are subject is impersonal and general.' That notion of 'compulsion' comports with the concept of law in the natural-law tradition.

Frankel goes on to describe the free monetary order as having 'principles, enforced by custom, convention and law, which ensure that its operation will not be arbitrarily, capriciously, or lightly altered in favour of particular groups, individuals, or interests'. Quoting A.I. Melden,[24] he argues that a free monetary order implies 'the maintenance of the moral structure of the relations between all of the parties concerned'.[25]

Following Simmel, he is making an essentially moral case for a free monetary order. The order 'implies that contracts freely made in money do, as such, carry society's guarantee that the measuring-rod of money in terms of which they are made will not be deliberately tampered with by anyone, *not even by the Government itself*'.[26] That guarantee is an essential part of the rule of law.

Frankel contrasts a free monetary order with a system of monetary discretion in which 'money increasingly becomes an *instrument* of sectional political or economic action'.[27] He attributes monetary discretion to the rise of the State Theory of Money under the spread of Keynesian economics, but that is perhaps too facile an interpretation of how the change in the philosophy of money came about. Knapp had no catallactic theory of the demand for money, and despite endorsing Knapp's approach, Keynes understood the demand for money to be derived from market behaviour (a distinction ably drawn by Roger Garrison in comments on this paper).

Nevertheless, Frankel accurately draws the sharp contrast between the classical, liberal view of money and the modern, or contemporary view:

> Thus for Simmel and for Menger, as also for most liberal economists of the nineteenth century, the monetary order was not something to be left to the whim of the Government or the State. Indeed, Menger pointed out that Governments had so often and so greatly misused their power that it was forgotten that a coin is nothing but a piece of metal the fitness and full weight of which was guaranteed by the mint. The fact that Government had treated money as if it were merely the product of the convenience of men, and part-

icularly of their legislatures, simply multiplied errors about its nature.[28]

The issue Frankel raises here, in the name of classical liberalism, already had been analysed within the natural-law tradition. Can the state 'declare what things should be used as money', and legitimately alter its value to suit the state's needs? This question was addressed most directly by one of the Spanish late-Scholastic thinkers, Juan de Mariana, SJ (1536–1624).

Can the King Debase Money?

Mariana's 1609 work, *De Monetae Mutatione,* eventually led to his imprisonment and the seizure of all of his papers.[29] But for this, he would have been most known for his history of Spain, *De Rege et Regis Institutione,* published in 1599, which, although it defended tyrannicide, was not proscribed by either the civil or religious authorities.

Mariana proceeds in classic Scholastic style. In the 'Argument', he set out the facts: 'The treasury was completely exhausted by long and drawn-out wars in many places and by many other problems.' In other words, the king needed additional revenue. How could it lawfully be obtained? Mariana next asks, 'Does the King Own His Subjects' Goods?' Citing Aristotle, the treatise *Novellas Constitutiones,* and the Old Testament, he answers, 'No'.

He then poses the next question, 'Can the King Demand Tribute from His Subjects Without Their Consent?' He concludes that 'The established principle' is that 'the prince is never permitted to oppress his subjects with new burdens, without the consent of those concerned, at least of the leaders of the people and State'. To this end, he referred to a chapter from the Papal Bull *In Coena Domini* (1364) that condemned those who imposed new taxes without the consent of those being taxed.[30]

Mariana's strong conclusion may seem at odds with our notion of royal absolutism. But there had been a period of parliamentary ascendancy in Spain, and although parliamentary powers had been eroded by Mariana's time, they had left a powerful intellectual legacy. By the fourteenth century, writes Richard Pipes, 'the *cortes* of Castile, Aragon, Catalonia, and Valencia won the right to approve all extraordinary taxes as well as to participate in the drafting and implement-ation of laws'. The Aragon oath of allegiance to the king went: 'We who are as good as you swear to you who are no better than we, to accept you as our king and sovereign lord, provided you observe all our liberties and laws; but if not, not.'[31]

Perhaps Mariana had a 'vehement character' that led him to take strong positions.[32] But his reasoning was the cul-mination of a long line of enquiry on political and economic issues, beginning with Aquinas and continuing down through Aquinas's Scholastic successors.[33] Mariana reminds the reader that 'here we are discussing not what is happen-ing, but, rather, what right reason demands'. That is classical natural-law reasoning.

The king cannot tax without consent. Nor can he engage in subterfuge. He cannot 'fraudulently establish a monopoly without consent of the people'. For a monopoly accomplishes precisely what taxation does by taking revenue from citizens without their consent. Mariana folds in political economy with his moral reasoning.

Finally he arrives at his central question: 'Can the King Debase Money by Changing Its Weight or Quality Without Consulting His People?' He answers:

> One concludes, therefore, that if the king is the director – not the master – of the private possessions of his subjects, he will not be able to take away arbitrarily any part of their poss-essions for this or any other reason or any ploy. Such seizure occurs whenever money is debased: For what is declared to be more is worth less. But if a prince is not empowered to levy taxes on unwilling subjects and cannot set up mono-polies for merchandise, he is not empowered to make fresh profit from debased money. The strategies aim at the same thing: cleaning out the pockets of the people and piling up money in the provincial treasury. Do not be taken in by the smoke and mirrors by which metal is given a greater value than it has by nature and in common opinion. Of course, this does not happen without common injury.[34]

Mariana here employs political economic argument to buttress a moral case against debasement and inflation. The positive and normative analysis is conceptually separate but practically intertwined.

Our historical excursion brings us full circle back to Menger's concern that governments had so abused their power that it had long been forgotten that government, by its stamp on coins, was guaranteeing the fineness and full weight of the coin and not defining its worth. That captures Simmel's sense that money is built on trust. Violating that trust disturbs all the economic and social relationships established on that trust.

We have abandoned any concept of trust in money, or perhaps in government guarantees whatsoever. In such a world, there isn't any morality in money. That is the consequence of passing from the world of evolved money, money built on trust, to one in which money is an artefact to be manipulated by the prince, or his agents, to suit his purposes. 'Money increasingly becomes an *instrument* of sectional political or economic action.'[35]

Keynes understood that entering 'the Age of Chartalist or State Money' entailed abandoning morality in money. Here Hayek reminds us of Keynes' famous line in his *Two Memoirs*: 'So far as I am concerned, it is too late to change. I remain, and always will remain, an immoralist.'[36]

Money Today

Today we have moved far from the world of Menger, not to mention Mariana. Monetary policy is viewed as the province of technocrats and central bankers. The monetary order is no longer abstract, permitting individuals to coordinate their activities within it. Money is now consciously controlled by government in pursuit of specific policies and identifiable interests. Only after a longer period of monetary abuse do investigators go back to basics. Hayek once said that historically the best monetary theory has been the product of the worst monetary practice.

It is paradoxical, to say the least, that economists almost casually concede dominion over money to the state. In modern times, a few classical liberal economists have felt the need to question why government should be involved with money.

In *A Program for Monetary Stability*, Milton Friedman asks 'whether monetary and banking arrangements cannot be left to the market, subject only to the general rules applying to all other economic activity'. He first points out 'that monetary arrangements have seldom been left entirely to the market, even in societies following a thoroughly liberal policy in other respects' and reasons that paper money will inevitably come to displace a pure commodity standard. Competition cannot be relied upon to limit the supply of paper money. That justifies government intervention.[37]

In 1986, in an article for the *Journal of Monetary Economics*, Friedman and A.J. Schwartz had revisited government's monetary role and reconsidered the case for gold and free banking,[38] but twenty years later, Friedman seemed to favour a monetary rule and central banking.[39] Hayek, in *The Constitution of Liberty* (1960), accepted the state's involvement, although in *Denationalisation of Money* (1976) he questioned it. Others, including the economist and monetary theorist L.H. White, challenged Friedman's reasoning.[40] But Friedman's 1960 view generally holds sway among even free-market economists.

If you ask the average economist about the effects of fixing the price of bread, establishing minimum wages, or imposing usury laws, you will generally get an analysis of shortages and surpluses in the affected markets. Ask about the desirability of government establishing a monopoly on food distribution or producing automobiles, and you will get a lecture on incentives and the role of free prices and profits in allocating resources. But ask most economists today why governments should control money, and they will look at you as if you were daft. Yet money is the most significant good in a market economy. It is one side of every trade. To control money is to influence *every* price.

And the control of money affects not just the price of goods and services, but through its influence on interest rates, monetary policy inevitably affects the allocation of capital. 'The interest rate' is shorthand for a complex array of inter-temporal prices that guide the allocation of capital and production across time.[41] The temporal allocation of capital is a vital function in a market economy. Mises argued that command economies cannot rationally allocate capital, which, he correctly predicted, would be a major reason for their failure.[42]

Ceding money to the state does not just abandon the monetary order; it disorders the market economy. A disordered monetary (and banking) system has been the source of great disorder in the broader economy. Monetary excess has historically sown episodes of booms and busts, including the current one.[43]

Many monetary theorists have placed their hope for sound money in the independence of central banks. But central banks were never independent *of* government. Their 'independence' was operational. Government set the goals of monetary policy. In the European Union and elsewhere, the central bank was given the mandate to control inflation. In the United States, the Federal Reserve System has the dual mandate of maintaining full employment and controlling inflation.

The Federal Reserve System was designed as a bankers' bank, and the twelve regional reserve banks are legally owned by their commercial bank members. The employees of the reserve banks are not US officials. The Fed has consequently retained a certain legal independence, which has helped preserve its operational independence.

In the current economic crisis, however, the Fed has increasingly coordinated its actions with the Treasury. Its special lending programmes involve credit allocation and constitute a form of fiscal policy. Independent central banks are not supposed to engage in fiscal policy, that is, the allocation of resources for specific purposes and to aid specific groups. Anna Schwartz and Walker Todd argue that the Fed is on a 'slippery slope' that will politicize monetary policy.[44]

The Fed perhaps still possesses nominal operational independence. But it is independence in name only. So the government today has further extended its domain over money.

Money Tomorrow

While Mises accepted the workings of the laws of nature in positive economics, he rejected the notion of natural-law reasoning in the area of morality. In the context of economics, that can sometimes be a fine distinction. As he himself observed, man must accept certain regularities 'if he wants to succeed'.

This essay has not focused on the technicalities of monetary policy but on whether there is a law of monetary development, and it has presented an affirmative case. And it has examined whether there is a morality of money. It presented a case for the presence of morality in a free monetary order built upon trust. In so doing, the essay follows the approach of Harold James on globalization.[45] The present essay has further suggested an absence of trust and morality in the current monetary system.

Some economists believed they had discovered a new period of economic stability and 'Great Moderation' in the volatility of housing and the broader economy beginning in the 1980s.[46] Instead, we have reaped a whirlwind of volatility and economic decline. In the United States, the economic disorder has not spilled over into political and social disorder. But in other countries, even Western European countries, it has. As this is written, there have been major marches, demonstrations, hostage takings, and even riots in Greece, Britain, France, Ireland, and Iceland. All are partly the fault of failed monetary policy and flawed monetary institutions. That suggests that it is time for a fundamental monetary reform that aims at the restoration of monetary order.

1   The author thanks Alejandro Chafuen, Maralene Martin, Douglas den Uyl, Walker Todd, and Roger W. Garrison for their comments and assistance.

2   S. Herbert Frankel, *Two Philosophies of Money: The Conflict of Trust and Authority* (New York: St. Martin's Press, 1977): 12.

3   See Bruce Caldwell, *Hayek's Challenge: An Intellectual Biography of F.A. Hayek* (Chicago, IL: University of Chicago Press, 2004): 51.

4   Carl Menger, *Principles of Economics*, trans. James Dingwall and Bert F. Hoselitz (New York: New York University Press, 1981).

5   Caldwell, *Hayek's Challenge*: 47.

6   Ludwig von Mises, *Human Action: A Treatise on Economics*, 3rd rev. ed. (Chicago, IL: Henry Regnery, 1966): 720, 761.

7   Joseph A. Schumpeter, *History of Economic Analysis* (New York: Oxford University Press, 1954): 111.

8   Alejandro A. Chafuen, *Faith and Liberty: The Economic Thought of the Late Scholastics* (Lanham, MD: Lexington, 2003): 20.

9   Carl Menger, *Problems of Economics and Sociology*, ed. Louis Schneider, trans. Francis J. Nock (Urbana, IL: University of Illinois Press, 1963): 146.

10   *Ibid.*: 158–9.

11 Gerald P. O'Driscoll, Jr., 'Money: Menger's Evolutionary Theory', *History of Political Economy*, 18 (Winter 1986): 601–16, 606.

12 Menger, *Principles of Economics*: 260.

13 O'Driscoll, 'Money: Menger's Evolutionary Theory': 608–9.

14 See *ibid.*: 609–10.

15 Frankel, *Two Philosophies*: 12.

16 Ludwig von Mises, *The Theory of Money and Credit* (Irvington-on-Hudson, NY: Foundation for Economic Education, 1971): 73, 463–9.

17 As quoted in Frankel, *Two Philosophies*: 43.

18 *Ibid.*: 43.

19 F.A. Hayek, *Law, Legislation and Liberty I: Rules and Order* (Chicago, IL: University of Chicago Press, 1973): 36.

20 Gerald P. O'Driscoll, Jr. and Mario J. Rizzo, *The Economics of Time and Ignorance* (New York: Routledge, 1996): 86.

21 Frankel, *Two Philosophies*: 4.

22 Michael Polanyi, *The Logic of Liberty* (Indianapolis, IN: Liberty Fund, 1998): 159.

23 F.A. Hayek, *The Constitution of Liberty* (Chicago, IL: Regnery, 1960): 160.

24 A.I. Melden, *Rights and Right Conduct* (Oxford: Basil Blackwell, 1959): 13.

25 Frankel, *Two Philosophies*: 4.

26 *Ibid.*: 40.

27 *Ibid.*: 39.

28 *Ibid.*: 33.

29 Augustinus Lehmkuhl, 'Juan Mariana', *The Catholic Encyclopedia*, 9 (New York: Robert Appleton, 1910). Accessed February 15, 2009 at http://www.newadvent.org/cathen/09659b.htm.

30 Juan de Mariana quotations are from his 'De Monetae Mutatione', as quoted in Alejandro A. Chafuen, ed., 'A Treatise on the Alteration of Money' (excerpts), *Journal of Markets & Morality*, 5 (Fall 2002): 533–93.

31 Richard Pipes, *Property and Freedom* (New York: Alfred A. Knopf, 1999): 152–3.

32 Lehmkuhl, 'Juan Mariana'.

33 See Joseph A. Schumpeter, *History of Economic Analysis*: 73–122; and Murray N. Rothbard, 'New Light on the Prehistory of the Austrian School', in *The Foundations of Modern Austrian Economics*, ed. Edwin G. Dolan (Kansas City, KS: Sheed & Ward, 1976): 52–74.

34 As quoted in Chafuen, 'A Treatise on the Alteration of Money' (excerpts): 543–5.

35 Frankel, *Two Philosophies*: 39.

36 As quoted in Hayek, *Law, Legislation and Liberty*: 26.

37 Milton Friedman, *A Program for Monetary Stability* (New York: Fordham University Press, 1960): 4–9.

38 See Milton Friedman and Anna J. Schwartz, 'Has Government Any Role in Money?', *Journal of Monetary Economics*, 17 (January 1986): 37–62.

[39]   See Milton Friedman, 'The Greenspan Story: He Has Set a Standard', *Wall Street Journal* (31 January 2006): A14.

[40]   See Lawrence H. White, *Free Banking in Britain: Theory, Experience, and Debate, 1800-1845* (Cambridge: Cambridge University Press, 1984); *Competition and Currency: Essays on Free Banking and Money* (New York: New York University Press, 1989).

[41]   See Gerald P. O'Driscoll, Jr., *Economics as a Coordination Problem: The Contributions of Friedrich A. Hayek* (Kansas City, KS: Sheed Andrews and McMeel, 1977).

[42]   See Ludwig von Mises, 'Economic Calculation in the Socialist Commonwealth', in *Collectivist Economic Planning: Critical Studies on the Possibilities of Socialism*, ed. F.A. Hayek (Clifton, NJ: Augustus M. Kelley, 1975): 87–130.

[43]   See Axel Leijonhufvud, 'Monetary and Financial Stability', *Centre for Economic Policy Research Policy Insight*, 14 (October 2007); 'Wicksell, Hayek, Keynes, Friedman: Whom Should We Follow?' presented at the *Mont Pelerin Society Conference*; 'The End of Globalizing Capitalism? Classical Liberal Responses to the Global Financial Crisis', *New York City* (5-7 March 2009). See also Gerald P. O'Driscoll, Jr., 'Money and the Present Crisis', *Cato Journal*, 29 (Winter 2009): 167–86; John B. Taylor, *Getting Off Track: How Government Actions and Interventions Caused, Prolonged, and Worsened the Financial Crisis* (Stanford, CA: Hoover Institution Press, 2009).

[44]   See Anna J. Schwartz and Walker F. Todd, 'Why a Dual Mandate is Wrong for Monetary Policy', *International Finance*, 11 (Summer 2008): 167–83, 171.

[45]   See Harold James, 'Globalization, Empire and Natural Law', *International Affairs*, 84 (May 2008): 421–36.

[46]   Taylor, *Getting Off Track*: 2.

Harold James

The Financial Crisis and the Disciplinary Challenge of Natural Law

One of the fallouts of the global financial crisis, especially in its post-September 2008 or post-Lehman phase, has been a questioning of the value of economics, whether as delivered by the mathematical adepts of sophisticated financial modelling in the business world or by academia. The principles of empirical economics — establishing relationships among masses of data — appeared so successful that the approach became the prevailing methodology of the social sciences. This kind of economics promised a rational world of ever-increasing predictability as well as happiness and stability. But by now, the analytical toolbox appears to be rather empty.

Some of the accusations against the discipline of economics are that it lent itself to misleading calculations of probabilities, it is based on too-limited data ranges, it found difficulties in explaining the logic of institutional responses, and the explicit eschewal of values necessarily precluded an analysis of policy choices.

But there is a more basic objection. Gillian Tett begins her compelling account of the financial crisis with a picture of a 2005 conference on credit derivatives on the French Riviera. She contemplates a 'dominant ideology' in which Power-

Point presentations 'reinforced unspoken, shared assumptions about how finance worked, including the idea that it was perfectly valid to discuss money in abstract, mathematical, ultra-complex terms, without any reference to tangible human beings'.[1]

The criticism thus runs in two directions: the first fundamental, the second empirical. The fundamental challenge asserts that the economic approach is premised on a very shallow conception of human personality, or an overemphasis on an imprecisely defined calculus of rationality, with the result that many phenomena are inexplicable. The further the approach attempts to comprehend complex or enigmatic behaviour, the more confused it appears. Thus spectacular and highly popular attempts to explain everyday life, such as Steven Levitt and Stephen Dubner's *Freakonomics* and its sequel, confront an ultimate impasse. Explaining why prostitution can be very profitable, for instance, these popularizers of an ambitious economics conclude, 'The real puzzle isn't why someone like Allie becomes a prostitute, but rather why *more* women don't choose this career'.[2] There is no way, apparently, to explain the character of moral choice.

The increased popularity of approaches involving behavioural analysis and behavioural economics appears to solve one problem—that of the subrationality of outcomes or the possibility of reaching multiple equilibria—but leaves open a further set of problems and challenges. How, for instance, can rationality produce bubbles, as well as bubbles in which there is a partly limited rationality?[3] Roman Frydman and Michael Goldberg have tried to develop an answer based on imperfect knowledge.[4] The imperfect rationality of outcomes explained by phenomena such as aversion to loss still assumes a world in which—in an optimal setting—a participant would want to judge the outcome in terms of a specific set of criteria, such as income or wealth maximization. The task of the analyst lies in explaining why these outcomes are not achieved. But is this really a characteristic way of judging results? And is it the best way? Those are questions that cannot be so easily answered.

Perhaps since many economists deny any professional concern with morality, this first, fundamental problem raises no great difficulties. The second—the empirical—problem is more obviously painful and central to the disciplinary crisis. Many observers have commented that much of conventional economics has failed empirically in that it ignored themes such as financial instability or the possibility of multiple equilibria, leading to suboptimal outcomes. Many prominent economists followed the maker of the rational-choice revolution, Robert Lucas, in erroneously claiming that macroeconomics had simply solved the central problem of depression prevention.[5] Consequently many people, including many economists, have complained that 'economic theories failed just when we needed them most'. Prominent figures such as Paul Krugman have joined in the orgy of recrimination and castigation (though rarely in self-castigation).[6]

Actually, this tradition of critique is quite old. It long has been a source of frustration that we can evolve very accurate predictive tools for dealing with many aspects of complex human interaction, involving millions of individual choices — for instance, in discussing why traffic or telephone systems freeze up in certain conditions — but not the economic process. Wassily Leontief, a Nobel Prize winner who as a young man worked with the Soviet Gosplan to try to establish a rational guide for economic planning, complained in 1982:

> Page after page of professional economic journals are filled with mathematical formulas, leading the reader from sets of more or less plausible but entirely arbitrary assumptions to precisely stated but irrelevant theoretical conclusions… Year after year economic theorists continue to produce scores of mathematical models and to explore in great detail their formal properties; and the econometricians fit algebraic functions of all possible shapes to essentially the same sets of data without being able to advance, in any perceptible way, a systematic understanding of the structure and the operations of a real economic system.[7]

The discipline of economics was not always like this. For much of the nineteenth century, it involved a concern with institutional analysis, and it revolved around controversies of how value was determined. The economists who worked in this tradition recognized that the framework for market activity was given by specific institutional design and that the market does not generate price-setting or value-determination simply by itself. These directions were literally marginalized — by the marginal revolution. Is there a case for the revival of the older concerns, and how should that enquiry be mounted?

An associated issue involves the legitimacy of institutions and the ability to assess the legitimacy of a social science that critically depends on being value-free. This is not primarily the domain of modern economics, but in a parallel exercise to that of the economists, many political scientists evolved an optimistic picture of an international order whose increasing functionality derived from the simple fact of interconnectedness. The literature self-consciously avoided dealing with issues of legitimacy, since it was clear to its practitioners that the system functioned well.

The problems in the functioning of processes (markets) and institutions raise questions about the relationship of positive and normative analyses. To be clear, the argument presented here is not that modern economics or social science is useless but that they need to be placed in a context that explains why some preferences exist, why we value some things but not others. This paper thinks about the current crises in some very important and apparently pre-eminently successful ways of doing social science. Why has a severe economic crisis also become a methodological crisis, and what are the ways out? In particular, will there be — can there be — a return to some of the older perspectives that depend on a more complex view of human personality, human problems, and human potential?

Values and Deglobalization

In financial crises, assessments of the future, which form the basis of monetary valuations, change very quickly. An inability to put a correct price on an asset leads to the breakdown of markets and the erosion of confidence. Banks, businesses, and people in general no longer trust each other. Collapsing material values fundamentally change immaterial values as well, and the globalization collapse becomes a story of changing values in both the usual senses of the term, as monetary and ideal values are shaken.[8] The consequence is profound vulnerability, with a devastating effect on social cohesion. Trust depends on a wide range of institutional arrangements, on states, on corporations, but both governments and business become vulnerable when values change abruptly and unexpectedly. At the 2009 G-20 London summit, world leaders asserted 'the desirability of a new global consensus on the key values and principles that will promote sustainable economic activity'.[9] How can this pledge become more than a conventional platitude? We need an explanation of how those values and principles evolve.

The breakdown of globalization in the past was associated with financial crises and a shifting of the geo-political balance. Financial flows are closely correlated with the geography of power: a powerful country attracts capital and re-exports this capital in a way that bolsters its international position. Small-scale financial crises may strengthen the link between security and dominance of the capital markets, but large-scale crises lead to a breakdown. Smaller-scale events such as 1929 may look very dramatic, but they do have quite easy and obvious policy answers. Catastrophic meltdowns, such as the Central European banking crisis of 1931, which ricocheted around the world, do not have such readily available solutions.

The connections of finance and the character of power and authority work not just at a level of high politics and the arcane calculations of security experts. They also influence the way in which people think about the myriad connections that link people across long distances and make globalization possible.

Complex transactions and relations in a globalized society and economy require an element of certainty that is provided by a simple capacity to make equivalences. The most obvious form of this security is the stability provided by a secure monetary standard, and upswings in globalization always have had a widely recognized and shared international measure of value. The late nineteenth century was characterized by Charles de Gaulle in retrospect as the *époque du trois pour cent*, the absolute confidence that government and other high-quality bonds would produce a stable and predictable return of 3 percent. The foundational belief in these eras of confidence is that market prices send an intelligible signal, and this belief has political implications. Markets limited the capacity of governments to behave badly. In the late twentieth century, price stability became a major objective of policy. Because the experience of the twentieth century had indicated that politicians could not be trusted, this task was delegated to increasingly independent central banks. Inflation-targeting led to the same kind of confidence in monetary stability that had characterized the gold-standard era. In each case, this basis for trust was a long-term phenomenon — but not a permanent one.

The confidence that was at the core of the belief in universal connectedness led many people to extend credit and take larger and larger risks. In short, the expectations aroused by globalization set off credit booms, and the downswing of deglobalization came with the disappointment of bubbly expectations and then with financial collapse. Raised expectations produced the sense that anything and everything is possible, a euphoria that lacked rational foundations. The power of markets in this case means that alternative disciplinary methods, in the form of state regulation or in the imposition of a complex non-state system of authority in a corporation, also begin to be eroded. There is then a universal questioning of every type of value.

In credit booms, there is not necessarily a synchronized upward movement of all prices. Speculative bubbles develop in some sectors but not everywhere. Take a well-known example: in the bubble that preceded the current crash, values for contemporary art exploded, but prices of old masters remained more or less stagnant. The bust was consequently larger for the contemporary market, while 'traditional' paintings did not fall as much.

There is further uncertainty because periods marked by technological transformation and structural breaks in the economy also see very radical breaks in the pattern of demand. Both the bubble and the technical change mean that the relations of prices become radically unstable.

There are then consequences for policy of radical price instability in times of stress. The instability of prices means that it is hard to find a single guideline for judging monetary policy. The weapon that destroys a broad range of values is price instability.

Severe financial crises of the 1931 type do their damage by dramatically heightening monetary uncertainty and eroding or destroying the idea of a common way of measuring value. Even technical terms such as inflation or deflation do not capture what is happening well, because values shift dramatically relative to each other. When monetary uncertainty prevails, trust and confidence are destroyed. The monetary uncertainty also corrodes institutions that previously had developed in order to eliminate additional uncertainty — companies that internalize some transactions or states that offer a guarantee of stability. People in these circumstances will cast around desperately, seeking some better or truer measure of value and hence a guide to conduct.

Economics and Natural Law

Responses to the latest crisis have given much greater room to policy initiatives. There is a new attention to the role of the state in managing crisis, preventing panic, or stabilizing expectations.[10] The mid-twentieth-century recommendations of John Maynard Keynes have a new degree of actuality.[11] Many aspects of the new policy are worrying: will temporary surges in state spending to deal with the aftermath of banking crises lead to permanently higher levels of government spending and indebtedness? How can the resulting deficits be financed? Is there a danger of inflationary developments as a consequence of ballooning public-sector deficits?[12]

There is a danger of an overextension of expectations about what politics and politicians can do. When states get into the business of assessing values — in particular, in determining currency values — the likelihood is of increased competition between states that produces and exacerbates uncertainty. In the 1930s, this was reflected in the fear of states undertaking competitive devaluations; and in the second phase of the current economic crisis, we also are seeing increased political pressure on exchange rates, notably on the dollar-renminbi rate.

Citizens should ask precisely what is worrisome in the new policy initiatives; only with an articulation of that concern will it be possible to formulate legitimate policies. Very often, complaints about the inadequacy of economics are linked to a very strong advocacy of some policy position in response to the crisis. Such policy positions are fiercely contested, and many of them appear linked to particular and powerful interests; banks and financial services, lawyers, automobile producers, and automobile trade unions have tried to assert that a general good depends on the subvention and rescue of their particular kind of activity.

One particular distributional issue has for a time dominated national and international debates: what sorts of compensation levels are appropriate, and how should these levels be determined? What criteria can be used in setting levels of compensation? Or is this an activity that the state should not be involved in at all and that should be left to market processes? The most divisive issue at the 2009 G-20 Pittsburgh summit concerned precisely the appropriate response to the problem of remuneration in the financial sector. Most Americans are prepared to argue that high pay levels are not appropriate where losses mean that financial institutions need to be bailed out with public money. More generally, it is plausible to argue that even if the government gave no explicit guarantee, the belief that major banks were too big or too interconnected to fail established an implicit guarantee, and as a consequence, the high rewards for taking risk were effectively underwritten by the government. Some others argue that a distorted incentive system in the past led bankers to take inappropriate risks and that consequently, for pragmatic reasons, the incentives should be better adjusted to mirror long-term performance (and also the long-term social or general gains). By contrast, some European governments and thinkers suggest that excessive pay levels were in themselves wrong—even if they did not lead to losses and inappropriate gains.

The controversies do not really address the causes of the perceived failure of conventional economics. The question remains whether this is simply a technical failure or derives from some more basic problem. Is there a more general failure because of an unwillingness of economists to discuss fundamental questions concerned with value? What is the value of public goods such as currency stability? Why should we place a value on open markets? For what reasons should people have the opportunity to undertake employment? Sometimes discussions of such motivations revolve around concepts of natural rights: a right to employment, to a fair income, or to access to markets. What is the source of such rights, and how can conflicts of rights be arbitrated?

It is not surprising that there is a new concern of some economists with justice—note Amartya Sen's 2009 book, *The Idea of Justice*—and with ways of interpreting justice that do not necessarily involve the clash of two or more conflicting rights but rather develop potentials inherent in human beings. One interesting consequence of this new concern has been a revived interest in how different cultures have handled clashes of interest. Often the idea of precepts that can be derived from reason is traced back to Greek philosophy, especially to Aristotle as mediated by medieval philosophy in the writings of Averroes and Aquinas. But Sen has pointed out how Indian thinkers evolved a rather parallel discourse to that of Aristotle. And Arthur Waldron has identified the same debate in China over two millennia ago.[13] Ancient and medieval writers found no problem in combining empirical economics with an ethical orientation, but this tradition largely disappeared.

It is reasonable to think that the crisis in empirical economics and the broader crisis in values are connected. Financial crisis is linked to other sorts of crisis inasmuch as the language and the thinking that produced financial disorder has spread to other domains of life.

Some analysts, for instance, have argued that modern finance simply corresponded to contemporary art, which experienced a remarkable asset price bubble parallel to the financial markets, especially after 2004. In both cases, a fundamentally unintelligible product was being marketed to a wide audience who could not understand the underlying value. Some modern artists and their patrons pointed to the parallel between contemporary art and new financial products. Two Swedish management gurus, in their book, *Funky Business Forever*, wrote that bankers should learn from experimental art: 'If you want to do something really interesting and revolutionary, learn to ignore your customers. Most customers function as rearview mirrors. They are extremely conservative, boring, lack imagination, and don't know their own minds.'[14] Deutsche Bank, a pioneer in the field of corporate cultural engagement, explained a new project (called 'Moment') by saying that 'Moment mirrors developments in the increasingly virtual banking business as well as tendencies in contemporary art'.

After financial implosions such as the collapse of the dot-com bubble in 2000 or the subprime meltdown of 2007–08, the parallel between bewildering and apparently meaningless art and unintelligible financial products is damning rather than reassuring.

The language of finance not only affected art (and vice versa), but it also has affected personal relationships. A study of dating and sexual practices in New York found that users of a candid website explained that they avoided any permanent relationships and instead sought to establish a pattern of put and call options in their private lives. Potential partners were ranked according to degrees of social attractiveness, and the less attractive were held in reserve in case a superior relationship did not materialize. The personal life thus came to resemble a trading floor. The chronicler of this process explains: 'They use their cell phone to disaggregate, slice up, and repackage their emotional and physical needs, servicing each with a different partner, and hoping to come out ahead. This can get complicated quickly, however, and can lead to uneasy situations.'[15]

Natural-law thinking, in which a body of guiding principles can be derived from the application of reason, can be a powerful corrective to the distortion of values in economics. One outstanding problem, however, is that the two traditions of analysis presently haven't any way of speaking directly to each other. Natural-law philosophy is normative. By contrast, economics self-consciously avoids the creation of norms and instead analyses the relationships inherent in empirical data. Economists systematically refrain from making judgments of moral value, supposing that individuals will define their own goods or preferences. The task of the social scientist or the economist is held to lie in the calculation of the consequences of people acting to attain these goods or preferences. As a result, the different approaches look like endless parallel bars, inviting impossible intellectual and moral gymnastics between is and ought.

Both disciplines, then, have their own very distinct version of the crisis. For many natural-law philosophers, the world of the market does not behave as they hold it should; economists have discovered that the market does not behave as they think it will. The two disciplines also have different views of the time framework for analysis, each of which presents its own peculiar problems. Natural-law reasoning maintains that the concepts of justice are eternally valid, with the result that many will ask how they should adjust to a world that is constantly changing and generating new problems that require new analyses. Economists note that utility may be a very short-term concept. Indeed, much of the literature on happiness has been devoted to showing that many forms of consumption generate only a short-term surge in happiness without leading to a long-term increase in well-being. As a result, there is a widespread sense that a truer measure of felicity would need to examine long-term contentment. Latin distinguishes very clearly between the short-term state of happiness (*felix*) and the longer-term state (*beatus*).

The most basic issue in the debate on the contribution of natural-law thinking to economics is the question of the realization of human freedom. Over the past thirty years, a prominent theme of much analysis has been that political and economic freedom produces benefits in the form of particular gains in well-being. Sophisticated measures such as those provided annually by Freedom House are used to establish the empirical veracity (over fairly narrowly defined time periods) of this social-science claim. A parallel stream of thought claims that religious practice is desirable and beneficial because—again, as demonstrated empirically—it also produces gains in income and wealth.[16] But in both cases, the thinking behind the empirical argumentation is deeply distorted and quite destructive. Do we just view freedom or truth as an instrumental mechanism? Or is it rather a question of fundamental good that cannot be justified in simply instrumental terms—and indeed is perverted, undermined, and ultimately destroyed by such an attempt? Freedom has a value—or represents a truth—in itself. Religious values are not derived from their potential material benefits but from a transcendent order. Even though it may be true that faith and love represent a powerful tool in tackling poverty, they do that because of their intrinsic value as an expression of what is truly human. The greatest contribution that the natural-law tradition provides is its powerful insistence on a hierarchy of value in which value as such is recognized rather than appearing as an instrumental tool for some other purpose.

Debt and Crisis

Debt is at the heart of the current crisis, and it raises acute moral issues. Is there a solution to the problem of debt, of the vast expansion of financial assets and liabilities — debts of households, of financial institutions, as well as of governments that attempt to guarantee or to take over the debts of households and banks in order to assuage the panic? Why should burdensome obligations come with a duty to repay? Is it good to be in debt?

Deflation produces radical anti-capitalism and a demand for a cancellation of debt. Revulsion against the market economy often takes the form of a specific condemnation of debt and debt instruments. Saudi Grand Mufti Abdul Aziz al-Sheikh made the case that the cause of the crisis is interest on debt and that the *sharia* principle of risk participation would eliminate the problem. This is a very old answer. The Old Testament famously recommended a cancellation of debt every forty-nine years as a 'jubilee'. And the medieval Christian Church attacked usury. Such arguments are not built on simple obscurantism. Both the Church and Islam distinguish between debt that is exploitative, in which individuals are tied to debt servitude, and the relationship that arises out of a sharing of entrepreneurial risk. The old answers invite us to think about the circumstances in which debt may inhibit free choice or the free development of the human personality.

The theological interpretation of modernity is that we borrow from one another on an increasingly grand scale for a reason, and that reason stands as a condemnation of modern life. We borrow because we are convinced that our utility schedule is more important than someone else's. If I see a beautiful piece of jewellery or a bright new car in a shop, I am convinced that it should be mine and that it can be more usefully employed in my possession than in that of someone else. In this way, greed feeds on a kind of pride or self-regard. The problematical character of debt is captured in an ambiguous phrase of the Lord's Prayer that refers not only to spiritual offence but to actual debt (and was often in the past translated as 'forgive us our debts'): *dimitte nobis debita nostra*.

Solutions to the crisis include a simplification of finance, a return to lower levels of debt, and a reduction of flows across long distances. The quasi-nationalization of banks is already producing some of these effects in that the new government-owned institutions are unlikely to be willing to let their funds flow across national frontiers, where they would be used to the benefit of citizens of a different political entity. Sometimes this package is discussed as a move to 'retro finance'.[17]

Some natural-law traditions point in a very radical direction and demand regular cancellations of debt as in the Old Testament jubilee. Islamic finance, in its original form at least, is sometimes regarded as offering an alternative and more stable basis for economic exchange.[18]

A less radically intrusive approach would demand the end of those incentives that created powerful motives for households and corporations to increase their debt. In particular the tax deductibility of mortgage interest payments led to an excessive level of household debt; and tax deductions for interest led to high levels of corporate leverage. There is a widespread recognition that a major cause of financial-system weakness lay in the high levels of leverage. Before the First World War, US banks had capital ratios of 15–20 percent; by the 1990s, these had fallen to 5 percent. This was conventionally interpreted as a sign of a desirable economizing on capital and of the development of financial maturity. In the aftermath of the crisis, it has been re-diagnosed—notably by Andrew Haldane, the Bank of England's executive director with responsibility for financial stability—as producing a 'doom cycle', in which banks became dependent on implicit guarantees of the government and hence of taxpayers.[19]

There are possible solutions to excessive debt-dependence. Some countries, including the United Kingdom, already have experimented with ending or reducing the levels of permissible mortgage-interest deduction, but patterns of behaviour that built up when mortgage payments provided a substantial element of tax relief have continued to persist. A progressive ending of this distortion would in general remove an economic and psychological burden. In terms of the financial system, an increase in capital requirements or the introduction of contingent capital requirements (a mechanism for converting debt into equity when capital increases are needed) would offer an alternative to the implicit dependence on state guarantees. A more radical proposal involves the restriction or removal of limited liability and a return to nineteenth-century financial principles.

An alternative direction thinks more generally in terms of measures that would increase confidence. There might be a more direct relationship of individuals to financial activity that leaves them more empowered and that does not place them in the hands of people they do not and cannot trust. But trust is not something that simply can be created at will by governments or ordered by legislative fiat. Trust depends on a delicate social infrastructure.

Trust is also intrinsically related to a capacity for empathy, putting oneself in the perspective of another when contemplating a business transaction. This is a tradition of thought that on the one hand derives from Adam Smith's reflections in *The Theory of Moral Sentiments* and on the other from religious and perhaps specifically Christian thinking about compassion or *misericordia*. But it was largely marginalized because of the development of powerful institutions, corporations, and state regulation that seemed to obviate the need for a moral imagination.[20]

Benedict XVI's third encyclical, *Caritas in Veritate*, tries to push even further, calling love (*caritate*) rather than *misericordia* the basis for economic life. But, as some commentators have pointed out, this may for some religious traditions be a step that goes too far into the mystical and transcendental.[21]

The projection of moral thought into business relations runs against a powerful stream of recent thinking that detaches financial matters from the rest of the world, making them a sort of mathematical abstraction. One of the most reflective and self-critical modern masters of finance, George Soros, once wrote, 'If I had to deal with people instead of markets, I could not have avoided moral choices and I could not have been so successful in making money. I blessed the luck that led me to the financial markets and allowed me not to dirty my hands'.[22]

At this stage, there arises the most fundamental problem in regard to values in economics. Many analysts have suggested that a market society cannot live simply on the basis of the values it generates itself as a result of its own commercial activities and exchanges. The fundamental values derive from some other source. A powerful current of interpretation suggests a religious origin of such basic values regarding human dignity, motivation, and conduct. In his famous tract, Max Weber tried to suggest that the ethic that drove modern capitalism had originated with a cultivation of a very unbusinesslike asceticism in the world of the Reformation: the idea of renunciation and a denial of consumption then produced an accumulation of surpluses. The initial asceticism of the business elite gradually eroded as it was replaced by what Weber called the 'iron cage' of rationalistic calculation. The original motivation disappeared, generating a feeling of emptiness.

Conduct in a market society needs to be guided by some external source of commonly defined and commonly held values. If those values erode, instability ensues. Globalization does not automatically establish a self-sustaining set of values. On the contrary, the continual change and uncertainty — driven by new encounters, new possibilities, and new technologies — tends to subvert. A crisis then produces the demand for a return to older values. In the current circumstances, there is even nostalgia for the Weberian conception of a Protestant work ethic. At his inauguration in January 2009, President Barack Obama appeared to be explicitly setting aside the late twentieth-century obsession with happiness and the measurement of 'pleasures' as a way of judging the value of economic activity:

> In reaffirming the greatness of our nation, we understand that greatness is never a given. It must be earned. Our journey has never been one of shortcuts or settling for less. It has not been the path for the faint-hearted, for those who prefer leisure over work, or seek only the pleasures of riches and fame.[23]

The President's declaration coincided happily with the themes of Asian frugality and Asian values that framed the Governor of the People's Bank of China's attack on American hegemony. Zhou Xiaochuan emphasized the importance of

Confucianism, which values 'thrift, self-discipline, Middle Ground, and anti-extravagancy'.[24] Such appeals still raise the Weberian question of how and why the work ethic is motivated and in what ways it corresponds to basic human proclivities. We cannot simply understand economic life by observing its operation; we need to think about an inner logic and about how that logic corresponds with the nature and development of human character. In that sense, the financial crisis has brought us back to basics.

1   Gillian Tett, *Fool's Gold: How Unrestrained Greed Corrupted a Dream, Shattered Global Markets, and Unleashed a Catastrophe* (London: Little, Brown, 2009): xii–xiii.

2   Steven D. Levitt and Stephen J. Dubner, *SuperFreakonomics: Global Cooling, Patriotic Prostitutes, and Why Suicide Bombers Should Buy Life Insurance* (Illustrated Edition) (New York: HarperCollins, 2010): 56.

3   See Jean Tirole, 'Asset Bubbles and Overlapping Generations', *Econometrica*, 53 (September 1985): 1071–100, which began the literature. See also Dilip Abreu and Markus Brunnermeier, 'Bubbles and Crashes', *Econometrica*, 71 (January 2003): 173–204.

4   See Roman Frydman and Michael D. Goldberg, *Illusions of Stability: Financial Markets, the State, and the Future of Capitalism* (Princeton, NJ: Princeton University Press, forthcoming).

5   See Robert Lucas, 'Macroeconomic Priorities', presidential address of the *American Economic Association* (10 January 2003). Available online at http://citeseerx.ist.psu.edu/viewdoc/download?doi=10.1. 1.85.3363&rep=rep1&type=pdf

6   See Paul Krugman, 'How Did Economists Get It So Wrong?', *New York Times Magazine* (6 September 2009): 36; Francis Fukuyama and Seth Colby, 'What Were They Thinking? The Role of Economists in the Financial Debacle', *American Interest*, 5 (September–October 2009): 18–25.

7   Wassily Leontief, 'Academic Economics', in 'Letters', *Science*, 217 (9 July 1982): 104, 107. For a long list of these old complaints, see Tony Lawson, 'Really Reorienting Modern Economics', lecture at *Institute for New Economic Thinking inaugural conference*, Cambridge, England (April 2010). Available online at http://youtu.be/Kes9fRWN0sw

8   See Benjamin M. Friedman, *The Moral Consequences of Economic Growth* (New York: Knopf, 2005).

9   'Leaders' Statement', *G-20 London Summit* (2 April 2009).

10   See Harold James, 'Die Krise der Finanzmärkte und die Rückkehr des Staates', Berlin Academy Lecture, *Zeitschrift für Staats- und Europawissenschaften (ZSE)*, VII (January 2009).

11   See Robert Skidelsky, *Keynes: The Return of the Master* (New York: Public Affairs, 2009).

12   See Carmen M. Reinhart and Kenneth S. Rogoff, *This Time is Different: Eight Centuries of Financial Folly* (Princeton, NJ: Princeton University Press, 2009).

13   See Amartya Sen, *The Idea of Justice* (Cambridge, MA: Belknap, 2009); Arthur Waldron, 'The Dialogue of Salt and Iron', in *Natural Law and Economics*, ed. Harold James, forthcoming.

14   Jonas Ridderstråle and Kjell Nordström, *Funky Business Forever: How to Enjoy Capitalism* (Harlow: Pearson, 2008): 150.

15   Wesley Yang, 'A Critical (But Highly Sympathetic) Reading of New Yorkers' Sexual Habits and Anxieties', *New York Magazine*, 'News and Features' (25 October 2009), http://nymag.com/news/features/sexdiaries/2009/60297/

16   See Robert J. Barro and Rachel M. McCleary, 'Religion and Economic Growth' (8 April 2003), http://www.economics.harvard.edu/faculty/barro/files/Religion_and_Economic_Growth.pdf; Rachel M. McCleary and Robert J. Barro, 'Religion and Economy', *Journal of Economic Perspectives*, 20 (Spring 2006): 49–72; Luigi Guiso, Paola Sapienza and Luigi Zingales, 'People's Opium? Religion and Economic Attitudes', *NBER working paper 9237* (September 2002), http://www.nber.org/papers/w9237

17   See Amar Bhide, 'In Praise of More Primitive Finance', *Economists' Voice* (Berkeley Electronic Press, February 2009).

18   See Felix Salmon, 'Shrinking Banks', post to blog, *Felix Salmon* (26 August 2009), http://blogs.reuters.com/felix-salmon/2009/08/26/shrinking-banks/

19   See Andrew G. Haldane and Piergiorgio Alessandri, 'Banking on the State', *BIS Review*, 139 (2009).

20   See John Paul II, *Dives in Misericordia*, encyclical letter (1980): 'The present-day mentality, more perhaps than that of people in the past, seems opposed to a God of mercy and in fact tends to exclude from life and to remove from the human heart the very idea of mercy. The word and the concept of "mercy" seem to cause uneasiness in man, who, thanks to the enormous development of science and technology never before known in history, has become the master of the earth and has subdued and dominated it. This dominion over the earth, sometimes understood in a one-sided and superficial way, seems to leave no room for mercy.'

21   See Benedict XVI, *Caritas in Veritate*, encyclical letter (2009), http://www.vatican.va/holy_father/benedict_xvi/encyclicals/documents/hf_ben-xvi_enc_20090629_caritas-in-veritate_en.html; David Nirenberg, 'Love and Capitalism', *New Republic*, 240 (23 September 2009): 39–42.

22   George Soros, *The Crisis of Global Capitalism: Open Society Endangered* (New York: Public Affairs, 1998): 197.

23   Barack Obama, *Inaugural Address* (transcription) (20 January 2009), http://www.nytimes.com/2009/01/20/us/politics/20text-obama.html

[24] Zhou Xiaochuan, 'On Savings Ratio', speech for People's Bank of China (24 March 2009), http://www.pbc.gov.cn/publish/english/956/index.html (scroll to 'Zhou Xiaochuan: On Savings Ratio').

Part 2

ECONOMICS AND THE

COMMON GOOD

Philip Booth

The Crash of 2008
A Discussion of its Causes & their Relationship to Ethical Issues[1]

The common perception regarding the causes of the financial crash of 2008 is that unregulated laissez-faire capitalism was allowed to let rip and that the greed of bankers, motivated by bonus packages, led them to an unprecedented degree of risk taking. This has seemed to many economists, journalists, and others to be obvious. The market had failed, and that failure proved the need for extensive government intervention. That is almost exactly what people believed in the immediate aftermath of the 1929 Wall Street crash, although subsequent reflection proved that view to be largely mistaken. That being the case, it would be wise to explore alternative hypotheses with regard to the crash of 2008—specifically the ways in which government action contributed substantially to, if not caused, that crash.

It is impossible to untangle the many factors that caused the crash, and this paper is not an attempt to evaluate the empirical evidence in this way. Instead, it will be argued that there was a tide in financial markets and that the US government in particular and regulators more generally swam strongly with the tide and encouraged it. Nothing in the behaviour of government, regulators, or monetary policy-makers suggests that by giving them more discretionary power, we will make future financial crises less likely.

Loose Monetary Policy—Boom and Bust

It is now widely accepted that the boom and bust culminating in the Great Depression of the 1930s arose as a result of catastrophically mismanaged monetary policy. The same was true of the Japanese boom, bust, and malaise of the late twentieth century. Was monetary policy an important cause of the crash of 2008? It probably was. For six years from the year 2001, the US Federal Reserve seemed to send the message to participants in financial markets that if the markets were to fall, the Fed would underpin them. Loose monetary policy led to a financial bubble and asset-price boom, low saving, and a boom in consumption. Higher asset prices raised the value of collateral against secured loans, thus encouraging more lending and—combined with mark-to-market accounting—raising accounting profits. Low interest rates encouraged unsustainable borrowing, consumption, and investment in the housing market and exacerbated the problem of global imbalances. There also seemed to be an excessive desire on behalf of the Fed to prevent corrections in financial markets (the so-called 'Greenspan Put').

In this regard, there are some key figures worth mentioning:

- In the United States, the federal funds rate was cut from 6.25 to 1.75 percent in 2001.
- The rate was then cut further and was held at 1 percent until mid-2004.
- The real federal funds rate was negative for two-and-a-half years during the period of 2002–04.
- A Taylor Rule would have led to a federal funds rate of between 2 and 5 percent during the period of 2001–05.
- Money-supply growth in the United Kingdom was 14.1 percent per annum in September 2007.

This was not an easy time to conduct monetary policy, although criticisms of policy were made at the time. A rise in consumer price inflation failed to materialize (partly due to the fall in prices of tradable goods), central banks were arguably looking at price indices that were too narrow (the relevant price index in the United Kingdom excluded housing costs altogether), and the high level of savings in Asia made it difficult to determine whether low interest rates were a real or a monetary phenomenon.

However, it could be argued that there was too little emphasis on the role of the money supply in causing price inflation, and economic and financial distortions more generally. Both Austrian economic theory and some monetarist descriptions of the transmission mechanism suggest that loose monetary policy does not necessarily manifest immediately as higher consumer prices but works first by distorting asset markets, leading to both an asset price boom and an investment boom. There is substantial evidence that these forces were at play during the late 1920s in the United States, in Japan at the height of its boom, and in recent events.

Bailouts and Moral Hazard

In addition to these problems, moral hazard built up within the financial system. First, on both sides of the Atlantic, there were deposit insurance schemes. These are not industry-run schemes or schemes that charge proper risk-related premiums. In reality, they compensate for bad decision-making on behalf of banks and their customers. Indeed, most banks didn't pay any premiums into the US scheme in the run-up to the crash.

Second, a series of incidents in the conduct of US monetary policy convinced market practitioners that financial markets would be underpinned by accommodating monetary policy (see above). These incidents included several special rate cuts such as after September 11th, after the bursting of the dot-com bubble, and after the failure of Long-Term Capital Management. It is possible that these cuts might have been justified, but their length and frequency suggest that the objective was to put a floor under the markets. As Thomas Woods pointed out, *The Times* had suggested in 2000 (eight years before the crash) that Alan Greenspan had encouraged a destructive tendency toward excessive risky investment supported by hopes that the Fed would step in to help by loosening monetary policy if things went bad.[2]

Other bailouts were less subtle. In the 1980s and 1990s, the failure of the savings-and-loans institutions cost the US government $126 billion. The government also underpinned a large part of the American mortgage market. Fannie Mae and Freddie Mac guaranteed payments on mortgage-backed securities, and investors believed — as can be seen from the pricing of its capital—that if Fannie Mae and Freddie Mac failed, the government would bail them out. Personal bankruptcy law in the United States is also weak, and it is often difficult for a lender to have recourse to other assets when a borrower defaults on a mortgage.

Over a period of years, a pattern was built up in the markets that conveyed the message that individuals were protected from the consequences of risk taking. This was reinforced by the events following the crash, and specifically some of the key bailouts:

- the US-government's Troubled Asset Relief Program,
- the government-sponsored enterprise (GSE) stock purchase programme, where the government bought Fannie Mae and Freddie Mac preferred stock,
- the government mortgage-backed securities purchase, and
- the money-market mutual funds bailout.

The United Kingdom also bailed out a number of banks, their depositors, and unsecured creditors, although their shareholders had also generally lost money.

Incentives to monitor are reduced significantly when markets expect bailouts, and this is particularly true of providers of credit. Guarantees also mean that markets do not send price signals in terms of widened bond spreads, so crucial information is lost. The too-big-to-fail problem is then self-fulfilling, as government-backed institutions find it easier than other institutions to raise capital and so they expand more rapidly. As we underpin the financial system with guarantees, people are insulated from the consequences of their own actions and so take riskier actions. Prudence comes to have public-good qualities, and incentives to monitor risk are reduced for creditors, depositors, and providers of debt capital. In the nineteenth century, banks competed with each other to demonstrate how sound they were, and they often had double shareholder liability. Before the American deposit insurance scheme began, banks usually had equity capital of 20 to 30 percent of total assets; during the rest of the twentieth century, this figure never reached more than 10 percent, and indeed, Fannie Mae and Freddie Mac had only 1.2 percent equity capital at the end of 2007.[3]

We cannot insure risk in the whole financial system without dramatically increasing moral hazard. This then simply leads to the risks growing and to the costs — when those risks materialize — being imposed on taxpayers.

Encouragement of Subprime Lending

Many also have blamed the complex securitization instruments for the crash. But there are some pertinent questions we should ask. Why was there so much subprime lending? And why was so much of it obscured by securitization? Securitization itself can be very helpful for diversifying risk and making it less systemic. This will be discussed below, but first it is worthwhile to examine the push toward subprime lending and securitization that came not from the market (which is now being blamed) but from government and regulators.

The Community Reinvestment Act, backed up by progressively tightening state regulation, more or less forced banks to lend to bad risks. In addition, there were substantial implicit subsidies for people to buy houses. These were particularly targeted at the subprime mortgage market:[4]

- By 2005, the mortgage giants had explicit targets to provide over 50 percent of their financing to people on or below median incomes.
- A Boston Fed manual instructs lenders, 'Special care should be taken to ensure that standards are appropriate to the economic culture of urban, lower–income, and nontraditional consumers'. Banks were warned that they would be fined $500,000 if they were sued for discrimination.[5]
- In 2004, Greenspan encouraged credit institutions to move away from fixed-rate mortgages toward variable-rate mortgages, which they did; the rise in short-term interest rates then helped trigger the subprime crisis.
- It is estimated that the abolition of capital gains tax for residential real estate alone led to a rise in house prices of 17 percent.
- In half of US states, mortgages are non-recourse, so the borrower can walk away from the property if it is

worth less than the mortgage. This largely happens because bankruptcy laws are too lenient.

- Fannie Mae had a commitment to spend $2 trillion, expanding home ownership among low-income earners and minorities. Forty percent, then, of loans that Fannie Mae bought and securitized in 2007–08 were subprime or Alt-A loans, mainly without documentation.
- As noted, by the end of 2007, Fannie Mae had equity capital of only 1.2 percent of its assets.
- Government policy of low interest rates encouraged borrowing and unrealistically high asset prices.

These well-meaning policies were designed to help the poor have access to better housing without direct intervention through the tax system. The government and its agencies were at the heart of the push toward subprime lending and the particular techniques of securitization. Astonishingly, the policies were apparently regarded as very low-risk. Joseph Stiglitz and colleagues wrote a report in which it was stated that Fannie Mae faced a risk of less than 1 in 500,000 of having to be bailed out by the government.[6]

One cannot blame the Community Reinvestment Act alone for the crash—the figures do not bear it out. However, a whole range of sources strongly encouraged subprime mortgages, and securitization and government institutions were at the heart of it. The government-backed securitization machines underwrote the risks on mortgages granted by banks that then had little incentive to monitor properly.

Regulation and Tax Policy

International regulation also played its part. The Basel Accord in 1988 and its successor, Basel II, led banks to take on gearing in more complex ways and then to the adoption of similar risk models in much of the rest of the banking system. First, the accords radically distorted the activities of banks, encouraging them to take on more complex gearing — and to give the impression that they had off-loaded risk through securitization. Banks could reduce their regulatory capital ratios by securitizing loans, even if risk was kept on the balance sheet. A bank could securitize a tranche of loans and buy securities backed by a set of loans similar to those they had previously securitized, and still reduce their capital requirements significantly if the securities they bought were triple-A securities. This encouraged the rating agencies to overrate securities. The gap was plugged in the United States by requiring penal capital if banks kept risk exposure when they undertook securitizations; banks then responded by moving the risk off the balance sheets altogether and lost the incentive to monitor loans.[7] The activities of rating agencies also were seriously distorted by the regulatory capital advantage banks gained from holding better-rated securities.

Second, through the Basel II process, international regulators strongly encouraged the adoption of similar risk models throughout the banking system. This was the case even before full implementation. When those risk models turned out to be flawed, it affected the whole system simultaneously. Intended to reduce the probability of failure of individual banks — which is not really the job of the regulator — these models encouraged banks to have similar business models, thus raising the probability of the whole system failing. It has to be said, in defence of the regulatory institutions, that such models had been evolving as an industry standard for a number of years, and a strong case can be made that industry practitioners over-relied on quantitative models parameterized using historical data. Arguably, businesses did not heed Friedrich Hayek's warnings about over-reliance on quantitative information.[8] The whole point of a competitive process is to ensure that businesses that use inappropriate methods either fail or adapt. But as we have seen, the political and economic background discouraged failure or adaptation.

In addition, government policy across the Western world has provided strong tax incentives for companies — including banks — to gear their balance sheets and become more risky. This situation arises as a result of the way different forms of corporate capital are taxed. Almost without exception, when a company raises capital by issuing equity capital, its tax burden is considerably higher than when it raises capital by borrowing. This does not explain why financial institutions lent out too much with insufficient capital, but it does help explain the explosion in debt markets in general and the increased gearing in financial-sector balance sheets. Also, the regulation of long-term investment institutions such as life-insurance companies and pension funds increasingly encouraged them to invest in debt rather than equity instruments. This raised the demand for securitized debt instruments — especially those that were rated more highly by rating agencies.

Financial markets are heavily and closely regulated in minute detail. To give an example from the United Kingdom, the Financial Services Authority (FSA) regulatory handbook contains ten sections. The section titled 'Prudential Standards' is divided into eleven subsections. The subsection 'Prudential Sourcebook for Banks, Building Societies and Investment Firms' is made up of fourteen sub-subsections. The sub-subsection 'Market Risk' is divided into eleven sub-sub-subsections. The sub-sub-subsection on 'Interest Rate PRR' has sixty-six paragraphs. This is often described by the FSA as 'principles-based, light-touch regulation'. There are probably over 1,100,000 paragraphs in the rule book. Essentially, regulators are trying to do a job that cannot be done — closely regulate the investment-banking system through detailed rules.

It is probably true to say that in the early twenty-first century, banks have been permitted to undertake a wider range of activities than they were for most of the twentieth century — although financial markets were extraordinarily free in the United Kingdom in the nineteenth century. However, the way in which those activities are undertaken is now regulated in incredible detail to an extent that no one would have anticipated thirty years ago. This regulation has encouraged the creation of the new opaque financial instruments to 'arbitrage' regulatory systems.

Other Suspects and Red Herrings

Much has been made of how other factors, not considered hitherto in any detail, supposedly caused the crash. Three of those suspects are most often advanced: ethical failure, departure from traditional models of banking, and the paying of excessive bonuses to bankers. These factors were important and caused significant problems, but either they did not cause the system *as a whole* to fail or they were endogenous and affected by other upstream causes.

Ethical Failings

It has been suggested that the crash, at its root, was an ethical failure. There were, no doubt, ethical failings, and they were not confined just to highly paid workers in large banks. Mortgage applicants lied about their income; bank branch managers oversold loans; traders created new products that did not provide long-term value for shareholders; senior managers did not monitor junior managers; directors did not properly manage senior managers on behalf of shareholders; and so on.

But it is difficult to conclude that these things caused the crash, as such. If so many people had not failed ethically, it is *possible* there would not have been the crash of 2008. More likely, though, the crash would have manifested itself in other ways, given how markets had been distorted by regulation and the operation of monetary policy. If ethical failings are to blame for the failure of the financial system as a whole, we have to ask ourselves whether, somehow, ethical behaviour was worse in 2008 than in 1968, or whether it was worse in 1929 than 1959. I do not think this is the case.

More generally, a financial system cannot be built around the assumption that participants in it are saints. The financial system as a whole must be relatively impervious to ethical failure. In *Centesimus Annus*, Pope John Paul II wrote that it is important for self-interest and the interests of society as a whole to be brought into fruitful harmony.[9] This requires that individuals who make decisions are held financially accountable for them. If the impact of financial decisions is socialized through bailouts, widespread state-provided deposit insurance, and accommodating monetary policy, then the pursuit of self-interest will not lead to the pursuit of the general interest: people will be encouraged to make reckless decisions, imposing potentially huge losses upon others.

Furthermore, as Samuel Gregg has noted, we use the phrase *moral* hazard and not simply *risk* hazard to describe the situation where the financial decisions of one individual are underwritten by society more widely.[10] This is because people face incentives to act less prudently—in a way that is intrinsically unethical—if we underwrite their actions. Indeed, the financial system is more likely to attract unethical people to work in it if ethical behaviour is not seen to be beneficial. It may be thought that this reflects badly on people who work in the financial sector and that it should be addressed by a renewal of ethics. Such a renewal would be desirable — both for its own sake and for its beneficial consequences. However, we cannot build the system on the assumption that such a renewal takes place.

An analogy can be drawn with the welfare state. There is, at the moment, great concern about the effect that the welfare state has on work incentives, marriage, and so on. These problems involve ethical aspects. It is wrong for a person to claim incapacity benefit when he is fit for work, but the incentives are such that many are strongly tempted to do so. In the same way, economic incentives and ethical issues come together in governing behaviour in the financial system, with people acting against their better instincts because of the incentives they are given. Indeed, the analogy between the welfare state and the banking system goes further. As has been noted, there wasn't any shortage of regulation of the banking system. Firms generally complied with it, and having done so, they felt they had discharged their ethical responsibilities. In the same way, someone might feel that if he ticks all the right boxes on the incapacity benefit form and successfully passes the doctor's examination, then he should claim the benefit and not worry about looking for work. A more conscientious person may realize that although he can, technically, qualify for the benefit, he should go out looking for work all the same. In both cases, the ethical compass is distorted by socializing the costs of a person's unethical actions. This may happen among people who are weak-willed or in cases where prudent thought is required to determine the correct ethical course.

Ethical behaviour also often requires careful discernment, and to discern what is and what is not ethical behaviour can become genuinely difficult when price signals are distorted by government action. If credit spreads are depressed because of loose monetary policy, is lending money to a marginal borrower immoral profiteering, or is it helping that person to establish a business? Is securitization creating a shady financial product to generate fees for the bank, or is it reducing mortgage spreads for poor home owners? If interest rates are held down by the central bank, do we take this as a signal of a permanent reduction so that individuals can increase their long-term borrowing, or do we treat it as a temporary phenomenon that will leave over-borrowers dangerously exposed? If asset prices are inflated, do we treat net wealth as artificially caused by loose monetary policy, or has it genuinely increased so that any given person can increase his or her borrowing? In many respects, the price system lost its coordinating function in the financial system in the early twenty-first century, and in such circumstances, it can be very difficult to make prudent and ethical judgments.[11]

Financiers respond rapidly to price signals to drive wealth creation in financial markets. Ethical behaviour will help promote more stable markets. The problem is that once governments interfere to the extent that they have, we simply do not know what behaviour creates wealth and what behaviour simply feeds the boom. A moral sense might help somebody judge what they ought to do ethically, but it may not help very much when they do not have the information they need to apply their ethical principles effectively.

There isn't any question that a financial system populated by ethical people would be desirable. But it is difficult to know how public policy can directly and beneficially improve the situation. Government can, however, change structures so that individuals and firms bear responsibility for their financial decisions and unethical behaviour is not encouraged. A side effect of this is that the market would then run with the grain of self-interest, a self-interest that encourages ethical behaviour, so that the pursuit of self-interest would be less likely to evolve into imprudent actions.

Product Complexity and Departure from Traditional Modes

Pawel Dembinski makes his case powerfully in his 2009 book rooted in Christian social thinking.[12] In recent years, banks have tended to fund their loans not through savers' deposits but through securitization. This has meant, it is argued, that they have less concern for 'relationships' with customers and might not properly monitor those who borrow from them. If a customer defaults on a loan, it does not affect the bank that makes the loan, because the loan has been sold on to another investor.

Of course, if banks sell securities backed by poor-quality loans, investors will not buy them — if they know the risk. However, risky loans often have been bundled into complex securities, and the risk of those loans has been obscured and measured by complex models built on assumptions that may have been naïve. Dembinski argues that in this whole process, 'transactions' (the buying and selling of securities) have become more important than relationships (a direct relationship between a bank and a borrower). However, while much is made of the widespread exposure to American subprime mortgages and the interconnectedness that created, if these mortgages had not been securitized but had been held by traditional banks that then failed, the consequences would have been different but equally serious.

It is not possible, *a priori*, to dismiss complex financial products as wrong or dangerous. As late as April 2007, a now deputy governor of the Bank of England, Paul Tucker, commented: 'So it would seem that there is a good deal to welcome in the greater dispersion of risk made possible by modern instruments, markets and institutions.'[13] The welcome for securitization was not just coming from the market participants who were making fees for creating the products.

Any particular securitization might bring lower mortgage rates for poor borrowers or spread risk around the financial system, making that risk less systemic. On the other hand, widespread securitization and the development of financial products based on the trading of credit risk may bring the sort of systemic problems that the crisis produced. There is little evidence to suggest that governments, regulators, and tax authorities should be anything other than neutral about the process. It seems strange to blame so-called unregulated financial markets for subprime lending and securitization when it was encouraged by bank capital regulation, the tax system, the regulation of pension funds and insurance companies, and the participation of the mortgage giants Fannie Mae and Freddie Mac.

In fact, it is normal for financial markets to punish complexity by demanding higher rates of return. It is interesting that this did not seem to happen before the recent crisis. This may have been the product of simple market error and complacency, but regardless of the cause, we need to reverse the situation whereby complex transactions are encouraged by government and regulators and also address the problem that risks arising from complexity are not properly priced because of government underwriting of risk in the financial system.

Excessive Bonuses

A third suspect is the bonus packages paid to bankers, which encouraged risk taking. Bonuses certainly have increased in recent years. Total bank-bonus payouts on Wall Street and in the City of London in selected years are shown in the table below:[14]

Year	Wall Street Bonuses ($ billion)	City of London Bonuses (£ billion)
2002	9.8	3.3
2004	18.6	5.7
2007	33.2	10.2
2008	18.4	4.0
2009 (est.)	27.5	6.0

Remuneration packages, it is said, cause managers to focus too much on short-term profits and the pursuit of beta (systematic risk). Academic work certainly suggests that bonuses can affect executive behaviour in this and other ways, but there is a fatal weakness in the argument of regulators and politicians who are calling for bonus structures to be regulated. Bonuses are, in fact, endogenous and not exogenous. Bonuses simply respond to the incentives facing firms. Recent academic work suggests that 83 percent of the variation in relative compensation premiums in the financial sector is explained by how free the banking sector is.[15] As regulation of the banking sector is loosened, financial-sector remuneration rises.

This is not an argument for more regulation of banks — it is simply evidence that bankers' bonuses are a rational response to the incentives facing banks. Bonuses are not an exogenous variable: they are therefore not the lever to control if we want to control the risks taken by banks. I would argue that the approach that should be taken is one that would ensure banks bear the costs of the risks that they take. There then wouldn't be any need to regulate bonuses – a practice that in any case is likely to be ineffective if they are an endogenous variable.

Public-Choice and Austrian Economics

The main intellectual problem in much of the post-crash analysis is that commentators have been overconfident in their beliefs about what regulators can achieve. Many of the problems that led to the crash were caused by well-meaning responses to previous financial crises. This included, for example, the creation of the mortgage securitization ware-houses – but also the many particular aspects of international financial regulation and accounting regulation. There are several reasons not to put trust in regulation, many of which are suggested by public-choice and Austrian economics. Public-choice economics predicts the following result from regulation:

- Regulation will tend to be diverted away from its proper economic objectives as a result of incentives within bureaus. This leads to a number of effects:
  - Regulators will tend to discharge their duties by writing rules.
  - There will be too much detailed regulation because the costs of regulation are dispersed but its benefits are often experienced by a rel-atively small group (including politicians and employees of the regulatory bureau).
  - Regulators will be risk-averse and will try to reduce the number of failures on their watch.
  - Regulators may treat firms favourably if they expect to work for the firm at some stage in the future.
  - Paradoxically, if a failure does happen, the regulator may be slow to act, in the hope that the failed institution will recover and that the failure does not have to be revealed.
- Regulators also may well be captured by those whom they are trying to regulate.

There also are lessons from Austrian economics. It is simply not possible for regulators to gather all the information necessary to regulate the market effectively. Indeed, that is precisely what they were trying to do in the run up to the 2008 crisis. The regulatory system before the crash was extensive, but it failed. Indeed in many senses, as we have seen, it actively — if unintentionally — encouraged the behaviours that led to the crash. Whatever regulators try to do, there will be unintended consequences — and these unintended consequences may be very serious.

What Should We Do?

Given these public-choice problems and the impossibility of accumulating dispersed market information within regulatory bureaus in order to regulate markets to produce optimal outcomes, it is necessary to look to other approaches to try to prevent future problems in financial markets of the type seen in 2008.

The obvious approach is to make financial institutions responsible for the financial decisions they make and to ensure that borrowers also are held fully accountable for their financial decisions. This will have a dramatic effect on risk-taking behaviour — we know this from the study of the financial system in the past. Yes, individual banks may be more likely to become insolvent, but the system will be more stable. Banks will be more careful, and their counterparties who provide credit or capital will have enhanced incentives to monitor. In so far as we do have further regulation in order to reduce the externalities that arise when an individual financial institution fails, it should take a form that enhances market discipline rather than replace it with regulatory discipline: for example, the requirement to have a layer of preference share capital,[16] double liability for shareholders, and/or contingent equity capital. And there are other methods of restoring market discipline that should be considered:[17]

- the use of risk-based deposit insurance — preferably organized by the market,
- a requirement for depositors to be senior creditors in a bank that is being wound up,
- a requirement for 'living wills', to ensure that banks can be wound up in the event of a failure with all creditors (except insured depositors) suffering losses,

- a requirement for banks to publish more detail of their exposures to the market—currently their key relationships are with regulators, and
- better legal certainty in terms of the way in which complex financial contracts are treated.

Unless we abolish centrally provided deposit insurance, there is always going to be a need for some sort of regulation. This is better administered within a central bank than within a special regulatory bureau. Regulation within a bureau such as the United Kingdom's FSA produces perverse incentives,[18] while regulation by a central bank better aligns incentives—it is their capital that is at risk if a lender-of-last-resort's loan fails. And if the capital of the central bank is provided by the clearing banks themselves, so much the better. It is not necessary to extend regulation farther out into the financial system, as the EU has proposed, on the grounds that any institution could be systemic if it contracts with a bank (as AIG had done). This would, in any case, be an impossible task. If retail banks have their capital regulated, then their capital requirements can depend upon the counterparties with which they are connected. It is not necessary to regulate the counterparties themselves.

Ensuring that banks can fail will help. However, other 'win-win' policies should be pursued for their own sake, as well as to make the financial system more stable. Discrimination against equity capital in the tax system should cease, and the American government's support for housing loans should end.

In summary, there are many ways in which governments and regulators were at fault for the crash. There are many ways in which private-sector actors were at fault as well. It is not possible to perfect regulatory systems. However, it is possible to ensure that private-sector actors are held responsible for the decisions that they make. If that is done, many substantial economic and ethical benefits will follow.

---

1   Much of this discussion summarizes ideas in Philip Booth, ed., *Verdict on the Crash: Causes and Policy Implication*, Hobart Paperback 37 (London: Institute of Economic Affairs, 2009). Specific examples and figures quoted are not fully referenced but in a number of cases are taken from Johan Norberg, *Financial Fiasco: How American's*

Infatuation with Home Ownership and Easy Money Created the Economic Crisis (Washington, DC: Cato Institute, 2009); Booth, *Verdict*; Philip Booth, ed., *Christian Perspectives on the Financial Crash* (London: St. Paul's, 2010); and Thomas E. Woods Jr., *Meltdown: A Free-market Look at Why the Stock Market Collapsed, the Economy Tanked, and Government Bailouts Will Make Things Worse* (Washington, DC: Regnery, 2009).

2 See Woods, *Meltdown*.

3 See Norberg, *Financial Fiasco*.

4 These examples are discussed in a number of sources, including Woods, *Meltdown*; Norberg, *Financial Fiasco*; and Booth, *Verdict*.

5 Federal Reserve Bank of Boston, *Closing the Gap: A Guide to Equal Opportunity Lending* (April 2003): 13.

6 See Joseph E. Stiglitz, Jonathan M. Orszag and Peter R. Orszag, 'Implications of the New Fannie Mae and Freddie Mac Risk-based Capital Standard', *Fannie Mae Papers*, 1 (March 2002).

7 See Norberg, *Financial Fiasco*.

8 See, for example, Friedrich August von Hayek, 'The Pretense of Knowledge', *Nobel Prize lecture* (11 December 1974), http://nobelprize.org/nobel_prizes/economics/laureates/1974/hayek-lecture.html

9 See John Paul II, *Centesimus Annus*, encyclical letter (5 January 1991).

10 See Booth, *Christian Perspectives*.

11 Prudence involves appraising a situation and obtaining the necessary information before making a decision. It is easy to see how prudence is undermined if the price mechanism is sending faulty signals as a result of government action.

12 See Pawel H. Dembinski, *Finance: Servant or Deceiver? Financialization at the Crossroads* (Basingstoke: Palgrave Macmillan, 2009).

13 Paul Tucker, 'A Perspective on Recent Monetary and Financial System Developments', speech to *Merrill Lynch Conference for Hedge Funds* (26 April 2007).

14 Source: Kent Matthews and Owen Matthews, 'Controlling Bankers' Bonuses: Efficient Regulation or Politics of Envy?', *Economic Affairs*, 30 (March 2010): 71–6.

15 See Matthews and Matthews, 'Controlling Bankers' Bonuses'.

16 At the moment, this is very strongly discouraged by the tax system.

17 Many of these are under active consideration by regulators and legislators.

18 Financial regulation in the United Kingdom, as it happens, is returning to the central bank.

Amity Shlaes

The Limits of Cardiology
Forgotten Factors in the Great Depression and the Current Period

The main metaphor that policymakers have chosen to describe the financial events of 2008 is 'cardiovascular emergency'. Richard Fisher, president of the Federal Reserve Bank of Dallas, sketched out this image most deftly in a presentation at the Council on Foreign Relations:

> In an economy, the central bank is the heart, money is the lifeblood, and financial markets are the arteries and capillaries that provide critical sustenance to the muscles that are the makers of goods and services and the creators of employment. A properly functioning cardiovascular system fosters healthy growth; if that system fails, the body breaks down and the muscles atrophy. That is what happened in the most recent crisis... The economy, starved of the lifeblood of capital, shut down.[1]

The assumptions inherent in Fisher's choice of image are as follows. Someone—the treasury secretary, the senator, the president, or the Federal Reserve chairperson—is chief surgeon. That surgeon requires emergency powers and ought not be questioned by lesser figures (Mr. Fisher spoke of keeping government authority 'free from short-term political pressures').[2] With the patient unconscious upon the table, the surgeon may order a transfusion (have the Fed pump money into the banking system) and also shock the heart back into action (with a fiscal stimulus). Finally, and within hours, the surgeon will operate on the heart or the arteries. There is always a premium on action.

The economic theories underlying the cardiological metaphor are monetarism and Keynesianism. Observers do not always see these two theories as similar. Monetarism is associated with the great free-market economist, Milton Friedman. Keynesianism is associated with John Maynard Keynes, with whose ideas Friedman so often disagreed. Yet the two theories do bear a striking similarity: as practised, they both place enormous faith in the discretion of experts at the top, especially monetary experts. The monetary leader of a country—whether at the Bank of England, the United States Treasury, the Federal Reserve, or the White House—is the surgeon in charge of crisis.

This surgeon shoulders moral responsibility beyond any other economic actor and is responsible not only for individual rescues but also for the business cycle itself. Those who dare to question his primacy or his remedies in the operating theatre endanger the patient. (President George W. Bush insisted that the House and the Senate endorse large spending or face responsibility for 'global economic meltdown'.)[3] The chief sin ascribed to President Herbert Hoover and Treasury Secretary Andrew Mellon is that they failed in their roles as surgeon and did nothing for the agonized patient on the table: the American economy in the early 1930s. Federal Reserve Chairperson Ben S. Bernanke's public promise to Milton Friedman at one of Friedman's last public appearances was that the Fed would never repeat the error of failing to supply liquidity to address a depression. 'Regarding the Great Depression,' Mr. Bernanke said to the Nobel laureate, 'you're right, we did it. We're very sorry. But thanks to you, we won't do it again.'[4]

To this one might respond, all of this is well and good and certainly a compelling story. Immediate action is necessary when someone suffers a massive heart attack.

But what if the patient's complaint is endocrine?

It is quite possible for a hypothyroid patient to go into a coma, to experience heart failure, and even to die due to a shortage of thyroid hormone. A surgeon might have to take quick action at the beginning to pull the patient back to consciousness or restore the heart. But effective treatment would need to be prolonged and overseen by a very different sort of medical response, by non-surgical gradualists who aim for consistency and results over years, not minutes. Or perhaps the patient's problem is both cardiological and endocrine. To treat the patient's heart in isolation is to fail to treat his different, perhaps multi-causal, illness and sets the stage for another, and possibly deadly, health crisis.

The mainstream understanding of the Great Depression has been that of the surgeon treating a heart attack when the patient's problem was in fact multi-causal. This paper posits two things. First, the crisis-oriented monetary analysis of the Great Depression patient led those in charge of the post-mortem to overlook important policy errors committed by Washington in the 1930s. Some of these are familiar, though not all are well defined in academic language. These five trouble areas are, loosely, hostility to enterprise, increasing taxation, favouring unions and rising wages, violation of property rights, and government arbitrariness. Of these, it is arbitrariness that did the most damage. Second, whether we describe it as such or not, our approach to the 2008 financial crisis and subsequent economic downturn was similarly Washington-centred and surgical, overlooking the same factors neglected in the remedies and studies of the 1930s. As a result, we may have postponed addressing important economic troubles of the current time.

The Standard Analysis

The standard analysis of the early 1930s emphasizes monetary, or money-related, error. Policymakers at the Treasury and the Federal Reserve saw inflation, or inflationary tendencies, where there was actually disinflation, or deflation. This caused them to pursue a monetary policy that was too tight: to raise interest rates, sustain them, or cut them too slowly and so sterilize needed inflows of capital. Additional interpretations, such as those of Allan Meltzer, emphasize the fractured nature of the American banking system, the fragile condition of banks, and credit or banking policy such as the real bills doctrine. The perverse effect of this doctrine was to make money scarcer, just when credit could have done the most good. Yet other interpretations have emphasized the 1931 decision by the United Kingdom to go off the gold standard, an event that moved American depositors to withdraw their own cash or gold, subsequently draining banks of reserves.

The sheer drama of this perfect storm of the early 1930s has drawn scholars for decades. Preoccupied with the scintillating period of 1929 to 1933, historians and economists alike have neglected the latter half of the 1930s. Those who have studied the years after 1935 often have framed them as part of the pursuit of monetarist or monetary explanations, using models that prioritize the early days of the Depression as subject. In the 1970s, for example, Michael Darby noted that the high unemployment of the second half of the 1930s weakened the central monetarist argument that the economy moves toward full employment in the absence of severe shocks. His explanation for this was not a problem with the model (any fallibility of the surgeon) but rather that traditional unemployment modelling by Stanley Lebergott and the US Bureau of Labor Statistics (BLS) had under-counted employment.[5]

Similar explanations include the increase in reserve requirements and its contractionary effect; the vetoing by Roosevelt of the veteran's bonus, which would have increased cash on hand for lower earners; and the Roosevelt administration's decision to spend less subsequent to the election of 1936. In addition, scholars emphasize the unpredicted effect of Social Security payments, first collected in 1937: citizens paid Social Security from the first dollar earned, and this new regressive tax took its toll on consumer demand. In a noted 1991 paper, Christina Romer assigns an overwhelming role to monetary expansion, arguing that 'nearly all of the observed recovery of the U.S. economy prior to 1942 was due to monetary expansion'.[6]

These analyses may be right, as far as they go. But a new review suggests that the five other factors mentioned above, subtle but real, contributed to the duration and severity of the Great Depression. While the monetary factor clearly dominates in the early years, in the gruelling extra half decade from about 1934 to 1940, the other factors, taken in total, counted more. Although government spending may have done some good, the aggregation of power that attended likewise proved destructive. Washington, growing and unpredictable, resembled, if not an elephant in the room, then at least a tiger. Let us consider the five factors.

Hostility to Enterprise

The standard take on Washington's hostile attitude toward private enterprise after the crash is that Wall Street existed but was not important. This attitude overlooks the strength and duration of the attacks. President Hoover has a reputation for friendship with business, but in fact (perhaps because of his background in mining), he steadily nursed a suspicion of financial markets. He repeatedly expressed, for example, hostility to shorting stocks and 'speculation'.[7] The Pecora Commission, which was assembled to uncover the cause of the crash, also operated during his presidency, though it was not the president's personal project.

Roosevelt assailed business more systematically, beginning with aggressive campaign rhetoric. Most chilling perhaps was his line in the Commonwealth Club speech in 1932 describing business as the 'Ishmael or Insull whose hand is against every man'.[8] More impactful attacks came later.

One such attack, noteworthy for its violence and success, was the assault upon the economy's most promising industry: utilities. Utilities were the internet or cell phones of the day; demand for them was strong, in recession years as well as in prosperous ones. The New Deal went after this potential source of growth on four fronts. The first attack involved creating competing entities in the public sector, such as the Tennessee Valley Authority (TVA) or the Rural Electrification Administration (REA). The administration described these new entrants to the market place (especially the TVA) as a 'yardstick' necessary to establish a fair, low price level in what it alleged was a heretofore unfairly priced marketplace. The price competition that these two subsidized entities represented put private-sector companies, which did pay taxes, at a market disadvantage. As executives commented at the time, the yardstick proved not an innocent measuring device but a weapon to beat utilities about the head with.

The second attack was regulatory: passage of the Public Utility Holding Company Act. New industries are capital intensive, but this law severely constrained the utility companies' ability to raise capital. The third attack was in the courts, where the administration routinely fought the utilities' right to serve the markets in which they were located or into which they were expanding. Last came vilification. The most spectacular version of this was the vilification of Samuel Insull, the great Chicago innovator. Thousands of Insull shareholders were wiped out in the crash, and federal prosecutors followed Roosevelt's lead and ramped up investigations of Insull that had begun in the Hoover era. Despite long years of effort, the administration's lawyers found it difficult to prove that the magnate had violated the law.

Increasing Taxation

Though there isn't any longer much awareness of the tax environment of the 1920s, it is worth recalling that it was taxpayer and business friendly. Even after the dramatic increases in World War I and further increases pushed through by Treasury Secretary Andrew Mellon, the top marginal rate was still only 25 percent. The reversal that began in the Hoover period (with the cooperation of a reluctant Mellon, at least at the very beginning) raised that rate from 25 to 63 percent, and then to 79 percent in the last half of the 1930s. The administration also repeatedly experimented in new forms of taxation. Following the repeal of Prohibition, liquor and other excise taxes widened the tax load of lower earners. In 1935, a new tax law targeted not only top earners but entrepreneurs. In the 1930s, the Roosevelt administration also planned and succeeded in passing a new levy, the Undistributed Profits Tax, which ate at the essence of businesses that chose not to disgorge capital in the form of wages or dividends.

Roosevelt and his Treasury secretary, Henry Morgenthau, opted for aggressive tax prosecution. Most notable were the show trials of Mellon himself. Morgenthau told his prosecutor, Robert Jackson, that with Mellon all democracy was on trial and that Jackson must go after Mellon with all his energy. Like Insull's trials, Mellon's had enormous symbolic effect, and like Insull, Mellon found himself under suspicion until he died. Walter Annenberg's paper, the *Philadelphia Inquirer*, printed editorials sceptical of Roosevelt. The administration silenced Annenberg with tax prosecution, and he landed in jail. Meanwhile, the Roosevelt Treasury and its

Bureau of Internal Revenue opted to throw out many of the old distinctions between tax avoidance on the one hand and tax evasion on the other.

Favouring Unions and Rising Wages

A third area in which the economic patient suffered (and perhaps the least studied) is labour price. Here it may be recalled that, prior to the crash, wages were relatively flexible.[9] President Hoover made wages stickier when, as early as late autumn in 1929, he called business leaders to Washington to exhort them not to cut wages, notwith-standing the market crash. Hoover codified his desire to see higher wages when he decided to sign the 1932 Davis-Bacon Act into law (the act mandated that public-works projects pay 'prevailing wages' in the regions they were undertaken, which tended to put upward pressure on wages).

Roosevelt and Congress expanded enormously on Hoover's small start with the passage of the National Indus-trial Recovery Act (NIRA). Minimum wages in multiple sectors were a result of the industrial codes that came out of the act. In addition, as Harold Cole and Lee Ohanian point out, with the NIRA law, 'the government only approved these codes if [a given] industry agreed to raise wages con-siderably and to engage in collective bargaining with labor'.[10] As early as December 1933, they report, there was a 20-percent gap between those industries tightly covered by the NIRA and those industries that were not.

When the Supreme Court threw out the NIRA in May 1935, the upward pressure on wages did not cease. That is because within months Roosevelt signed the Wagner Act — the basis of modern American collective bargaining. Though we tend to forget it today, the Wagner Act was a lion of a law that created not only the closed shop and the ability of ind-ustrial labour to organize but also the possibility of the sit-down strike. (Taft-Hartley, America's post-war labour legis-lation, neutered the Wagner Act, making a pet pussycat of the lion, so the Wagner Act's militant side has faded in memory.)

Union membership rose from one in ten men in 1935 to three in ten men in 1939.[11] The number of strike days rose from 14 million in 1936 to 28 million in 1937. Employers in unionized fields raised wages. Cole and Ohanian calculated that wages were 25 percent higher than they otherwise might have been. They also point to an emerging disparity between wage increases in unionized and non-unionized jobs as evidence that unions were what was making the difference. The deflationary tendency of the economy in the 1930s meant that workers and employers may not have known, analytically, the scale of these wage increases. They were nonetheless there, anomalously high for a downturn.

Violation of Property Rights

Another trouble area is as significant as rising wages. It is the erosion of property rights. Here, the most famous example is the removal of the gold clause in bond contracts. The clause guaranteed the lender the right to payment in gold or the gold equivalent and offered an effective and widely used inflation hedge. Gold clauses were used widely before the Great Depression, including by the federal government with the Liberty Bonds, which helped to finance World War I. Roosevelt retroactively invalidated such clauses with the Gold Reserve Act of 1934. The Supreme Court subsequently affirmed Roosevelt's move. In traditional histories, this is portrayed as a rough but necessary move taken in the name of a legitimate goal: reflation. Still, the act gave government the ability to expropriate private property. It does not matter so much that bond holders lost an inflation hedge for those years—there was not much inflation in the 1930s—but that they lost an ability to protect property.

A similar erosion of property rights occurred in the area of residential real estate, when in 1934 the Supreme Court upheld a Minnesota law that abridged contracts by lengthening the period when strapped borrowers had to make mortgage payments before foreclosure. Speaking for the majority in *Home Building and Loan Association v. Blaisdell*, Chief Justice Charles Hughes subordinated private contracts to the more general social contract in a manner new to American jurisprudence. Hughes opined that 'the question is no longer merely that of one party to a contract as against another, but of the use of reasonable means to safeguard the economic structure upon which the good of all depends'.[12]

Government Arbitrariness

A final trouble area, the hardest to quantify but to my mind the most important, was the damage caused by what might be called the culture of arbitrariness that prevailed in government in the 1930s. The Roosevelt administration acted both inconsistently and unpredictably over the course of the decade.

One example of such unpredictability—this one has drawn the attention of monetary scholars—is Roosevelt's currency policy. The president's emissaries to a London monetary conference travelled on the assumption that they were to negotiate an agreement with European governments on how to adjust the gold standard. Even as they sought to coax foreign leaders into agreement, Roosevelt changed course and sent out telegrams announcing the United States had no intention of subordinating domestic concerns to international monetary arrangements.

The president's gold experiment was likewise wildly unpredictable. In the spring, he elected to take the United States off the gold standard, using emergency powers granted him. He then decided to drive up the price of gold through a discretionary purchase programme adjusted daily and personally by him. Then he proceeded, with the advice of economist George Warren, personally to pick the level of increase of that price. As Morgenthau wrote in his diary, 'If anybody ever knew how we really set the gold price through a combination of lucky numbers, etcetera, I think they would be frightened'.[13] Finally, having mocked gold, Roosevelt returned to the gold standard after a significant devaluation. The problem was not the monetary direction in which Roosevelt moved—there is a case for 'loosening' at this point—but rather the methodology and unpredictability that was problematic.

Less famous, but equally stunning, were repeated shifts in the administration's attitudes toward the optimal size of businesses. Early on in the administration, influenced by thinkers such as Stuart Chase and Rex Tugwell, it conducted a romance with the economy of scale. The appreciation for the economy of scale informed the design of the National Recovery Administration, which gave leading roles to larger companies at cost to smaller firms. Anti-trust activity was often suspended. Later, the administration turned to the opposite approach, seeing a Brandeisian 'curse of bigness' afflicting the economy. Later there was talk of a 'breathing spell' for big industry and signals that the administration sought its respect and cooperation again. Yet later, the administration urged on a fiery orator, Harold Ickes, in his attacks on the wealthy and big business.

Similarly, when it came to stimuli, Roosevelt seemed to have two brains. He instinctively disliked spending, due to what journalist Anne McCormick called the 'Dutch House-holder' in him.[14] As is well known, he campaigned in 1932 on a balanced-budget plank. Less well known is that Roosevelt actually cut federal wages upon taking office. Later, Roose-velt let the country in, raising government spending from millions to billions. Yet even later, he turned householder again, the result of which was the budgetary retrenchment of 1937.

But where did Roosevelt get the license to act so arbit-rarily? And why did he tell himself, as he did, that any action helped the economy to recovery? Though the idea is what we today would call Keynesianism, it did not come from Keynes, who was still formulating his theory that action, nearly any action, is a multiplier and useful stimulant to growth. Roosevelt's sense that any action is better than none may have come from Waddill Catchings and William Trufant Foster, whose *Road to Plenty,* published in the 1920s, depicted spending and fine tuning as keys to recovery.[15] (Roosevelt, the governor, wrote in the fly leaf of his copy, 'too good to be true'.) His sense of the need to reflate, to recalibrate, also may have come from Catchings—and per-haps Irving Fisher of Yale, though Fisher grew appalled at Roosevelt's style of implementation.

But to ascribe Roosevelt's tendency to act erratically to economic theory would be an error. Rather his license der-ived from two sources. The first is the Progressive convic-tion, which he inherited from his cousin Teddy Roosevelt, that government action is usually good—and certainly better than private-sector action. This was simple faith. The second source was his essential discomfort with economics. Roose-velt had broad areas of mastery. He was a seasoned sailor who knew every crack and crevice in the East Coast. He was a world-class naval strategist. He understood how to fight the right side of a World War and win. He had an innate ability to cheer people in trouble. His domestic coalition-building skill has been matched by no other American president.

But Roosevelt was not certain about economics. Nothing convinced him. Nothing quite made sense to him. Rather than delve, he shifted. It is perhaps most useful to see him as a collection of sometimes competing economic impulses. Advisers, not to mention Congress and the rest of the country, struggled in vain over the course of the decade to find coherence in the president's policy. The absurdity of the effort was described most eloquently by an adviser who left the Roosevelt administration mid-decade in despair, Raymond Moley:

> If this aggregation of policies springing from circumstances, motives, purposes, and situations so various gave the observer the sense of a certain rugged grandeur, it arose chiefly from the wonder that one man could have been so flexible as to permit himself to believe so many things in so short a time. But to look upon these policies as the result of a unified plan was to believe that the baseball pictures, school flags, old tennis shoes, carpenter's tools, geometry books, and chemistry sets in a boy's bedroom could have been put there by an interior decorator.
>
> Or, perhaps it would be more apt to say that the unfolding of the New Deal between 1932 and 1937 suggested the sounds that might be produced by an orchestra which started out with part of a score and which, after a time, began to improvise. It might all hang together if there were a clear understanding between the players and the conductor as to the sort of music they intended to produce. But nothing was more obvious than that some of the New Deal players believed that the theme was to be the funeral march of capitalism; others, a Wagnerian conflict between Good and Evil; and still others, the triumphant strains of the Heldenleben.[16]

The Prolonged Downturn

The quantifications of such damage exist and warrant more review. In *The Forgotten Man*, I focus on enormous casualties of the anti-utilities war. That war had the effect of chilling an industry that might have helped pull the economy through recovery. As evident in the chart below, utilities stocks performed even worse than the Dow Jones Industrial Average in the 1930s.

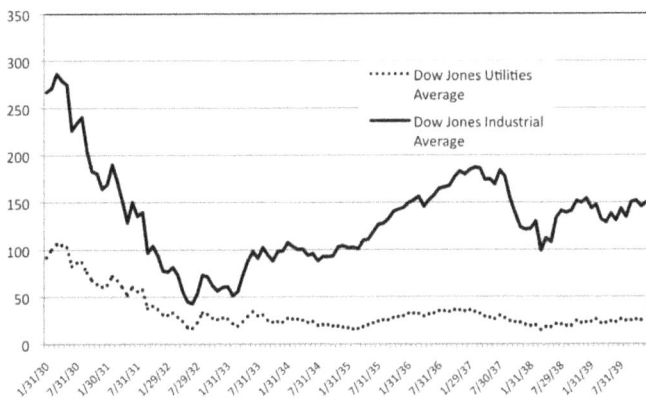

The evidence of trouble prolonged is also clear in unemployment outcomes. Lee Ohanian and Harold Cole note that private hours worked in 1939 were 21 percent below the level of 1929, an astounding figure given the wage increases and increases in working-age population during this period.[17] Quantifying unemployment for the decade is a source of controversy even in 2010, with bloggers trading barbs and attacking each other's data sets, whether these are the Census sets; the old BLS sets; the sets of Stanley Lebergott, who worked with the BLS; or those of Darby and those who followed him. What the blogosphere tiffs obscure is that the data are not all that different. Unemployment averaged 14 percent for the decade by Darby's math and 18 percent by Lebergott's.[18] In modern terms, when an unemployment rate of 10 percent is viewed as untenable, the difference is the difference between terrible and awful.

The peculiarity of a recession market with high labour prices shows up in the culture and the way the troubles of the period were described. Most Americans can recall their parents or grandparents saying, 'It was all right if you had a job' or 'A dress was cheap. A maid was cheap'. In short, citizens were 'stimulating the economy' when they shopped with their wages. But they were doing so in a cruel way: by cutting others out. A 1937 musical featured the wistful song,

'Nice Work If You Can Get It'. The song was actually referring to prostitution, but it resonated because of the general
wistfulness of the underemployed. The explanation of Cole
and Ohanian thus seems as plausible as, or more plausible
than, the monetary explanations for the later 1930s slowdown.

This is especially so because there also is evidence of a
similar outcome to a similar labour-price experiment in the
United Kingdom. Those who work in the monetary area tend
to think of the United Kingdom's case of Depression as less
virulent than that of the American, and tend to ascribe some
of the difference to the nation's decision to leave the gold
standard in 1931. But this obscures an unemployment tragedy, less known: joblessness averaged 14 percent for two
decades, not one, from 1921 to 1938, never going below 9.5
percent. The work of Daniel Benjamin and Levis Kochin in
the 1970s suggests that the relatively attractive unemployment payments and their relative cost contributed to joblessness.[19] Roosevelt himself sensed what was going on in the
United Kingdom. He spoke pejoratively of the dole and
resisted, at every turn, efforts to replicate it in the United
States. He saw the British experiment as an epic policy failure whose stated purpose was to be humane.

Another quantifiable consequence of New Deal errors
was the capital strike. The *New Yorker* cartoon image of the
wealthy retreating to their country house living rooms to
pout among the pieces of dusty furniture is accurate. Not
only hiring but investment slowed. Business did not declare
war on Roosevelt; it simply decided to 'sit this one out'. The
scholar whose original work makes this clear is Robert
Higgs.[20] He notes that gross, private investment did not
reach its 1929 level until World War II, plummeting more
sharply than the gross domestic product (GDP) during the
'Depression within the Depression' and generally lagging the
GDP's recovery. The 'idle money' that Roosevelt's staff dep-
lored was not idle out of spite, as they surmised, but out of
fear. As Eleanor Roosevelt summed up the problem, 'They
are afraid'.[21]

And beyond the evidence as we uncover it now, there is
another reason to think these under-studied areas of trouble
caused significant pain: people in the period believed they

did. Critique of unions, abuse of property rights, and government arbitrariness in particular appeared often in the press (probably because of the Keynes-Schlesinger filter of modern education, we forget that the press in the 1930s was more conservative than it is today). Foreshadowing Benjamin and Kochin's insights, for example, a Depression-era editorialist in Muncie, Indiana, asked, 'Who is the "forgotten man" in Muncie? I know him as intimately as I know my own undershirt. He is the fellow that is trying to get along without public relief and has been attempting the same thing since the depression that cracked down on him'.[22]

These quantifications were not entirely overlooked by the economists from the period. Even Keynes made a point of singling out for criticism Roosevelt's treatment of utilities and his hostility toward business executives. Roosevelt might nationalize utilities, he allowed — he supported that — or he might leave them alone. But the episodic bullying of the industry was counterproductive: 'What's the use of chasing them around the lot every other week?' Of businesspersons, Keynes said, 'It's a mistake to think that they are more immoral than politicians'.[23]

The most consistent and articulate of the economists addressing issues such as taxes or high wages is one we scarcely study today; Benjamin Anderson of Chase National Bank, editor of the *Chase Economic Bulletin,* offered a diary of frustration over taxes and labour prices. He also pinpointed the arrogance of power and arbitrariness in his 1949 book that included a bitter review of 1930s events: 'The Great Depression of 1930 to 1939 [was] due to the efforts of the governments and very especially the government of the United States to play God.'[24]

To disregard these analyses as consistently as scholars have done in the post-war period is hubris. Equally destructive is the habit of ignoring current non-Keynesian, non-monetarist analyses of the 1930s. Even if we do not want to concede yet that scholars such as Robert Higgs or Lee Ohanian are correct, their work is worthy of our attention.

The Trouble Areas Today

But what do spotlights on these neglected factors help us to discern today? First, hostility to business of the sort on show at the recent hearings on financial reform is not productive. There is a concern that too many banks and companies are parking money instead of investing it in productive new ventures. If we want to increase employment, we might make clearer the possible cost of prosecutorial actions and anti-business crusades.

Second, taxes cannot be subordinated too far below monetary policy or treated merely in the Keynesian context as cyclical tools. The extent of the coming tax increases must be taken seriously rather than considered *en passant* in discussions of interest rates at the Fed. Most observers know that raising interest rates and raising taxes do similar damage. Yet the two are not treated as the parallel costs that they are.

The third 1930s takeaway is that increases in labour prices are not necessarily benign. The Obama administration may lack the enthusiasm for cooperating with radical labour leaders in wage combat with heavy industry, but the government's 'wage clout' exists in another form due to the government's now-large presence in the economy. When President Obama says, as he did, that he hopes that government-funded projects (which fall into the purview of Hoover's Davis-Bacon law) ought to give their workers generous pay and benefits, his message affects millions more jobs than a similar statement by Hoover might have. This factor deserves recognition.

Fourth, the erosion of property rights can reduce the quality of recovery. This will be especially true due to the scale of foreign investment in US real estate, equities, bonds, and currency. Outsiders do not acquire these assets out of a sense of affection for the United States; they acquire them because they regard them as the property least likely to lose value. Should succeeding administrations erode property rights too cavalierly, foreigners may decide to move their investments elsewhere.

But to my mind, the least-appreciated factor is the fifth one: potential damage of government arbitrariness. The most flamboyant examples of arbitrariness have come in the bold changes to the Troubled Asset Relief Program (TARP). Though it promoted the TARP idea as funding for the purchase of toxic assets, the Treasury made it clear within just weeks of TARP becoming law that the goal actually had been increased discretion for the Treasury and the Federal Reserve. The Fed under Chairman Alan Greenspan was already an arbitrary institution, making its calls on interest rates according to its analysis of the business cycle. The Bernanke Fed has expanded that discretion and unpredictability by expanding its presence in the banking arena so many times.

In short, it may be time to take models beyond monetarism or Keynesianism more seriously. My own view is that old, classical economics and modern public-choice theory can help provide a fuller picture both of the 1930s and the present day. Some already extant meters seek to ask questions about arbitrariness and uncertainty—and to make them primary. One is the VIX, the Chicago Board Options Exchange Market Volatility Index. Another is the new Chicago Booth/Kellogg School Financial Trust Index. This index, created by Paola Sapienza and Luigi Zingales, measures how much people trust the private institutions into which they can invest their money. As such, it monitors the response to property erosions and an uncertain general environment.

Setting aside whether there can or should be a wholesale shift in attitudes toward economic illness, we can at the very least say it is time to add such measures to our medical kit: the more variety in our outlook, the better the understanding of the patient. The patient may, after all, be suffering from more illnesses than just a heart attack—even if the average doctor following the established diagnosis sees only the heart problem. And if we are going to save the patient, we have to know exactly what is wrong with him.

---

1   Richard W. Fisher, 'Lessons Learned, Convictions Confirmed', *Remarks before the Council on Foreign Relations*, New York (3 March 2010).

2   *Ibid.*

3   President George W. Bush, 'Speech on the Financial Markets and World Economy', *Manhattan Institute* (13 November 2008). Transcript available online at http://www.clipsandcomment.com/2008/11/15/full-text-president-george-w-bush-speech-on-the-financial-markets-and-world-economy-manhattan-institute-november-13/

4   Ben S. Bernanke, 'On Milton Friedman's Ninetieth Birthday', *Conference to Honor Milton Friedman*, Chicago, IL (8 November 2002).

5   See Michael R. Darby, 'Three-and-a-Half Million U.S. Employees Have Been Mislaid: Or, An Explanation of Unemployment, 1934–1941', *Journal of Political Economy,* 84 (February 1976): 1–16.

6   Christina D. Romer, 'What Ended the Great Depression?', *National Bureau of Economic Research Working Paper No. 3829* (September 1991). Accessed May 2010 at http://papers.nber.org/papers/w3829.

7   See 'Hoover Reveals He Demanded Curb on Short Selling: President Warned Exchange Heads They Must Adequately Protect Investors', *New York Times* (20 February 1932). Accessed May 2010 through ProQuest Historical Newspapers database.

8   Franklin Delano Roosevelt, Commonwealth Club address, San Francisco (23 September 1932). Accessed May 2010 at http://www.americanrhetoric.com/speeches/fdrcommonwealth.htm

9   See Bryan Caplan, 'Wage Adjustment and Aggregate Supply in the Depression of 1920–1921: Extending the Bernanke-Carey Model', *Princeton University Paper* (1996).

10   Harold L. Cole and Lee E. Ohanian, 'Where the New Deal Went Badly Wrong', *Milken Institute Review*, third quarter (2009): 16–25, 22.

11   Harold L. Cole and Lee E. Ohanian, 'New Deal Policies and the Persistence of the Great Depression: A General Equilibrium Analysis', *Research Memo, UCLA* (February 2003). Accessed May 2010 at http://hlcole.bol.ucla.edu/NewDealucla.pdf.

12   *Home Building and Loan Association v. Blaisdell*, 290 U.S. 398 (1934).

13   John Morton Blum, ed., *From the Morgenthau Diaries* (Boston, MA: Houghton Mifflin, 1967): 70.

14   As quoted in Amity Shlaes, *The Forgotten Man: A New History of the Great Depression* (New York: HarperCollins, 2007): 341.

15   William Trufant Foster and Waddill Catchings, *The Road to Plenty* (Pollak Foundation for Economic Research No. 11, 1928).

16   Raymond Moley, *After Seven Years* (New York: Harper & Brothers, 1939).

17   See Cole and Ohanian, 'Where the New Deal Went Badly Wrong'.

18   See Darby, 'Three-and-a-Half Million'.

19   Daniel K. Benjamin and Levis A. Kochin, 'Searching for an Explanation of Unemployment in Interwar Britain', *Journal of Political Economy,* 87 (June 1979): 441–78.

20   See Robert Higgs, 'Regime Uncertainty: Why the Great Depression Lasted So Long and Why Prosperity Resumed After the War', *Independent Review,* 1 (Spring 1997): 561–91, 565.

21   David M. Kennedy, *Freedom From Fear: The American People in Depression and War, 1929–1945* (New York: Oxford University Press, 1999): 360.

22   Robert S. Lynd and Helen Merrell Lynd, *Middletown in Transition: A Study in Cultural Conflicts* (New York: Harcourt, Brace and Co., 1937).

23   John Maynard Keynes, 'Letter of February 1, 1938 to Franklin Roosevelt', *Collected Works,* vol. XXI (London: MacMillan).

[24] Benjamin M. Anderson, *Economics and the Public Welfare: A Financial and Economic History of the United States, 1914–1946*, 2nd ed. (Indianapolis, IN: Liberty Fund, 1980).

Robert Skidelsky

The Great Recession
Causes and Cures

In my most recent book on John Maynard Keynes, I committed myself to the view that the present crisis was at root not a failure of character or competence but a failure of ideas; I quoted Keynes that 'the ideas of economists and political philosophers, both when they are right and when they are wrong, are more powerful than is commonly supposed. Indeed the world is ruled by little else'.[1] So any enquiry into policy failures—assuming that these were at least partly responsible for the Great Recession—inevitably turns into an enquiry into the ideas that were in the policymakers' minds.

As a matter of strict logic, diagnosis and cure should be part of a consistent set of ideas. In practice, this is not so. Economists whose models tell them that crises such as that of 2007 to 2009 cannot occur are nevertheless often to be found supporting or advocating stimulus measures which, according to those models, will be wholly ineffective or even make things worse. Policymakers are even more prone to such cognitive dissonance. Thus bad theory frequently trumps common sense.

In what follows, therefore, I exclude from consideration the hard-line version of the rational expectations hypothesis (REH) and the efficient market hypothesis. Hard-line REH assumes that outcome and expectation always agree: 'The probability distribution over economic variables that agents hold, cause them to take actions which in turn generate just this probability distribution. This is the idea of a rational expectations equilibrium.'[2] It excludes by assumption the possibility of a large-scale economic collapse. Robert Lucas's statement, 'I guess everyone is a Keynesian in a foxhole',[3] is a flag of surrender in terms of the REH model he is chiefly associated with.

I will confine this paper to the consideration of two models, or theories, which are in principle capable of explaining what has gone wrong. The first is the monetarist theory derived from the quantity theory of money (QTM), and the second is the Keynesian theory of effective demand. It is interesting to divide up the diagnosis in this way, because the two positions provide distinctly different emphases on the cure. Put simply, the monetarist diagnosis leads to quantitative easing, or 'printing money'; the Keynesian diagnosis, to fiscalism, or expanding the budget deficit.

The Monetarist Diagnosis

The QTM is familiarly expressed in the equation MV=pY. M is the supply of money; V, its velocity of circulation; and pY, the community's money income. This is simply an identity; the amount of money spent is equal to the total value of goods bought.

For the quantity of money equation to become a theory of the price level, three conditions need to hold: constant velocity of circulation, constant output, and exogenous money supply. More precisely, changes in V and Y are independent of changes in M.[4] We then have the quantity theory: a change in M produces a proportional change in p, and this is the only effect. This is equivalent to saying that money is 'neutral' in its effect on the level of activity.

By what mechanism(s) does an increase in money lead to a proportional change in prices? We can identify two mechanisms, direct and indirect.

In the direct mechanism, the new money is directly spent or distributed by those who produce it. When money was gold, it was the newly enriched owners of gold mines who paid out gold in exchange for goods. In modern conditions, it would be the central bank or the government. An example is Milton Friedman's 'helicopter money'.[5]

In the indirect transmission mechanism, the central bank injects the new cash into the banking system. The increase in banks' cash reserves enables them to lower the interest rate they charge on loans to customers. The customers borrow more and spend more, and prices rise.

The textbook presentation of the QTM is the 'cash balances', or helicopter money version. For convenience and precaution, people choose to hold a certain fraction of their income in cash. This is a demand for 'real balances': command over a certain quantity of goods and services. Now the government adds, say, 10 percent to each person's money holding. People will be holding more cash than they want to hold at that level of prices. So anticipating a 10 percent rise in the price level, they spend the extra 10 percent, making the anticipation self-fulfilling and leaving their real balances unchanged. Notice that correct anticipation is necessary for this effect. Formally, the price level is what equilibrates the supply of cash with the demand to hold cash.

How does a theory of the price level that treats money as neutral become a theory of the business cycle? Keynes, who started his professional life as an orthodox quantity theorist, gives the clue, which Friedman developed: the QTM is only true in the long run – 'and in the long run we are all dead'. Keynes argued that in the short run, changes in money would change the velocity of circulation (V) because of uncertainty about the future course of prices.

Consider the effect of a change of M on V, assuming uncertainty about future prices. When M increases, people will speed up their purchases, expecting prices to go on rising. The speed up in V will cause prices to rise more than proportionately to money. When M decreases, people will postpone their spending, expecting prices to go on falling. So the fall in prices will be less than in proportion to the reduction in M. This speed-up and postponement of spending decisions will have a 'real effect': trade will be brisker in the first case and more sluggish in the second.

In arguing thus, Keynes made the common sense assumption that there is always some slack in the economy that can be activated by monetary events. This leaves the relative changes of prices and output indeterminate within quantity of money equation. When M goes up, we get an inflationary boom; when M goes down, we get a deflationary recession. Money is not neutral.

In his influential restatement of the QTM, Friedman conceded Keynes' point that it was true only in the long run.[6] If one allows time to elapse between the injection of money and the effect upon prices, changes in M can affect both V and Y, disturbing the 'neutrality of money'. It is for this reason that Friedman proposed that the monetary authority follow a money rule: the annual increase of the money stock was to equal the trend growth in productivity. That way there wouldn't be any monetary 'surprises', capable of sending out false signals about 'real balances'.

This kind of apparatus can be readily adapted to explaining the crisis that developed in 2007 and 2008, and Martin Wolf has dubbed this explanation the 'money glut' theory.[7] Broadly speaking, the central banks of the Western world, led by the Federal Reserve Board, made credit too cheap and too plentiful in the years leading up to the crash. The injection of credit led to an increase in the velocity of circulation. This fuelled an asset boom based on houses and commercial property. A debt-fuelled consumption boom was built on the back of these rising asset prices, but this did not cause general inflation, because the supply of cheap, imported goods from East Asia more than kept pace with the increased demand.

The asset boom was bound to collapse as soon as credit was tightened. The collapse of the real-estate boom (residential and commercial) in 2006 and 2007 hit the banks that had over-lent to this market, firms that had over-invested in commercial property, and consumers who had borrowed for consumption on the back of rising house prices. The pile-up of bank losses led to a credit freeze. Velocity of circulation slowed down as everyone started 'deleveraging'. This brought about a collapse in the money supply, which spread recession to the whole economy. The story can be followed in the money-supply figures (M4 in the United Kingdom and M2 in the United States [2001–2010]):[8]

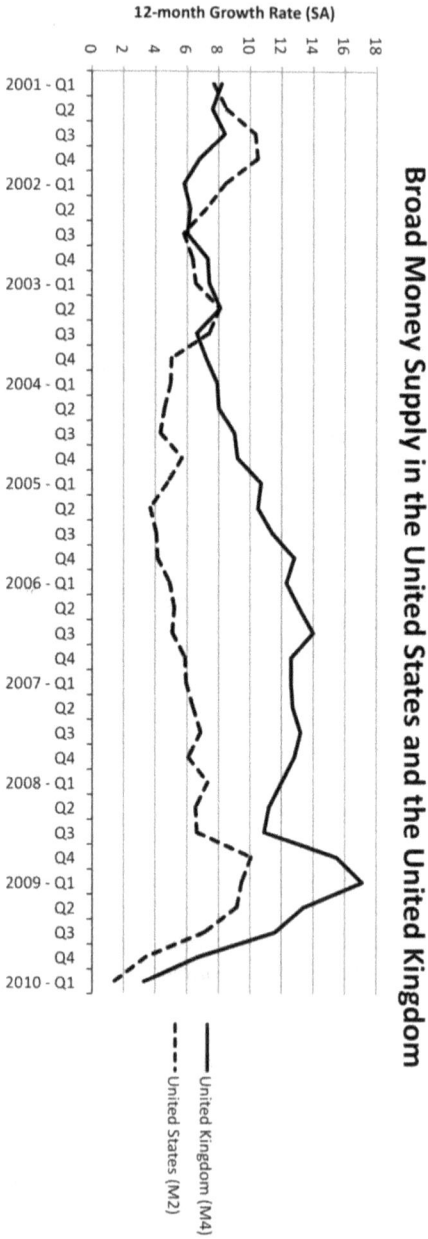

Source: Bank of England; Federal Reserve Bank

The Keynesian Diagnosis

The genesis of the Keynesian explanation for the 2007 to 2009 recession evolves from *A Treatise on Money* (1930). This can be read as an analysis of short-run changes in the velocity of circulation. The book offers two advances from the *Tract on Monetary Reform*: recognition that changes in 'opinion' can change the velocity of circulation independently of any money creation by the central bank, and the formulation of a new equilibrium condition — that saving should equal investment — to replace that of the stability of the price level. The analysis is still conducted, though, in terms of price levels — albeit disaggregated ones — with changes in output treated as part of the short-period adjustment from one price level to another. The equilibrium is still a full-employment one.

Keynes decomposes money holdings into two parts, each with its own velocity of circulation: that part which supports the 'industrial circulation' — the process of producing output — and that which supports the 'financial circulation'. The first velocity is a relatively stable fraction of money income. The second is the variable one. Money held for 'financial circulation' is defined more broadly than the 'speculative' motive for holding cash in *The General Theory of Employment, Interest, and Money*. Keynes defines it as money put aside for 'the business of holding and exchanging existing titles to wealth,... including stock exchange and money market transactions, speculation and the process of conveying current savings and profits into the hands of entrepreneurs'.[9] The point Keynes aims to bring out is that the demand for liquidity is not just a demand for cash but for liquid wealth. Thus a speculative boom based on the transfer of money from the 'industrial circulation' to the 'financial circulation' may conceal an underlying underinvestment in *new* capital equipment. He writes, 'The investment boom in the United States in 1929 was a good example of an enormous rise in the price of securities... which was not accompanied by any rise at all in the price of the current output of new fixed capital'.[10]

The duty of the central bank is to preserve the 'price stability of current output'. Its dilemma is that if it increases the quantity of money to prevent the 'financial circulation' from stealing money from 'industrial circulation', it will encourage bubbles, while if it refuses, it will create deflation. As Keynes writes, 'It may be that a rate of interest high enough to avoid prospective over-investment is calculated to produce present unemployment'.[11] The solution lies in letting both the Industrial and the financial circulations have all the money they want but at a rate of interest that exactly balances saving and *new* investment, but Keynes concedes that this 'may sometimes be... beyond the wits of man'.[12] Keynes' doubts about the efficacy of monetary policy to control booms or prevent slumps have already surfaced.

The *Treatise on Money* is an interim statement: it is also the nearest Keynes came to explaining the causes of the Great Depression. By the time his *General Theory* appeared in 1936, the Depression was seven years old. The *explanandum* was not why it had started but why the economy had remained depressed for so long. In *The General Theory*, Keynes set out to explain why there could be 'under-employment equilibrium'. Employment was made to depend upon aggregate demand. In the face of a shock, income adjusted, not prices. This income-adjustment mechanism established the possibility of a stable equilibrium short of full employment. Keynes could then say that his new book switched attention from the analysis of the causes of a change in the price level of current income/output to the analysis of its effects upon the equilibrium level of current income/output.

Keynes had abandoned the condition that the level of national income was an independent variable. It was directly determined by changes in the velocity of circulation. But in an economy with a central bank, money could not be completely endogenized. This is seen in Keynes' liquidity-preference equation, $M=L(pY,r)$: the demand for money is assumed to vary with the rate of interest and the level of money incomes, but the supply of money is exogenously given, as in the quantity theory. The reason is that $r=f(M,pY)$. That is, the rate of interest is what equilibrates the demand for cash with the supply of cash at a given level of money income. By varying the supply of cash, the monetary authority can offset fluctuations in the 'demand for money to hold' and thus exercise a stabilizing influence over the level of economic activity.

It is also important to notice that the QTM remains valid as an explanation of inflation at full employment. Keynes' less-than-full-blooded abandonment of the QTM is explained by the fact that he wanted to retain a role for the monetary authority in controlling the rate of investment. To the extent that investment is interest-elastic and that monetary policy can control the term structure of interest rates, it remains a powerful—although as we shall see, not sufficiently powerful—anti-slump weapon.

Moving from theory to explanation, Keynesian theory attributes the crisis of 2007 to 2009 to the instability of investment. In this story, the origins of the crisis are to be found in the excess of saving over investment—or a rise in liquidity preference—and not in the fall in M, as the monetarists would say. The crisis can be traced back to an autonomous fall in the demand for new investment following the collapse of the dot-com bubble in 2001. Greenspan's cheap money policy was insufficient to revive private-sector investment demand, but it did create a highly leveraged asset and consumption boom: the increased demand for liquidity went into the purchase of liquid assets. Since, however, too few *new* assets were being created, the private sector, by choosing to go on borrowing, became progressively over-indebted. The rise in the interest rate after 2005 to cut off the housing boom caused a fall in house prices. The collapse of the real-estate boom disclosed the extent of the over-indebtedness. The 'deleveraging' of households, banks, and companies brought about a collapse in consumption demand, which caused the great recession. The problem was not a money glut but an investment dearth.

From Explanation to Cure

The monetarist and the Keynesian stories are quite similar in their accounts of the development of the crisis; both emphasize the 'speculative' element in the pre-crisis boom. But there is a crucial difference in their explanation of its genesis. In the monetarist story, the causation runs from a collapse in the money supply to failure of the 'real economy'; in the Keynesian story, the causation runs from the failure of private-sector investment demand to the collapse of the money supply. Policy mistakes helped cause both crises, but they were different ones. According to the first story, the crisis was caused by the failure of the Fed to curtail credit sufficiently to cut off the build-up of asset inflation. The cause in the second case was the failure of the Fed to expand credit sufficiently to prevent the 'financial circulation' from stealing money from the 'industrial circulation'.

Within the monetarist's framework of the QTM, a sufficient cure for the recession is to increase the supply of money; within the Keynesian framework, the cure requires an increase in the amount of aggregate spending. This cannot be guaranteed by simply printing more money, since there is no guarantee that the extra money will be spent on buying currently produced output.

Which theory stands up better to experience of the recovery phase of the 2007–2009 recession?

Take the United Kingdom as an example. The monetarists argue that the main reason behind the current crisis is the decline in money-supply growth in 2008 and 2009. Behind this collapse stands the pressure for banks to reduce their holdings of risky assets. For monetarists the correct response to this was to print enough money to offset the fact that banks were no longer creating credit on the old scale. Under its programme of quantitative easing, the Bank of England started to inject cash into the banking and non-banking system in the spring of 2009, which over the year reached £200 billion, equivalent to 15 percent of the gross domestic product. It did this by buying gilts and high-grade corporate bonds.

The monetarist prediction was that restoration of the previous rate of money growth was a sufficient condition for the restoration of the equilibrium level of money national income. Money national income (pY) will expand proportionately to the increase of M through a combination of the direct and indirect mechanisms described above. These will be sufficient to give the recession a 'knockout blow'. So Tim Congdon, a leading monetarist, argues that 'an increase of 10, 20 or 30% in M2 [in the case of the United States] would raise equilibrium national income, if not by exactly 10, 20 or 30%, at least by a number that would be within striking distance of 10, 20 or 30%'.[13]

The idea was that the commercial banks, with their accounts electronically credited by the central bank, would find themselves with larger cash balances than they would want to hold at that level of nominal national income. They would increase their volume of loans and lower the price they charged for them. The corporate sector would be a direct beneficiary of the 'helicopter money'. Its deposits with the banks would swell; it also would want to increase its borrowing at the lower rate of interest. The result would be an expansion of deposits and more spending. Nominal national income (pY) would rise to bring actual balances into line with desired balances, which is by definition the equilibrium level of national income. The increase in 'broad' money, resulting from the initial cash injection, would be split between an increase in Y and p, with a rise in Y predominating in the early stages, and p in the later stages, of the recovery. This is why the monetary stimulus would have to be withdrawn as the economy recovered.

Keynes would accept that an increase in the money supply (cash issued by the central bank) was a necessary condition for an increase in money national income. But he would have denied that it is a sufficient condition. This is because if liquidity preference is increasing or has increased at the same time, the injection of cash by the bank may not lower the rate of interest sufficiently to restore a full employment level of aggregate spending. As Keynes put it, if money is the drink that stimulates the system to activity, 'there may be several slips between the cup and the lip'.[14] At the bottom of the Great Depression, he wrote:

> It may still be the case that the lender, with his confidence shattered by his experience, will continue to ask for new enterprise rates of interest which the borrower cannot expect to earn… If this proves to be the case, there will be no means of escape from prolonged and perhaps interminable depression except by direct state intervention to promote and subsidise new investment.[15]

In short, damaged expectations might cause the credit crunch to outlast the circumstances that gave rise to it. In such circumstances, fiscal policy needs to be the main agent of recovery.

So which policy recommendation was vindicated by the outcome in the United Kingdom? Despite an injection of £144 billion from March to August 2009, bank lending did not pick up. Money from bond sales remained stuck in the banking system. The commercial banks held on to the cash, either in the form of reserves at the Bank of England or by buying other gilts or corporate bonds. Commercial bank reserves at the Bank rose from £45 billion on March 4th – the day before the launch of quantitative easing – to £161 billion on July 29th. In July of 2009, balances available for lending to financial companies (net lending) fell at its fastest pace since records began in 1993, and the total amount of loans taken by households and non-financial companies remained anaemic. The corporate sector did not use its 'helicopter money' to expand its investments: it used it for deleveraging, or for buying securities. The injection of money caused a stock-market boom, but the recession was not given a knockout blow. The British economy contracted all the way through 2009, with a tiny pick-up in the last quarter. That is, despite a money injection of 10 percent, there wasn't any 10 percent increase in money national income as monetarists such as Congdon had expected.

For a Keynesian it is not difficult to understand why more money printed does not automatically translate into more money spent. As outlined above, another way to explain the absence of a knockout blow is to argue that a crisis brings down the velocity of money through increased uncertainty and also through higher debt ratios, leading to greater portions of wealth going to debt servicing. This argument corresponds with the experience in the United Kingdom in 2009. Steven Major, head of global fixed-income research at HSBC Bank, claimed that 'The vast majority of the liquidity is stuck in the banks in the form of reserves, but this is not about banks hoarding because they are afraid to lend. It is more about a weak economy, where households and corporates do not want to borrow'.[16] And similarly, John Wraith, head of sterling rates product development at RBC Capital Markets, stated that 'People are in no mood to borrow. It is not just banks hoarding. You can't lend if people don't want to borrow'.[17] In short, quantitative easing provides the fuel, but something is needed to ignite the economic engine, and that is confidence. Enter fiscal stimulus.

In a low-confidence economy running below full capacity, the government needs to step in to ensure that demand is sufficiently high to justify the re-employment of idle resources. Intervention can be financed in two ways: printing more money or raising debt from the public. Inflationary considerations limit the scope of financing by printing money alone. Rather, by raising debt from the public and then spending it, the government turns deposits into effective demand. While this expansionary policy necessarily implies a growing budget deficit, the increase in aggregate demand ultimately brings the deficit down *automatically* (the structural deficit, however, remains). And fiscal stimulus has an instantaneous effect on the real economy. Since the start of the crisis, the UK government's deficit has expanded by £125 billion. Part of this represents a discretionary increase in spending, but most of it results from the continuation of earlier spending programmes and increased spending on unemployment benefits, in the face of a fall in revenues. It is difficult to explain the flattening out of the recession without reference to the boost in aggregate demand brought about by this massive fiscal loosening.

It is impossible at this stage to judge the contribution to the flattening of the recession of quantitative easing relative to other factors such as fiscal policy, low interest rates, and the fall in the exchange rate. One conclusion, though, which might commend itself to both monetarists and Keynesians is that it is too early to withdraw the 'stimulus'. Whether the deficit is being financed by quantitative easing or by selling debt to the public, it is a life-support system that protects jobs, and until there is firm evidence that the private sector is picking up the slack, it should not be switched off. A final disquieting conclusion is that it may be necessary to increase the stimulus rather than reduce it, to overcome the contractionary forces still at work.

Conclusion

Underlying the monetarist and Keynesian approaches to the explanations and cures for crises are two different theories of the market economy. The monetarist theory draws on the whole tradition of economic theorizing from David Ricardo, which views the economy as a self-adjusting system. In the absence of monetary 'surprises', capital and labour always will be allocated to different uses in the proportions in which they are demanded. This is equivalent to saying that there can't be any 'general glut' or surplus of resources relative to the demand for them. This efficient system of allocation can only break down (temporarily) if people mistake money values for real values. Hence the only task of macroeconomic policy is to keep money *neutral* in its effect on allocation. This requires a general expectation of a constant price level. If it can be achieved—for example, by following some monetary rule—all goods and services, including future goods, will be traded at their correct, or barter, rates of exchange.

By contrast, the Keynesian theory views the economy as characterized by a more or less continuous surplus of supply over demand. This is because of the existence of irreducible uncertainty, particularly potent for investment behaviour. The Keynesian economy fluctuates around a 'normal' condition of 'under-employment equilibrium'. Full employment is only achieved, and that temporarily, in moments of excitement. And because subjective feelings of uncertainty wax and wane, such an economy is always prone to severe collapses as 'confidence' drains. The task of government is, minimally, to keep aggregate demand (or spending) sufficient to prevent large-scale collapses in economic activity and maximally, to ensure that actual output corresponds to potential output. The latter, in Keynes' view, would require a 'somewhat comprehensive socialization of investment'.[18]

At root, the difference between the two theories is epistemological. The first theory equips agents with objective probabilities for the relevant realizations of future variables; the second claims that over a wide range of future outcomes, such objective probabilities do not exist. In both theories, the task of government is to reduce uncertainty. But because the conditions of knowledge are more precarious in the Keynesian theory than in the monetary theory, the role of government will be correspondingly more extensive.

---

1   Quoted in Robert Skidelsky, *Keynes: The Return of the Master* (New York: Public Affairs, 2010): 28.

2   Frank Hahn, *Money and Inflation* (Oxford: Basil Blackwell, 1982): 3.

3   Quoted in Justin Fox, 'The Comeback Keynes', *Time* (23 October 2008), http://www.time.com/time/magazine/article/0,9171,1853330 2,00.html.

4   Mark Blaug, 'Why is the Quantity Theory of Money the Oldest Surviving Theory in Economics?', in *The Quantity Theory of Money:*

From Locke to Keynes and Friedman, ed. Mark Blaug *et al.* (Aldershot: Edward Elgar, 1995): 29.

5   See Milton Friedman, *The Optimum Quantity of Money and Other Essays* (Chicago, IL: Aldine, 1969).

6   See Milton Friedman, 'The Quantity Theory of Money — A Restatement', in *Studies in the Quantity Theory of Money*, ed. Milton Friedman (Chicago, IL: University of Chicago Press, 1956).

7   See Martin Wolf, *Fixing Global Finance* (Baltimore, MD: Johns Hopkins University Press, 2008).

8   John Slater argues that the M2 figures do not capture either the expansion or contraction of credit in the United States over the relevant period. He claims that 'effective money' — which includes money created by the shadow banking system — was three times larger at the 2007 peak than shown by M2. The collapse of the syndicated credit market led to a much larger fall in 'effective money' than the M2 aggregate shows. The collapse of structured investment vehicles alone took $400 billion out of the system worldwide (see John Slater, 'Did a Declining Money Supply Cause the Crash?', blog post to *Capital Matters: Funding Business Growth in an Age of Scarcity* [15 October 2008], http://capmatters.com/2008/ 10/).

9   John Maynard Keynes, *Collected Writings of John Maynard Keynes*, vol. V (London: Macmillan): 217.

10   *Ibid.*: 222.

11   *Ibid.*: 228.

12   *Ibid.*: 227.

13   Tim Congdon, 'Monetary Policy at the Zero Bound', *World Economics*, 11 (January 2010): 11–48, 41.

14   John Maynard Keynes, *Collected Writings*, VII: 173.

15   Robert Skidelsky, *John Maynard Keynes: The Economist as Saviour, 1920–1937* (London: Penguin, 1995): 441.

16   David Oakley, 'Critical Days Ahead for UK Quantitative Easing', *Financial Times* (4 September 2009). Accessed online at http://www.ft.com

17   *Ibid.*

18   John Maynard Keynes, *Collected Writings*, VII: 173.

Ludger Schuknecht

Booms, Busts, and Fiscal Policy
Public Finances in the Future

The financial crisis that became a deep economic recession after the Lehman Brothers bankruptcy in October 2008 followed a long boom period in most Western economies between the late 1990s and about 2007. During that time, rising prices in housing and stocks left both banks and households more highly leveraged and therefore vulnerable to a downturn in asset prices. The depth of the bust in housing and stock markets — and its virulent interaction with the financial sector, economic activity, and demand after the Lehman Brothers bankruptcy — also had an adverse effect on public-sector accounts within a very short period of time. Pressure on public balance sheets has become more and more visible: first in the very large public deficits and rapidly rising debt ratios, second in the very strong increase in the public expenditure ratio, and third in the significant contingent liabilities stemming from government rescue packages for the financial sector. This pressure on public balance sheets comes in addition not only to the considerable existing deficits and debt stocks at the end of the boom in many advanced economies, but also to the looming costs of population ageing.

If unchecked and uncorrected, these fiscal developments will prove unsustainable, a concern made evident in investors' charging increasing risk premiums to hold government debt from a number of countries. Even if the turmoil of the spring and summer of 2010 subsides, a vicious cycle looms in the long run, especially if growing debt is compounded by the adverse effects of higher spending and future ageing costs.

I consider here four central issues that those responsible for policy will need to tackle:

- First, significant fiscal consolidation will be needed to bring deficits and debt back on a sustainable path.
- Second, consolidation has to come largely from the expenditure side of budgets, thereby reversing the recent increase in public spending. This consolidation also would help reinvigorate long-term economic growth.
- Third, Social Security reform will be needed in order to contain fiscal pressures arising from the cost of population ageing.
- Fourth, structural reforms, including in the fiscal area, are needed to reduce incentives for the recurrence of booms and busts.

Central to these challenges is the task of reforming public expenditure. It is virtually inconceivable that fiscal sustainability and dynamic growth can be regained without major expenditure cuts in virtually all advanced economies. By the end of the crisis, public expenditure ratios will average broadly around 50 percent of the gross domestic product (GDP) in most industrialized countries. A desirable public-expenditure ratio, however, would require a reduction to below 40 percent and ideally even further, to 30–35 percent of the GDP in the future. Such a level would suffice to reach the core objectives of governments. The evidence shows that reforms to bring spending down have brought much benefit at limited costs in the past.[1] However, for many countries, even a return to pre-crisis spending ratios will be a major challenge and will require much political determination.

This study opens by considering what went wrong in the boom years in most Western economies. It explains that in the run-up to the present crisis, the credit-financed housing boom precipitated a very large private-sector debt build-up. During this period, public finances and underlying policies were also insufficiently prudent, so that when boom turned to bust, fiscal imbalances quickly became enormous. The boom legacy contributed to distorted economic structures, which in the future will require a reallocation of resources away from the boom's main 'profiteers', such as finance, real estate, and construction. All of this is likely to weigh on economic prospects in the coming years. The study continues with a discussion on where we stand, and it sets out the options for governments in Western economies (including the United Kingdom and the Euroarea) to deal with the main government finance-related policy challenges in the post-boom, post-bust decade.

What Went Wrong?

First, we will look at the private sector in boom and in crisis, which has moved from transient wealth to lasting debt. The period from the late 1990s up to 2007–2008 was characterized by a dramatic rise in house prices in many industrialized countries, along with associated growth in credit and debt to finance the housing boom. By 2007–2008, the trend of rising prices was reversing, leaving a highly indebted and less wealthy private sector in its wake.

Since the start of the financial turmoil or shortly thereafter, many industrialized countries have been in a period of asset-price, notably housing, bust. This period followed an extended boom, which lasted from the late 1990s up to broadly 2007.

Figure 1–4: House Price and Credit Developments in Selected Advanced Economies

Figure 1: Housing Prices Index (2005 = 100)

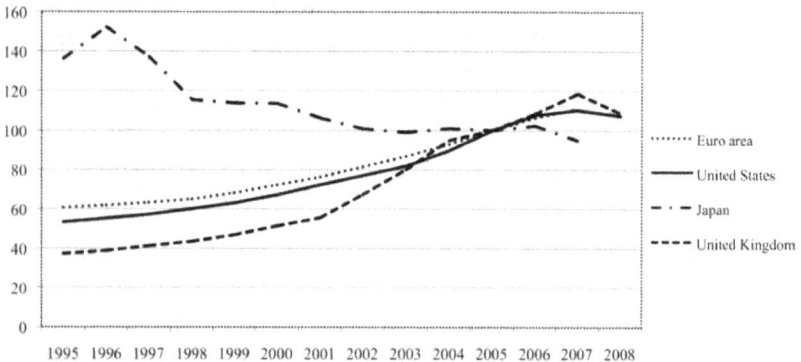

Figure 2: Housing Prices Index (2005 = 100)

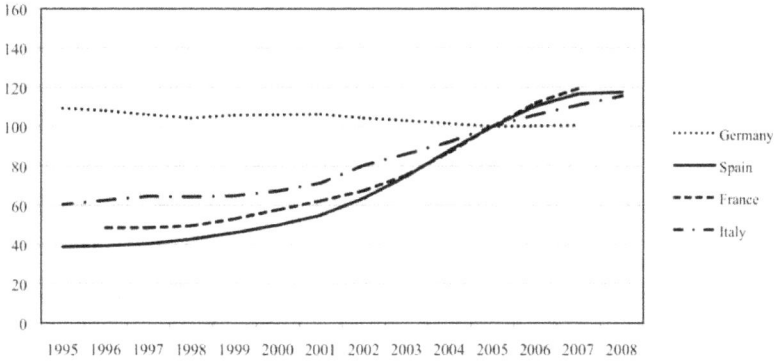

Figure 3: Credit Growth (Percent GDP)

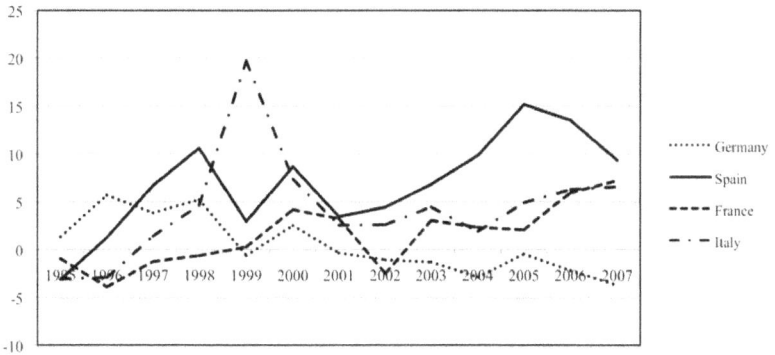

Figure 4: Credit Growth (Percent GDP)

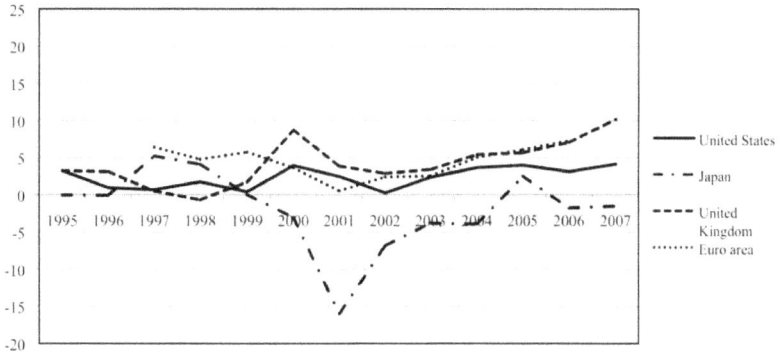

In the boom period, many industrialized countries saw house prices double or even triple within a decade (see Figures 1 and 2). The only notable exceptions among the larger countries were Japan and Germany, where real-estate prices were more or less flat. The British and Spanish booms were among the most pronounced.

The boom appears to have been built on a strong expansion in credit. In fact, real credit growth was rather high in all booming countries, while it was relatively low — and for several years even negative — in Japan and Germany. With the housing boom, housing wealth became the most rapidly increasing component of household wealth in the large, advanced economies — that is, the Euroarea, the United Kingdom, and the United States. Again, Japan and Germany were the exceptions. Financial wealth also increased, briefly interrupted by the stock-market bust of the early 2000s.

The strong credit growth that financed ever-more costly housing contributed to a much-increased household-debt ratio in 2007, compared to a decade earlier. Household debt to the GDP among the represented economies was largest in the United States, the United Kingdom, and Spain in 2007. But not only household debt increased; debt of non-financial corporations (NFCs) also went up strongly in a number of countries and among large, advanced economies, most strongly in Spain, France, and the United Kingdom. Japan and Germany, by contrast, saw little change in household and corporate indebtedness as a share of the GDP since the mid-1990s.

By 2007–2008, the housing boom had started to reverse, earlier in the United States and the United Kingdom and generally later in the other affected European countries. Real and even significant nominal reductions in housing prices started to emerge and continued into 2009. This went along not only with a significant reduction in credit growth but lately also with a reduction in household net wealth.[2] As a consequence, the boom period concluded with a much-increased private debt, especially among households in most advanced economies.[3]

Figure 5–6: Indebtedness of Non-Financial Corporations (NFCs) by Percent GDP. Source: European Central Bank.

Figure 5: NFCs Debt

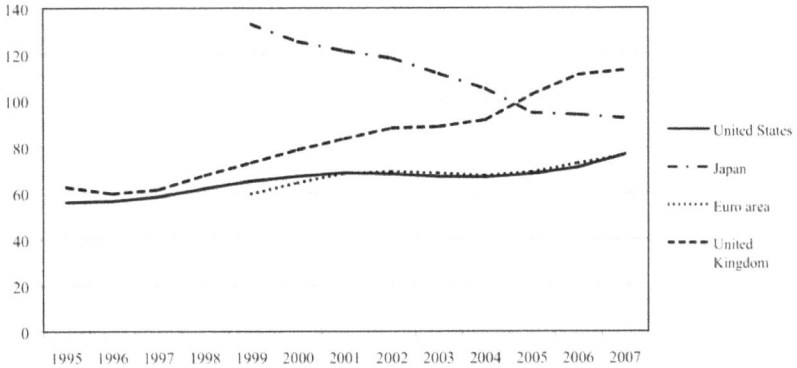

Figure 6: NFCs Debt

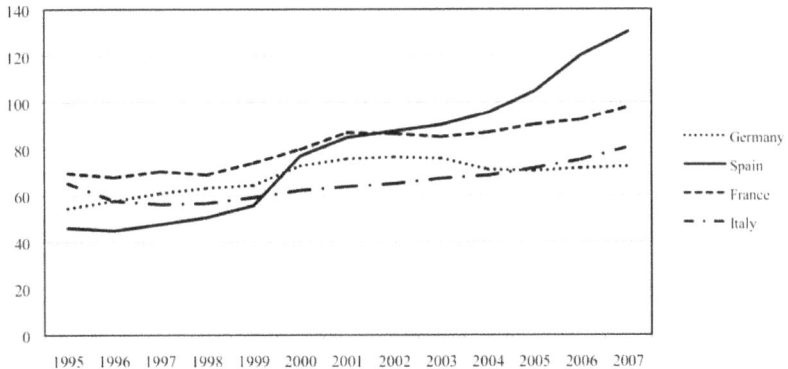

Second, public finances have gone from poor to worse. Despite some efforts to curtail spending and reduce imbalances, the boom years frequently saw a return of strong spending growth. As a result, the crisis caught many governments unprepared. If, however, governments had used the boom times to bring public finances onto a sound footing with surpluses, low debt ratios, and low expenditure ratios, the fiscal burden of the bust and crisis would have been easier to absorb.

Figure 7–8: Indebtedness of Households by Percent GDP. Source: European Central Bank.

Figure 7: Households Debt

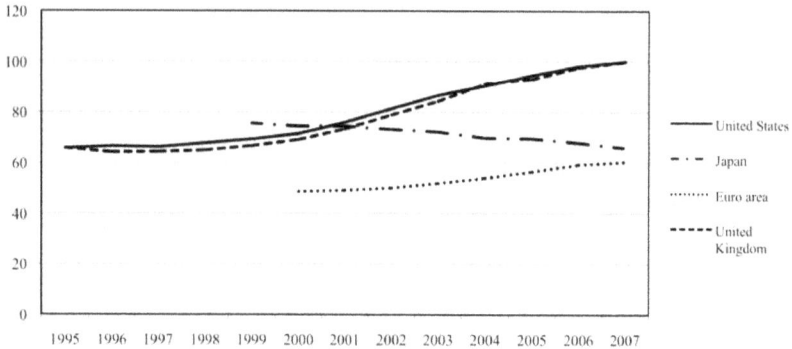

Figure 8: Households Debt

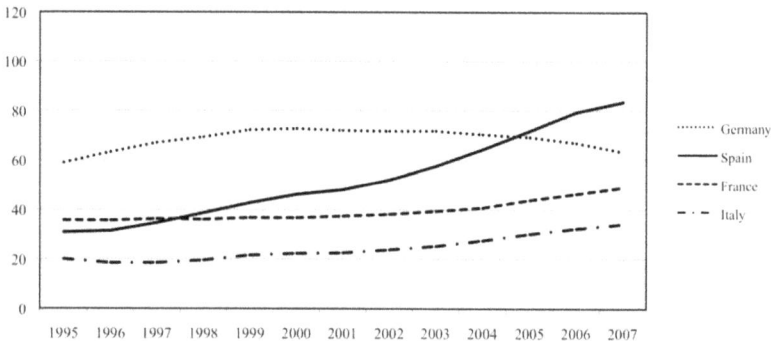

Advanced economies' fiscal balances had improved since the 1990s, but they were still in deficit in most countries at the end of the boom period in 2007. In fact, the United States, the United Kingdom, and France all reported deficits near the European Union's 3 percent of the GDP reference value, which is considered excessive even in less prosperous times. Public debt had declined somewhat in some of the boom countries, but it had increased in Germany and Japan (which, as mentioned, did not experience a boom over this period) and even France (see Table 1).

	Government Balance			Public Debt		
	1995	2007	2010	1995	2007	2010
United States	-3.1	-2.8	-14.2	71.3	63.1	91.1
Japan	-4.7	-2.1	-8.7	87.6	173.6	194
UK	-5.9	-2.7	-13.8	50.7	44.1	81.7
Germany	-3.2	-0.2	-5.9	55.6	65.1	78.7
France	-5.5	-2.7	-7.0	55.1	63.9	86.0
Italy	-7.4	-1.6	-4.8	121.5	104.1	116.1
Spain	-6.5	2.2	-9.8	62.7	36.2	62.3
Euro Area 12	-5.0	-0.6	-6.5	73.8	66.1	83.8

Table 1: General Government Balance and Debt, by Percent of GDP. Source: European Commission, *Economic Forecast: Spring 2009* (Luxembourg: Office for Official Publications of the European Communities, 2009).

To understand the origin of the poor starting position of public finances at the end of the boom, one has to consider public expenditure dynamics. Public expenditure had reached historic highs in most advanced economies at some point in the 1980s or early- to mid-1990s, before many countries introduced major expenditure reductions.[4] The average peak for Euro-area countries had been a staggering 53.7 percent before reforms in the 1980s and the 1990s brought the average spending ratio down. Euro-area spending, consequently, declined to about 47 percent of the GDP in 2000 – 6 percentage points below the average all-time highs in individual countries. By 2007, the spending ratio in the Euroarea had been brought down slightly further, which was mainly due to reforms in Germany and Austria (see Table 2).

In the high-growth countries, the expenditure ratios should have come down as tax revenue was booming, while spending commitments (for the unemployed, for example) even should have declined. This effect would be reached through the dampening effect of the so-called automatic stabilizers alone. Expenditure tends to grow more slowly than the GDP in boom times; hence the denominator of the expenditure ratio grows more slowly than does the numerator. At the same time, tax revenue booms in line with the GDP, hence the ratio stays constant. As a result, the deficit falls. The reverse holds during busts, when spending ratios rise because expenditure grows faster than the GDP and taxes grow in line with or even less quickly than the GDP.

	1999	2000	2007	2010	2000–10	2000–07	2007–10
Spain	39.9	39.2	38.8	47.1	7.9	-0.4	8.2
Germany	48.1	47.6	44.2	49.0	1.4	-3.4	4.8
Italy	48.1	47.3	47.9	51.1	3.8	0.6	3.2
France	52.6	51.6	52.3	56.4	4.7	0.7	4.1
Netherlands	46.0	44.8	45.3	50.2	5.4	0.5	5.0
Austria	53.5	52.4	48.5	52.1	-0.3	-3.8	3.5
Ireland	34.0	31.5	35.7	49.1	17.7	4.2	13.4
Euro Area 12	48.1	47.3	46.1	51.1	3.8	-1.1	4.9
UK	38.9	36.8	44.0	52.4	15.7	7.2	8.5
United States			37.4	43.7			6.3
Japan			36.4	46.7			10.3

Table 2: Total Public Expenditures, by Percent of GDP and Change in Percentage Points of GDP. Source: European Commission, *Economic Forecast: Spring 2009.*

But spending commitments did not come down, because governments adjusted their spending and benefits not according their own growth but according to the countries with even higher growth rates. Governments had been tempted to believe that high economic growth during the boom years was a permanent phenomenon, so more dynamic public-expenditure growth seemed financeable, but many observers also had warned about these temptations and dynamics (for example, the European Commission in 2006). While Spain's spending ratio went down minimally, those of France, the Netherlands, and Ireland even increased. Moreover, in many Euro-area countries, fiscal outcomes often were less prudent than were fiscal plans due to chronic overspending in the 'good times' up to 2007.[5]

An even less favourable picture emerges for the United States and the United Kingdom. The United Kingdom had reduced its public expenditure ratio hugely until the late 1990s, but then it reversed a significant share of that gain over the boom years, with spending ratios reaching a level not much below the Euro-area average. The American spending ratio in 2007 was relatively close to its peak of recent decades. Overall, this trend reflects rather imprudent spending policies in many countries during the boom period. Keeping expenditure ratios high made fiscal balances rather unfavourable, so public finances were not prepared when the housing bust and the economic downturn struck.

	Public Employment Growth (%)		Private Employment Growth (%)	
	1991–99	**1999–2007**	**1991–99**	**1999–2007**
Spain	16.5	36.8	17.0	49.8
Germany	-12.7	-5.4	0.4	2.3
Italy	-3.2	2.3	-1.5	21.1
France	5.6	7.0	9.7	9.6
Netherlands	-0.6	13.1	16.2	4.4
Austria	-3.0	-5.9	6.4	7.6
Ireland	8.9	46.5	48.1	36.7
Euro Area 12	-0.1	7.3	5.6	13.6
UK	-10.2	14.1	11.1	7.0
United States	9.5	9.4	16.3	10.5
Japan	5.0	-1.3	6.7	4.4

Table 3: Employment Developments in Selected Advanced Economies. Source: Organisation for Economic Co-operation and Development.

It is worth dwelling further on one element of expenditure policies. Table 3 shows that public employment policies in many countries had been very prudent in the 1990s, reflecting their expenditure-reform strategies. However, in the period from 1999 to 2007, fewer countries (notably Austria, Germany, and Japan) retained cautious employment policies. At the same time, Spain, the Netherlands, Ireland, and the United Kingdom started hiring strongly in the public sector, so that public employment grew more than private employment in these countries (with the exception of Spain, where private employment managed to grow even more than the huge gains in the public sector).

Third, we must consider the economic structures in the boom and the crisis, and the ways growing distortions hamper the prospects for output. The boom period led many countries to allocate too many resources to the financial and housing sectors. Although these practices contributed to higher growth in the boom years, the crisis has revealed that these sectors must change through a lengthy and costly re-allocation of resources. This change is dampening growth in the crisis, and looking forward, it will continue to do so.

In the late 1990s and early 2000s, the boom in the financial sector, real estate and related services, and construction drew an increasing share of national resources into these sectors. While the measurement of output is difficult, notably in the financial sector, Figures 9 and 10 nevertheless provide an illustration of this reallocation. The share of the broader 'fin-ancial sector' (financial services, real estate, renting, business activities) increased strongly in most advanced economies. Only in the two non-boom countries, Japan and Germany, and in the United States was this increase of resources to the financial sector relatively limited. These three countries also were those least affected by a shift of resources into cons-truction. In contrast, the share of Spain's and the United Kingdom's output increased strongly since the mid-1990s.

The boom-related growth of the financial and real-estate sectors has contributed significantly to the above-trend out-put growth during that period. However, given that this growth was unsustainable, it will not persist, and it will probably at least partly reverse. It is also noteworthy that, in some countries, a disproportionate share of profits (and thereby tax revenue) was generated in the financial sector over that period. The restructuring of the financial sector without the promise of equally high profits also will adv-ersely affect the government revenue outlook. In other words, the boom years have created an illusion of growth and fiscal revenue.

This resource misallocation is likely to hamper the econ-omic prospects for advanced economies.[6] Part of the capital in these sectors will have to be written off or reallocated, as the sectors are not likely to return to their pre-crisis impor-tance. Workers will need to find new jobs, which will take time and retraining. Difficulties in the financial sector and increased risk aversion may reduce the speed at which res-ources are reallocated and may impede new investment, thereby adversely affecting growth and innovation in the economy. Moreover, the need to reduce debt in the private sector should imply lower consumption and investment in the future as households and firms repair their balance sheets.

This should negatively affect consumption and investment for some time to come — with some potential adverse impact on the economic-growth outlook as well. All in all, one could argue that not only the level but also the speed of output expansion may be lower due to the boom-related distortions noted above and their unravelling in the crisis.

Figure 9–10: Share of Financial and Construction Sector in Selected Advanced Economies. Source: Eurostat, European Central Bank, Global Insight for the United States and Japan. Financial-sector data includes financial services, real estate, renting, and business activities.

Figure 9: Financial Sector, as a Percent of GDP

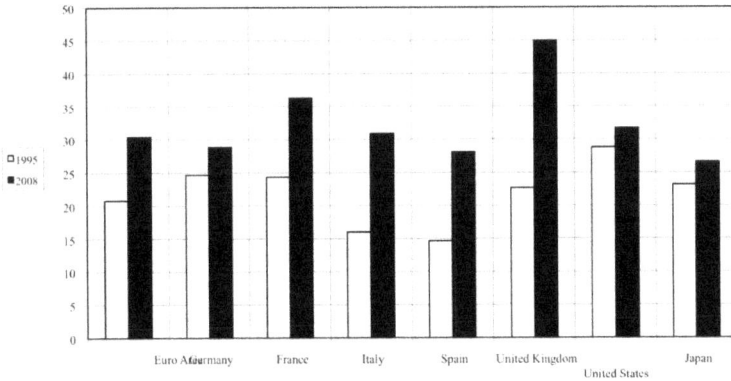

Figure 10: Construction, as a Percent of GDP

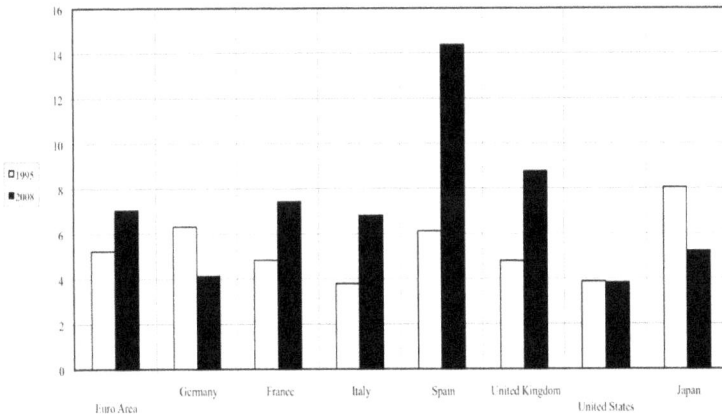

Public Finances at Risk

Advanced economies have seen a major deterioration of public finances, with double-digit deficits and a doubling of public-debt ratios projected in some countries. This is due largely to increasing expenditure ratios rather than to a fall in revenue. Meanwhile, public liabilities are being exacerbated by the impact of bank rescue operations and the additional costs of an ageing population. These factors put the sustainability of public finances at risk.

In the wake of the crisis, the European Commission projected worsening fiscal balances for 2010 that were staggering. Fiscal deficits were projected to increase by about 6 percent of the GDP in the Euroarea and Japan and by over 10 percent in the United States and the United Kingdom (see Table 1). This increase in deficits set in motion a very strong increase in the public-debt ratio, which was compounded in particular in 2009 by the expected strong decline in the GDP. Within only three years, public debt is projected to increase by about 30 percent of the GDP in the United States, almost 40 percent in the United Kingdom, and about 20 percent in Japan and the Euroarea. Moreover, as will be shown later, debt will continue to point steeply upward unless these countries reverse their deficit increases.

The rise in deficits was mainly due to an increase in public spending. This increase is partly the result of imprudent spending policies during the boom, as countries got used to more buoyant expenditure growth. It also reflects the impact of automatic stabilizers and, in addition, the activist measures most countries undertook, such as public-investment programmes, subsidies for scrapping cars, or employment-related spending. As a consequence, public spending started to increase very strongly. Tax revenue fell broadly in line with economic activity, even though in some countries the fall in taxes that was related to the financial and housing sectors also put pressure on public revenue. These factors and limited tax cuts also contributed to somewhat lower revenue ratios and higher deficits.

Table 2 reveals that the public-spending ratio will increase by, on average, 5 percentage points of the GDP in the Euroarea, 6 percent in the United States, and 8–10 percent in Japan and the United Kingdom. Not one country in this list had public-expenditure ratios below 40 percent in 2010, and most of them were near or above 50 percent of the GDP. In other words, many more countries and the whole of the Euroarea could be considered economies with 'big government' by 2010.[7]

The policy challenge of reverting to sustainable public finances with reasonable public-expenditure ratios will be compounded by two further factors: the potential impact of bank-rescue operations, and population ageing. Following the Lehman Brothers bankruptcy, governments extended significant financial support to the financial system. This includes guarantees, capital injections, asset purchases, and other measures (see Table 4). Up until the summer of 2009, their impact on public debt was 3.3 percent of the GDP in the Euroarea and 6.9 percent in the United Kingdom. At that time, the ceiling for further liabilities in the Euroarea was set at 20 percent of the GDP, contingent, for example, on guarantees being called. This figure was much higher for the United Kingdom, with guarantees alone amounting to about 50 percent of the GDP.

As regards population ageing, new projections by the EU Commission and the Economic Policy Committee of their ECOFIN (Economic and Financial Affairs) Council show that the long-term burden of population ageing is very significant, unless further decisive Social Security reforms are undertaken. Without further reforms, public expenditure would increase by about 5 percent of the GDP in Euro-area countries and the United Kingdom, half of which would come from pension and the other half from health and long-term care (see Table 5).

	Type of Intervention				
	Guarantees	Capital Injections		Asset Purchase	Asset Swaps/ Lending
		Acquisition of Shares	Loans		
Belgium	21.0	4.0	2.1	0.0	0.0
Germany	6.3	1.3	0.0	1.7	0.0
Ireland	214.8	4.2	0.0	0.0	0.0
Greece	0.6	1.6	0.0	0.0	1.8
Spain	3.1	0.0	0.0	1.8	0.0
France	1.1	0.8	3.2	0.0	0.0
Italy	0.0	0.0	0.0	0.0	0.0
Cyprus	0.0	0.0	0.0	0.0	0.0
Luxembourg	12.8	8.3	0.0	0.0	0.0
Malta	0.0	0.0	0.0	0.0	0.0
Netherlands	5.0	6.5	7.6	3.9	0.0
Austria	6.6	1.7	0.0	0.0	0.0
Portugal	3.8	0.0	0.0	0.0	0.0
Slovenia	0.0	0.0	0.0	0.4	0.0
Slovakia	0.0	0.0	0.0	0.0	0.0
Finland	0.1	0.0	0.0	0.0	0.0
Euro Area	7.5	1.3	1.2	0.9	0.0
UK	50.6	5.4	1.1	0.1	13.2

	Type of Intervention		Fiscal Impact		
	Debt Assumptions/ Cancellations	Other Measures	Government Debt	Government Contingent Liabilities	
				Provided	Ceiling
Belgium	0.0	0.0	7.4	21.0	34.6
Germany	0.0	0.0	2.9	6.3	18.7
Ireland	0.0	0.0	4.2	214.8	242.0
Greece	0.0	0.0	1.6	0.6	6.1
Spain	0.0	0.0	1.8	3.1	18.9
France	0.0	0.0	4.1	1.1	16.8
Italy	0.0	0.0	0.0	0.0	0.0
Cyprus	0.0	0.0	0.0	0.0	0.0
Luxembourg	0.0	0.0	8.3	12.8	0.0
Malta	0.0	0.0	0.0	0.0	0.0
Netherlands	0.0	0.2	18.2	5.0	35.0
Austria	0.0	0.0	1.7	6.6	27.8
Portugal	0.0	0.0	0.0	3.8	12.4
Slovenia	0.0	3.6	4.0	0.0	33.2
Slovakia	0.0	0.0	0.0	0.0	0.0
Finland	0.0	0.0	0.0	0.1	28.1
Euro Area	0.0	0.0	3.4	7.5	19.9
UK	2.0	-1.7	6.9	63.8	78.7

Table 4: Cumulated Interventions and their Fiscal Impact (as Percentage of 2009 GDP). Source: European Central Bank, *Monthly Bulletins* (2009).

	Pensions Change	Healthcare Change	Long Term Care Change	Total Change
Germany	2.3	1.8	1.4	4.8
Spain	6.7	1.6	1.7	9.9
France	1.0	1.2	0.8	2.7
Italy	-0.4	1.1	1.3	1.6
Netherlands	4.0	1.0	4.7	9.4
Euro Area	2.8	1.4	1.4	5.2
UK	2.7	1.9	0.5	5.1

Table 5: Expected Increase in Public Expenditure Due to Population Ageing, 2007–2060, by Percent of GDP. Source: European Commission and Economic Policy Committee, *2009 Ageing Report: Economic and Budgetary Projections for the EU-27 Member States (2008–2060)* (Luxembourg: Office for Official Publications of the European Communities, 2009).

These figures are conservative. Less-favourable assumptions and the impact of the financial crisis could drive them considerably higher. Ageing costs for the United States and Japan also are potentially very high, notably in the area of health and long-term care.

What Needs to Be Done?

The future course of policies must now be considered against this background of rising public expenditure, deficits, and debt — as well as potentially low economic growth for some time to come. As a matter of urgency, governments must decide how to revert to sustainable public finances. Four key policy challenges follow from the economic situation discussed above: to correct fiscal deficits so that debt dynamics do not explode, to reduce the public-expenditure ratio, to reform expenditure to reduce the future fiscal costs of the ageing population, and to reform fiscal and other policy to reduce the likelihood of future booms and busts.

The first challenge must be the ambitious correction of fiscal deficits so that debt dynamics do not explode. Scenario 0 in Figure 11 represents public-debt developments in Euro-area countries without any fiscal adjustment in the coming years. Given the higher deficits in the United Kingdom and the United States in 2009 and 2010, their dynamics could be even less favourable. The dotted line reflects the prospects for public debt if the Euro-area deficit on average declines by

0.5 percent of the GDP per year until it is in balance (in about 2020).

Figure 11: Simulation of Euro-Area Debt Ratio Under Different
Consolidation Scenarios[8]

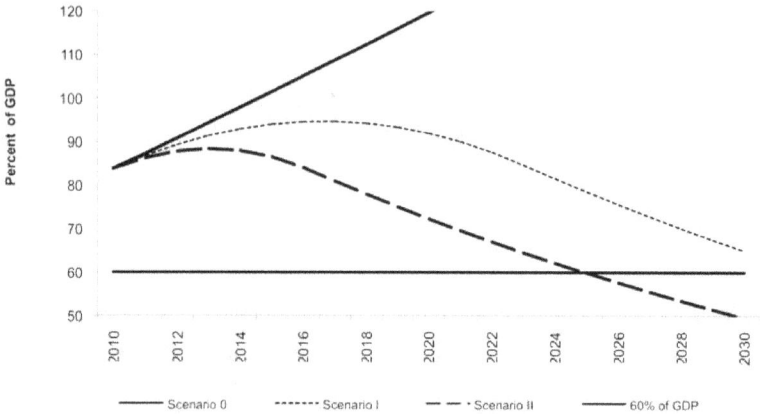

While this scenario would be consistent with a very minimalist interpretation of the Stability and Growth Pact, it is not comforting: public debt in the Euroarea would continue increasing until 2016, when it would peak near 100 percent of the GDP. Debt figures could be even higher if trend growth turned out to be lower or interest rates higher, and if significant further costs of banking support arose. Only an ambitious correction of deficits by 1 percent of the GDP or more per annum (and significantly more in countries with very high deficits) would bring the Euroarea back on a declining debt path relatively quickly. But even in that scenario, a balanced budget for the Euro-area average would only be reached in about 2015 and for the United Kingdom, even later. A reasonably safe debt ratio below the maximum value of 60 percent of the GDP, which all EU members have signed off to in the Maastricht Treaty, would on average not be reached before the year 2020, even in the best scenario.

Bringing down deficits and debt and returning to sound public finances will inevitably require a long process of fiscal belt tightening. The options are either higher revenue, lower spending, or a combination of the two.

	Single Earner, No Children, Average Income	Married, Two Children, Incomes of 100 and 67 Percent of Average
United States	43.3	34.0
Japan	33.2	30.5
UK	40.6	46.5
Germany	66.5	63.4
France	55.8	52.0
Italy	52.7	52.7
Spain	45.5	45.5
Euro Area (15)	52.8	52.3

Table 6: Marginal Tax Rates in Selected Advanced Economies. Source: Organisation for Economic Co-operation and Development (2008)

If a country wants to go the first route and generate a high revenue ratio, then average taxes must rise. And this also typically implies a higher marginal tax rate on each additional euro, pound, or dollar earned, which has a significant impact on decisions to work, innovate, and invest. Table 6 illustrates this, where the countries with (formerly) low spending ratios also typically feature lower distortive taxes (taxes that cause taxpayers to distort their behaviour). Marginal household income-tax rates for the represented income groups, for example, exceed 50 percent or even 60 percent in the traditionally high-spending continental European countries, while these rates are 'only' 30–45 percent in the United States, the United Kingdom, Japan, and Spain. However, with spending ratios in these economies to approach the Euro-area average, it is hardly conceivable that revenue ratios can be brought up to such levels without significantly increasing the tax wedge and thereby decreasing incentive.

In summary, all big-spending countries also will need to be high-taxing countries *if* they want to maintain fiscal sustainability *without* cutting spending. However, if history is a guide, tax-based efforts at creating economic sustainability have little chance of success.

The second, and probably pivotal, challenge, given the potentially dire consequences of much higher taxes, is to reduce the public-expenditure ratio. This reduction should bring spending ratios at least back to pre-crisis levels, but in many countries it would be desirable to reduce public expenditure even further. Experience has shown that a ratio below 40 percent, and ideally 30–35 percent, is sufficient.[9] Governments have been well able to produce good outcomes in terms of functioning markets, equal opportunity for market participants, essential public goods and services, infrastructure, economic stability, and income distribution with public spending in this range. I do not consider here the detailed possibilities for the reforms needed in individual countries and spending categories to reach lower spending ratios. But the evidence is that reducing spending on public employment and other public consumption, on transfers, and on subsidies has proven to be most beneficial for successfully bringing down public spending.[10]

Expenditure reform is pivotal, because first, deficit reduction and expenditure reform would be fully complementary objectives, and second, expenditure reform could have a positive effect on trend growth by reducing the number of tax- and spending-related disincentives to work and invest, and reducing rent-seeking. This in turn would speed up deficit and debt reduction; a virtuous cycle could emerge.

Expenditure reform is also key to the third (fiscal policy) challenge, reducing the future fiscal costs of ageing populations. Although reforms over the past decade have reduced the scope of future problems in some countries, welfare state-related spending now 'eats up' the lion's share of public budgets in many countries. And if policies are not changed, then the fiscal burden will continue to grow. The prospect of less growth and the fallout from the crisis on employment and fiscal balances make absorbing the costs of population ageing even more difficult.[11]

Many useful reforms identified in the vast literature deal with population ageing. An important reform would be to raise the statutory retirement age. Even if this caused a corresponding increase in pension entitlements, it would help indirectly, because a larger labour force would allow for a bigger GDP from which pensions would have to be financed. An increase in the effective retirement age through an elimination of early-retirement incentives would directly (through lower spending) and indirectly reduce the future fiscal burden of pension systems. As regards public health, increased competition, more copayments, more prioritization of services, and international trade in health services are only some of the reforms that could help contain costs. Non-fiscal measures such as labour and product-market reforms and the facilitation of private social insurance also could reduce sustainability risks from population ageing through higher growth.

The fourth challenge is to reform fiscal and other policy to reduce the likelihood of future booms and busts.[12] While fiscal policies may not be the most important policy domain for reducing asset price cycles, they can nevertheless play a role. In many countries, for example, the deductibility of mortgage interest payments from income tax is raising the incentive for households to indebt themselves. Similarly, tax policies have been found to encourage debt rather than equity financing of firms. When such measures are introduced, they are likely to boost real estate (and possibly other asset) prices, and when they are abolished, the reverse happens, thus potentially contributing to the volatility of asset prices. Changes in national fiscal institutions that contribute to saving rather than spending — the fiscal 'rents' of good times — also are likely to contribute to moderate boom-bust cycles. In particular, Germany and Switzerland have introduced fiscal rules in recent years that aim to keep fiscal positions sound while permitting some cyclical fluctuations. Such improvements in national rules would also make it easier to attain sound public finances and comply with the EU's Stability and Growth Pact.

Of course, fiscal policy is not the only area where important reforms are needed.[13] But all in all, reform of fiscal policies must be central to the restoration of economic fitness in the post-boom, post-bust economies. Re-establishing sound public finances with lean government will be pivotal in regaining economic stability and dynamism.

Conclusion

As Western governments decide on their future policy courses, their central task will be to return to healthy and stable economies, with sound and sustainable public finances. The best way to do this will be by reforming public expenditure. As matters stand, public deficits and debt trends risk being unsustainable, and government obligations to financial-sector and their ageing populations loom large.

With expenditure ratios averaging about 50 percent of the GDP in most industrial countries, neither fiscal sustainability nor strong economic growth is likely unless governments institute major fiscal policy reforms and reduce spending significantly. Due to their lack of trust in fiscal sustainability, investors charge increasingly high-risk premiums to hold government bonds from a number of countries with very high rates of deficit and debt. The EU/IMF (European Union International Monetary Fund) support programme for Greece and the creation of the European Financial Support Facility in spring 2010 added a new dimension to the European situation: the risk of a fiscal burden from international fiscal support. While the magnitude of problems differs across countries, policymakers almost everywhere must tackle four central problems.

First, *deficits and debts must be returned to a sustainable level.* Only if deficits are reduced by 1 percent of the GDP or more per annum (and significantly more in countries with very high deficits) will debt stabilize and decline relatively quickly. Even then, a balanced budget only would be reached in about 2015 for the average of the Euroarea and even later in the United Kingdom.

Second, *much lower spending is needed if deficits and debt are to be reduced and sound public finances restored.* Given the magnitude of deficits, a country would need to raise average and marginal tax rates enormously if it wanted to reduce debts and deficits by raising taxes. This most likely would have very adverse consequences for growth. The historical evidence is that mainly tax-based consolidation has little chance of success.

Moreover, spending ratios should be brought back at least to pre-crisis levels. Even this will be difficult, and much will depend on political determination. But there is a case for many countries to reduce more. A ratio below 40 percent of the GDP, and ideally 30–35 percent, should be sufficient and allow good outcomes in the areas judged to matter in Western economies: functioning markets, equal opportunity for market participants, essential public goods and services, infrastructure, economic stability, and income distribution. The evidence is that ambitious reforms that reduce government spending obligations on public employment and other public consumption, as well as on transfers and subsidies, is the best and most successful way to bring down public spending at little cost to economic growth and well-being.

In fact, reducing deficit and reforming expenditure are complementary objectives. Expenditure reform can have a positive effect on long-term growth by providing incentives to work and to invest, rather than to 'seek rents'. This in turn speeds up deficit and debt reduction and allows a virtuous cycle to emerge.

Third, *Social Security reform also should be introduced to contain fiscal pressures arising from ageing populations.* Despite some reforms, welfare state-related spending continues to absorb a major share of public budgets in many countries. Unless policies change, Social Security inevitably will increase the tax burden or crowd out other spending. For example, increasing the statutory retirement age and eliminating early-retirement incentives will be important. Health and long-term care reforms also could contribute to the affordability of services in the future.

Fourth, *structural reforms, including those in the fiscal area, are needed to reduce the likelihood of future booms and bust.* Fiscal policies, though not the most important way to stabilize the boom-bust cycles of asset prices, can play a part by eliminating excessive incentives to take on debt and by avoiding stoking housing markets that are already buoyant.

In addition, changes in national fiscal institutions that contribute to saving rather than to spending the fiscal 'rents' of good times also can help: they can contribute to moderate boom-bust cycles, healthier public finances, and compliance with the EU's Stability and Growth Pact. These national rules could include, for example, the fiscal rules introduced in Germany and Switzerland to keep fiscal positions sound while permitting some cyclical fluctuations.

To conclude, although fiscal policy is not the only area where important reforms are needed, fiscal-policy reforms are central to restoring economic fitness in the post-boom, post-bust economies. Re-establishing sound public finances with lean governments will be pivotal for regaining economic stability and dynamism.

1   Ludger Schuknecht and Vito Tanzi, *Reforming Public Spending: Great Gain, Little Pain* (London: Politeia, 2005).

2   This information on household assets, liabilities, and net worth is based on data from the Bank of Japan, the Cabinet Office (Japan), the European Central Bank, Eurostat, the Office of National Statistics, Haver Analytics, and IMF staff estimates.

3   For more detail, see International Monetary Fund, *World Economic Outlook* (May 2009).

4   See Schuknecht and Tanzi, *Reforming Public Spending*.

5   European Central Bank, 'Ten Years of the Stability and Growth Pact', *ECB Monthly Bulletin* (October 2008): 53–65.

6   See also the European Commission, 'Impact of the Current Economic and Financial Crisis on Potential Output', *European Economy Occasional Paper*, 49 (June 2009).

7   Vito Tanzi and Ludger Schuknecht, *Public Spending in the 20th Century: A Global Perspective* (Cambridge: Cambridge University Press, 2000).

8   Assumptions: All 2010 values from European Commission, *Economic Forecast: Spring 2009*. Nominal Euro-area GDP growth at 3.7 percent between 2011–2030. Nominal interest rates on outstanding government debt constant at 2010 level as forecasted by the EU Commission. Scenario 0: Unchanged primary balances. Scenario I: Minimum consolidation of primary balance by 0.5 percentage points (p.p.) of GDP each year until the total budget deficit reaches zero and then kept constant; structural consolidation is equal to nominal consolidation as growth is assumed to be at trend throughout; debt ratio reaches 94.6 percent of GDP in 2016. Scenario II: Consolidation of primary balance by 1 p.p. of GDP each year until the total budget deficit reaches zero and then kept constant; debt reaches 88.3 percent of GDP in 2013.

9   Tanzi and Schuknecht, *Public Spending in the 20th Century*.

10 A more in-depth discussion of experiences from past reform strategies can be found in Tanzi and Schuknecht, *Public Spending in the 20th Century*; Schuknecht and Tanzi, *Reforming Public Spending*; Sebastian Hauptmeier, Martin Heipertz and Ludger Schuknecht, 'Expenditure Reform in Industrialised Countries: A Case Study Approach', *European Central Bank Working Paper 634* (May 2006). European Commission *Forecast* (2006) reviews the literature on more- versus less-successful consolidation. For a measure of the efficiency of public expenditure, notably in relation to the size of total government spending and its components, see Antonio Afonso, Ludger Schuknecht and Vito Tanzi, 'Public Sector Efficiency: An International Comparison', *European Central Bank Working Paper 242* (July 2003) and forthcoming in *Public Choice*.

11 European Commission and Economic Policy Committee, *2009 Ageing Report: Economic and Budgetary Projections for the EU-27 Mem-*

ber States (2008–2060) (Luxembourg: Office for Official Publications of the European Communities, 2009).

[12] See for example Guido Wolswijk, 'Fiscal Aspects of Housing in Europe', in *Housing Market Challenges in Europe and the United States: Any Solutions Available?*, ed. Philip Arestis, Peter Mooslechner and Karin Wagner (London: Palgrave Macmillan, 2009).

[13] Discussing other reform areas that are key for mitigating the risk of future boom-bust cycles goes beyond the scope of this study.

Index

9 7 8 1 8 4 5 4 0 3 1 1 9